PHILOSOPHY OF ETHICS

PHILOSOPHY OF ETHICS

MURTAḌĀ MUṬAHHARĪ

Translated By
Mansoor Limba

Edited By
Seyyed Mohsen Miri

A catalogue record for this book is available from the British Library and the Australian National Library

Ordering Information:
Quantity sales. Special discounts are available on quantity purchases by corporations, associations, and others. For details, contact the distributor at the address below.

Shia Books Australia
www.shiabooks.com.au
info@shiabooks.com.au

ISBN 978-1-911361-01-5

This English edition first published in 2016
Second Edition 2021

Contents

Transliteration

Symbol	Transliteration	Symbol	Transliteration
ء	’	أ	a
ب	b	ت	t
ث	th	ج	j
ح	ḥ	خ	kh
د	d	ذ	dh
ر	r	ز	z
س	s	ش	sh
ص	ṣ	ض	ḍ
ط	ṭ	ظ	ẓ
ع	‘	غ	gh
ف	f	ق	q
ک	k	ل	l
م	m	ن	n
ه	h	و	w
ی	y	ة	ah
Long Vowels		Short Vowels	
آ	a	ـَ	a
ای	ī	ـِ	i
او	ū	ـُ	u
Persian Letters			
Symbol	Transliteration	Symbol	Transliteration
پ	p	چ	ch
ژ	zh	گ	g

At the end of Farsi words, 'eh', '-e', and '-ye' have been used.

Foreword

Considering necessity of preparing appropriate Islamic texts in English for the modern world and aiming at satisfying that need, Al-Mustafa International Research Institute (M.I.R.I.) decided to establish "Islam and West Research Centre" in 2009. This centre has accomplished that duty in the best way by producing, translating, and reprinting tens of such appropriate texts.

The present book, *Philosophy of Ethics,* which is a translation of the Persian book *Falsafeh-ye Akhlāq* by the great Muslim thinker and reformer Āyatullāh Murtaḍā Muṭahharī (which was initially lectures delivered by him, published by Ṣadrā Publications, Tehran, 2006), is among such invaluable books prepared and published by Islam and West Research Centre.

As for some basic references, the translation of Qur'anic passages is adapted from Sayyid 'Alī Qulī Qarā'ī's *The Qur'an with a Phrase-by-Phrase English Translation* (London: Islamic College for Advanced Studies, 2004); the translation of quotations from *Nahj al-Balāghah* is based on that of Syed 'Alī Raza (Qum: Foundation of Islamic Cultural Propagation in the World, 1995). For the poetic quotations from Sa'dī's *Gulistān*, *Būstān*, Rūmī's *Mathnāwī-ye Ma'nawī*, and the *Diwān* of Ḥāfiẓ, the translations of Edward Rehatsek [*Gulistan or Rose Garden of Sa'dī* (Tehran: Peyk-e Farhang, 1998)], Henry Wilberforce Clarke [*The Būstān of Sa'dī* (Tehran: Peyk-e Farhang, 2004)] and Reynold A. Nicholson, *The Mathnawī of Jalālu'ddīn Rūmī* (Tehran: Soad Publisher, 2002), and Henry Wilberforce Clarke [*The Divan of Hafiz* (Tehran: Aban Book, 2005)], respectively, are hereby adapted.

In a number of places, words or expressions marked by brackets were added to the text either to fill a gap or to render the meaning clearer.

Footnotes with the sign "[Trans.]" are not those of the author, and thus, not in the original Persian text, but provided by the translator to facilitate better understanding for the English readers. Footnotes in brackets are those of Āyatullāh Murtaḍā Muṭahharī's Works Supervisory Council or the publisher.

In the end, I would like to acknowledge the contribution of a number of experts, consultants and colleagues without whose efforts this project would have not been set up. First and foremost we are all deeply indebted to the great master martyr Muṭahharī, who delivered such invaluable lectures owing to his deep knowledge of Islamic teachings, and I have to thank Ṣadrā Publications for publishing for the first time the book in which those lectures were gathered.

A note of thanks goes to the translator, Dr. Mansoor L. Limba, who worked diligently to render the entry into English.

I would like to express my gratitude in particular to Professor Hamidreza Ayatollahy for his cooperation in starting this project and in general to Mohammad Meftah of the Qum-based International Institute of Islamic Studies for his most helpful translation consultancy, to Salahaddin Limba for proofreading the initial manuscript, and to the editor Amir Dastmalchian who went through the manuscript most meticulously.

I would also like to greatly appreciate the efforts of Ali Aranji and Leyla Majdani for supervising and facilitating the workflow of the present work.

I hope that this book would be an invaluable contribution to the Islamic thought and of great benefit for all readers in general and people of research in particular.

I take this opportunity to express our gratitude to "Islam and West Research Centre Ltd" for publishing this book and hope that the latter should form a link showing the way for those who seek advancement.

Seyyed Mohsen Miri

About the Author

Professor Āyatullāh Murtaḍā Muṭahharī (1298-1358 S.A.H) was born to a family of clergymen on Bahman 13, 1298 S.A.H.[February 3, 1920] in the village of Farīmān near Mashhad. At the age of 12, he went to Mashhad where he learned the basics of Islamic sciences and then moved to Qum where he attended the sessions of the great authorities of the theological center.

From 1319 S.A.H. [1940] Muṭahharī attended the sessions held by Imām Khomeinī and other famous teachers of the time. Moreover, he himself gave lectures in subjects like Arabic literature, logic, *kalām* (scholasticism), jurisprudence (*fiqh*), and philosophy.

In 1331 S.A.H. (1952) Muṭahharī moved to Tehran and in 1334 S.A.H.(1955) he was invited to teach Islamic sciences at the Faculty of Islamic Sciences, Tehran University. He was arrested at midnight on Khordād 15, 1342 S.A.H. (1963) and remained in prison for 43 days. After Imām Khomeinī's migration to Paris in France, Muṭahharī went to meet him, and the Imām assigned him the responsibility of organizing the Revolutionary Council.

On the night of Ordībehesht 11, 1358 S.A.H. (May 1, 1979) Muṭahharī was martyred by one of the agents of the terrorist Furqān group. He wrote more than 50 books and tens of articles, and delivered scores of speeches.

A cursory examination of the 22-volume *Ṣaḥīfeh-ye Imām*[1]—the largest ever compiled anthology of Imām Khomeinī's speeches, messages, interviews, religious decrees, permissions, and letters—reveals that the martyred Professor Muṭahharī undoubtedly occupied a distinct station in the sight of the Great Leader of the Islamic Revolution and the Idol-Breaker of the 20th Century.

Imām Khomeinī's communications with Āyatullāh Muṭahharī in the form of religious permissions (*ijāzāt*) and personal letters as well as descriptions of him in the Imām's letters, speeches, messages, statements, interviews, autobiography, and memorial note during and after Muṭahharī's lifetime as indicated in the encyclopedic authentic reference source suggest that the former considered the latter a trustworthy representative, compassionate teacher, erudite scholar, competent jurist, eloquent speaker, combatant *'ālim*, and an epitome of martyrdom in the way of truth and freedom of thought.

---

1. *Ṣaḥīfeh-ye Imām: An Anthology of Imām Khomeinī's Speeches, Messages, Interviews, Religious Decrees, Permissions, and Letters*, volumes 1-22 (Tehran: The Institute for Compilation and Publication of Imām Khomeinī's Works, 2007). [Trans.]

These benevolent views regarding him are consistent in an encyclopedic reference source of Imām Khomeinī's works—from the first volume of the anthology in which Professor Muṭahharī is indicated having been granted authority (*ijāzah*) on Dhu'l-Ḥijjah 24, 1388 S.A.H.(March 13, 1969) by the Imām in the financial and religious law affairs, up to the 21st volume (volume 22 being the indexes of the whole voluminous treatise) wherein he—in the Imām's message dated Shahrīvar 14, 1367 S.A.H.(September 5, 1988) addressed to the Muslim nation of Pakistan and the *'ulamā'* of Islam on the occasion of the martyrdom of Sayyid 'Ārif Ḥusayn Ḥusaynī—is mentioned as having been among "the freedom-loving *'ulamā'* of the Islamic world subjected to conspiracy and terrorism".

To the Imām, Shahīd Muṭahharī was more than a student, representative, associate, confidant, friend, or son. Indeed, it can be said that to him, Muṭahharī could not be confined to a single dimension as he embodied a totality of aspects. Muṭahharī is Muṭahharī.

***

A PhD holder in International Relations (University of Tehran) who also earned units in MA Islamic Studies, Mansoor L. Limba, the translator, has tens of written and translation works to his credit on such subjects as international politics, history, political philosophy, jurisprudence (*fiqh*), scholastic theology (*'ilm al-kalām*), Qur'anic sciences, *ḥadīth*, ethics, and mysticism.

Limba's English rendition of the Persian book *Shī'eh Pāsukh Mīdahad* (*The Shī'ah Rebuts*) by Dr. Sayyid Riḍā Ḥusaynī Nasab (Tehran: Ahl al-Bayt (A.S.) [1] World Assembly, 2007) was recognized as best translation of the year in the Shaykh al-Ṭūsī International Festival (Qum, 2008) while his paper "*Mahdawiyyah* as Final Vocabulary: A Postmodernist Reading of Islamic Iran's Foreign Policy Principles" was awarded "best paper" at the 5th International Conference on the Doctrine of *Mahdawiyyah* (Tehran, 2009).

The present volume is the fifth work by Āyatullāh Muṭahharī that the translator has translated into English, the others being the books *Iḥyā-ye Tafakkur-e Islām* (*The Revival of Islamic Thought*) (Tehran: Ahl al-Bayt (A.S.) World Assembly, *forthcoming*), *Naẓariyyeh-ye Shinākht* (*The Theory of Knowledge: An Islamic Perspective*) (Tehran: Institute of Humanities and Cultural Studies and Ahl al-Bayt (A.S.) University, 2012), *Ta'līm wa Tarbiyat dar Islām* (*Training and Education in Islam*) (Tehran: Institute of Humanities and Cultural Studies and Ahl al-Bayt (A.S.) University, 2012), and *Fiṭrat* (*Fiṭrah: Man's Natural Disposition*) (London: MIU Press, *forthcoming*). He is currently translating a booklet entitled *Akhlāq wa Farā-akhlāq* about the author's ideas on ethics and meta-ethics (Cotabato City, Philippines: SMERI Press, *forthcoming*).

---

1. The abbreviation, "'*a*" stands for the Arabic invocative phrase, *'alayhi's-salām*, *'alayhim'us-salām*, or *'alayhā's-salām* (may peace be upon him/them/her), which is mentioned after the names of the prophets, angels, Imāms from the Prophet's progeny, and saints (A.S.). [Trans.]

Preface

The present book consists of 13-session lectures by the martyred Professor Āyatullāh Murtaḍā Muṭahharī about the philosophy of ethics and it has two parts. The first part which constitutes the greater portion of the book consists of his 10-session lectures in the month of Muḥarram in 1351 S.A.H. (circa 1972) at Arak Mosque, Tehran. In this part, apart from the philosophy of ethics, Islamic ethics has also been discussed.

The second part consists of the professor's three lectures on the same subject on different occasions and venues.

The first lecture is entitled "The Criterion for Moral Action" delivered at the later part of his life before a group of Islamic seminarians in Qum.

The exact date of the second lecture in this part entitled "Communist Morality – Russell's School of Morality" is not determined, but it is obvious that it was delivered during the later part of the blessed life of this martyred thinker.

The third lecture entitled "The Issue of 'Self' in Ethics" was delivered in around 1339 S.A.H. (circa 1960) in the

Higher Training College of Tehran, and of course, its audio cassette recording is not available and its compilation is done through its transcript of the cassette recording at the time which was the disposal of the professor.

With the exception of the book's title (*Philosophy of Ethics*) and titles of two lectures – "Communist Morality – Russell's School of Morality" and "The Issue of 'Self' in Ethics," the rest of the lectures' titles are those of the compiler.

The martyred professor has relatively many notes related to the philosophy of ethics and Islamic ethics, which will be published in the thematic notes of the erudite scholar, God willing.

This book was first published in 1377 S.A.H. (circa 1998) and since then it has been much welcomed by the readers.

The earlier editions did not have the first lecture since its transcript became available afterward. Also, in this edition, subtitles are supplied in the text while meticulous editing and proofreading have been done after the typesetting, and since the book becomes thicker, it is hereby published in foolscap size. As a whole, this edition is presented in a thicker form and better quality. It is hoped that it is acceptable and approvable to those who are interested with the writings of this Islamic scholar and martyred combatant.

We beseech God, the Exalted, for more success.

Supervisory Council of Āyatullāh Murtaḍā Muṭahharī's Works

Bahman 1380 S.A.H.(February 11, 2000)

Part One:
Lectures in Arak Mosque, Tehran

Chapter 1: What is Ethics?

اعوذ بالله من الشيطان الرجيم

I seek refuge in Allah from the accursed Satan.

﴿هُوَ الَّذِي بَعَثَ فِي الْأُمِّيِّينَ رَسُولًا مِّنْهُمْ يَتْلُو عَلَيْهِمْ آيَاتِهِ وَيُزَكِّيهِمْ وَيُعَلِّمُهُمُ الْكِتَابَ وَالْحِكْمَةَ﴾

It is He who sent to the unlettered [people] an apostle from among themselves, to recite to them His signs, to purify them, and to teach them the Book and wisdom. (62:2)

The subject of discussion in the next few nights shall be "Philosophy of Ethics," God willing.

What is ethics and morality in general? How can we say that a human action is 'moral' or 'non-mortal'? And what constitutes an 'immoral' act? Similarly, how can we say that a person's trait can be considered 'moral', 'immoral', and neither 'moral' nor 'immoral'? The same question and classification are applicable to a person's thought or idea. What constitutes a 'moral' thought, an 'immoral' thought and that which is neither 'moral' nor 'immoral'? Although initially it seems that a moral action, trait or thought need no definition, *akhlāq* (ethics and morality) is a word which is prevalent in all people, nay in all people of the world. In every language, there is an equivalent word for it. All that are moral, therefore, and naturally, all that are immoral are known. They are no more in need of any definition. Yet, incidentally, like many other similar things, *akhlāq* is one of the things that while existing in the languages of all people and all people think that they know it and they can define it, is most difficult to define.

You will never believe that all these scholars, philosophers and scientists that exist in the world and all these scientific discoveries and philosophical unravelling on issues and on many of which they have consensus of opinion in the sense that the respective problems are solved – in mathematics, physics, natural sciences, philosophy, and logic, hundreds of problems can be identified which are already solved – yet, [the definition of] this common term is not yet solved in the sense that there is no consensus of opinion about it. If, for example, we ask Plato and Socrates what 'moral' action is, they will define it in a certain way. If we ask from Aristotle who was a student of Plato, he will define it in another way and regard Plato's definition as incorrect. If we ask Epicurus,[1] he will define it in yet another way. If we ask

1. Epicurus (341-270 B.C.): an ancient Greek atomic materialist philosopher, who believed that the greatest good was to seek modest pleasures in order to attain a state of tranquility (*ataraxia*) and freedom from fear, as well as absence of bodily pain (*aponia*) through knowledge of the workings of the world and the limits of one's desires. [Trans.]

the Stoics,[1] they will define it in their own way. If we ask the Cynics,[2] they will define it in their unique way. If we ask the Sophists,[3] they will define it in their distinctive way. If you travel to India and happen to study Hindu books and ethics, we can see that they define it in their exclusive way. Buddha has defined it in a specific way. Confucius has defined it in a particular way. Our own mystics (*'urafā'*) define it in a definitive way. In the modern world, every philosopher proposes a particular system of morality and *akhlāq* in his school is different from that one in other schools of morality. For instance, morality for Nietzsche[4] is basically repugnant to the other systems of morality. The Machiavellian morality is a unique morality in the

---

1. Stoics: adherents of Stoicism which is a school of Hellenistic philosophy founded in Athens by Zeno of Citium in the early 3rd century BC, and maintains that destructive emotions resulted from errors in judgment. [Trans.]
2. Cynics: adherents of Cynicism, a school of ancient Greek philosophy first outlined by Antisthenes, who had been a pupil of Socrates in the late 5th century BC, and for which the purpose of life was to live in virtue, in agreement with nature. [Trans.]
3. Sophists were a category of teachers in ancient Greece who specialized in using the techniques of philosophy and rhetoric for the purpose of teaching *arete* - excellence or virtue - predominantly to young statesmen and nobility. [Trans.]
4. Friedrich Wilhelm Nietzsche (1844-1900): a 19th-century German philosopher and classical philologist who wrote critical texts on religion, morality, contemporary culture, philosophy and science. [Trans.]

world. The Marxist morality is another unique type of morality in the world. Why is it so?

The source of difference of views on ethics

To some extent, the differences of opinion on the definition of ethics or morality emanate from the difference of worldviews. That is, the insight of every school about the world provides and proposes a specific system of morality for that school. The materialist school naturally proposes a kind of morality. Theistic school proposes another kind of morality. The insight on morality of those who regard the universe as originating from an eternal Intelligent Will and the human being as a Divine breath, is wittingly or unwittingly also different from that of those who regard nothing in the universe but darkness, accident, blind following, purposeless motions, and pointless actions. And basically, some schools of thought are in deadlock on the issue of ethics and morality. If God wills, we will discuss later on whether morality can have any concept or meaning – in whatever way it is defined – according to some schools of thought, or not. And this is a question in itself today: are morality and monotheism mutually independent? Can morality minus monotheism or minus God be able to exist in the world or not?

Now, we shall begin our discussion on definite questions among the people; we shall begin from the admitted opinions; from the issues on which all schools of morality have consensus of opinion. Later on, we will move forward to the question on whether we can be able to unravel a philosophy of ethics or not. And then [we will also address the question:] what is the Islamic system of morality? This is a very urgent and necessary subject; that is, we should exactly know our own Islamic system of morality.

The Holy Prophet (S)[1] has a statement which I have not seen in Shī'ah corpus *ḥadīth* in a popular expression I shall quote it. The Sunnī scholars (*'ulamā'*) have included it in their corpus of *ḥadīth* but it exists in the Shī'ah corpus of *ḥadīth* with the same meaning and only a slight difference. The popular statement is when the Holy Prophet (S) said:

بُعِثْتُ لِاُتَمِّمَ مَكارِمَ الْاَخْلاقِ.

> *"I was sent so as to perfect excellent pattern of morality."*

That is to say, "I have been chosen and sent so as to perfect excellent pattern of behaviour or *mukarramatī*[2] morality." The word *takmīl* and *tatmīm* implies that the Prophet (S) wants to say that "I am not only the Seal and Final Prophet; I have also the mission of perfecting

1. The abbreviation, "ṣ", stands for the Arabic invocative phrase, *ṣallallāhu 'alayhi wa ālihi wa sallam* (may God's blessings and peace be upon him and his progeny), which is mentioned after the name of the Holy Prophet Muḥammad (ṣ). [Trans.]
2. The word *mukarramat* is full of meanings and implications. When we reach the point of dealing with the criteria for Islamic ethics, we shall discuss this word which is a principal pivot in Islamic ethics.

excellent pattern of behaviour of the people. Each of the previous prophets had also the same mission. They have also come for the same purpose, but I have come in order to finish the unfinished business they had. *Khatm al-nubuwwah* (being the Seal of Prophethood) means that I have come at a time and circumstances when whatever is to be conveyed to mankind through Divine revelation (*waḥy*) must be conveyed by me. I have come in order to perfect or complete the excellent pattern of behaviour." This is the expression which Ghazālī[1] and his likes have narrated as a *ḥadīth*. We have searched for the exact expression in the Shī'ah corpus of *ḥadīth*. I have not found an identical wording but its paraphrase exists in our books of *ḥadīth*. In a *ḥadīth* recording in *Wasā'il al-Shī'ah*,[2] the Holy Prophet (S) said:

---

1. Ḥujjat al-Islām Abū Ḥāmid Muḥammad ibn Ghazālī al-Ṭūsī (1058 – 1111) is recognized by many as a great Sunnī theologian and authority. Starting his religious life as orthodox, Ghazālī soon turned to Sufism. He spent many years wandering from place to place before eventually going to Baghdad to preach and teach, where he composed what many see as his masterpiece, *Iḥyā' 'Ulūm al-Dīn* (The Revivification of the Sciences of Religion). His other well-known works include *Fātiḥat al-'Ulūm; Taḥāfut al-Falāsifah; Al-Iqtiṣād fī 'l-I'tiqād* and *Kīmyā-ye Sa'ādat* (The Alchemy of Happiness) which is an abridged *Iḥyā' 'Ulūm al-Dīn* for Persian readers. [Trans.]
2. Compiled by Shaykh Muḥammad ibn Ḥasan al-Ḥurr al-'Āmilī (d. 1693), *Wasā'il al-Shī'ah* is one of the best collections of traditions (*ḥadīths*) ever compiled in recent centuries. Including traditions quoted in the Four Books (*kutub al-arba'ah*) and in many other *ḥadīth* collections, it comprises more than fifty-one books from *Kitāb al-Ṭahārah* to *Kitāb al-Diyāt*. [Trans.]

عَلَيكُمْ بِمَكارِمِ الْاخلاقِ فَانَّ رَبِّي بَعَثَني بِها.

> *"May you have the excellent pattern of behaviour as I have sent for it."*

In our traditions, it is said in the above expression. Of course, there is no contradiction if ever the Prophet had said so in both ways on different occasions.

Natural action

Now, in general, what is *akhlāq* or, in the expression of the Noble Messenger, *akhlāq mukarramatī*? From where should we begin? We have said that we shall begin from the admitted opinions and indisputable facts. For the meanwhile, we are not concerned with doubtful issues which one school of thought may regard as 'moral' while another school of thought may not regard the same as 'moral'. What is certain is that most of the human actions are natural actions and they are called 'natural' and not 'moral'. In these actions, morality is not applied. For example, a person would leave this session and go home; he feels hungry so he eats; he feels thirsty and he takes a drink; he feels tired and he lies down and goes asleep. These actions are called natural actions; that is, common actions. Human nature necessitates such things. A child feels hungry and she suffers from this feeling; she also knows that eating food brings joy and comfort. In order to end this suffering and experience joy and pleasure, she eats food. When she grows up and realizes the benefit of food, she knows that her wellbeing and life depends on this food. If she does not take any food, her wellbeing and life will be in danger. So are sleeping and hundreds of other actions. All actions in life which a person does so as to live a normal life are 'natural' actions. A merchant is busy in his trading office, engaging in transactions in order to gain profits. This is a normal and natural activity for a person, and it stems from the desire for gain or profit and fear of loss which a person wants for himself. When a person feels sick, he consults a doctor in order to prevent any loss and harm, because getting sick is a loss. This is also a normal and natural activity in the level of animal actions.

To this extent, these actions are not worthy of praise or appreciation such that we say, "Bravo to so-and-so for eating food after getting hungry! Bravo to so-and-so for sleeping after getting tired! Bravo to so-and-so for looking for money!" Neither are they condemnable, reproachable and despicable such that we say, "Woe to so-and-so for eating food after getting hungry! Woe to so-and-so for taking a drink after getting thirsty!" Here, neither appreciation (bravos and hoorays) nor condemnation [is applicable]. None of them exists here. They are but natural and normal activities. Just as [natural] animal actions are worthy of neither appreciation nor condemnation, man's natural actions do not necessitate appreciation and praise, or condemnation and reproach so long as they are done with the natural motives and without any other purpose. We call them 'natural' actions. Traits or attributes which are also related to natural actions are 'natural' traits or attributes. Human desires which are also related to these actions such as desire for eating food, desire for sleeping, desire for drinking water, and sexual desire are 'natural' desires, and they are neither appreciable nor condemnable; they are normal; that is, they are in a normal level, not higher or lower. Ideas or thoughts related to such actions are also exactly like that; they are normal and 'natural' ideas. They thoughts are neither worthy of appreciation and praise, nor worthy of condemnation and reproach.

The human being, however, is uniquely such [that he has moral actions] and these are things which do not exist in non-humans. As such, if the human being is defined as a moral animal, this definition is not wrong; that is, moral action is a human action just as immoral action is also related to the human being. An animal can be able to do neither a moral action nor an immoral action. It is always in that normal level it has.

Moral Action

Now, what is a moral action? Its first indicator is that it necessitates appreciation, praise and acknowledgment; it requires honour and kudos. Everyone who can see or hear honours such an action, the trait which is the origin of that action as well as the idea which is related to it. The doer will be appreciated, praised or acknowledged. He will be told, "Kudos!" Let me cite an example. First of all, I will not cite stories of religious-moral figures, because such things exist in the human conscience of the whole humanity, including those irreligious persons.

Peter the Great[1] – who was the Russian Tsar that brought glory to Russia approximately two hundred years ago and perhaps a contemporary of Nādir[2] – is considered one of the great personalities in the world and even the current communists hold him in high esteem. In his *Histoire Générale* (a series of textbooks in history), Albert Malet[3] writes that this man died at the age of 53 due to pneumonia. In winter, in a month of January, he was standing near a river. A boat with some people riding on it was passing by. He sensed that the boat was sinking and there was nobody else there to rescue the passengers. He immediately threw himself into the river in order to rescue them. (I am not sure whether he succeeded in rescuing them or not.) As a result of this action, he was afflicted with pneumonia and died.

Now, what could anyone who hears it say? This person could have done one of two things. One was to be an

---

1. Peter the Great or Peter I (1672 - 1725) ruled the Tsardom of Russia and later the Russian Empire from 1682 until his death, whose cultural revolution and reforms made a lasting impact on Russia, and many institutions of Russian government traced their origins to his reign. [Trans.]
2. Nādir Shāh Afshār the Great (1688 or 1698-1747) ruled as Shāh of Iran (1736-47) and was the founder of the Afsharid dynasty. [Trans.]
3. Albert Malet (1864 – 1915) was a French historian and author of scholarly textbooks. [Trans.]

indifferent onlooker – to see whether the boat would really sink or not, with this idea in mind: "Shall I throw myself on water in this winter and frost in Russian winter at that in order to rescue others? Shall I endanger myself just to save some people? Why should I do this? On what basis should I do this?" Another option was to endanger himself and unconditionally do so without those questions – as he actually did. Anyone who would hear it will say that it was a humanitarian and moral act. This action was above the common level; it deserves appreciation. Anyone who would see or hear it will say, "Bravo! Hooray! What a man! He sacrificed himself in order to save others." This will be considered a 'moral' act.

Some years ago, our esteemed friend and great scholar, the late [Muḥammad Ibrāhīm] Āyatī [died in a car accident]. The cause of death of this man was that he was driving a car when a dog suddenly crossed the street. As he avoided hitting the dog, he bumped on something else and he died. If it were somebody else, he would just hit the dog. Now, anyone who would hear this story of a person who would not be pleased at endangering the life of an animal will appreciate the act. He will say, "Bravo! Kudos!" An action which is worthy of appreciation is called 'moral'. This act belongs to a lofty level.

Certain stories are narrated. This story has been written along with the same story of Peter [the Great] by one of our friends in the introduction to his book, and it is an interesting story. He says, "One day I was talking with a materialist person. I have cited these allegories to him and told him, 'How could these be reconciled with the logic of materialism?' and he gave no reply." He wrote that one day a young man was coming by walking from a far distance in a desert while he was extremely hungry, thirsty, tired, and his feet were wounded. Some individuals spread their table-spread near the highway. Just in order to survive, he told them, "I am hungry; please give me a morsel of your food." At that time, a dog was also littering around with the expectation that they would throw it some food. They told him, "We will throw some food over there. Anyone of you – either you or the dog – that gets it first will be his or its." They threw some bread and meat. Both he and the dog tried to get it first and he got it first. As he was taking the food, he was that the dog remained there standing and staring at him. He threw the food to the dog. That is, he gave preference to the dog over himself. "I am hungry and this dog is also hungry. As a human, I sacrifice myself for this dog which is an animal." Here religion and religious belief are not an issue either.

What can anyone who witnesses such an incident think and say? Will he take this act as something above normal or natural level, or not? Can he consider this act [just] 'natural'? It cannot be reconciled with the logic of nature. The logic of nature dictates that you have to strive and exert efforts for your own self. In the logic of nature, the centre is the 'I'; the centre is the 'self' – 'myself'. I work for myself. It is me. 'M' stands for myself. But here [in the story], the 'self' does not exist; what exists is other-than-myself. I prefer the non-self other than myself. What this act can be called? It is so clear that it is an act worthy of appreciation, praise and acknowledgment. Even someone, who could not do it in such a situation and has no determination to put it into action, will appreciate the one who did it, saying: "I am not such a man but I do salute and appreciate anyone who would do it."

In one of the battles fought by the early Muslims, some Muslims were lying on the ground wounded. As you know, whether the weather is hot or cold, a wounded person would feel much thirsty as blood is coming out of his body and he will immediately water and produce his own blood. One person came to these wounded companions. As he sensed that they were very thirsty, he immediately brought water to one of them. The wounded pointed his finger to another wounded companion. As the rescuing person approached the second wounded person, this one pointed to a third wounded companion. As he approached the third one, the latter would die due to thirst. As he approached the second one, this one would also expire. As he approached the first wounded person, this one would also breathe his last. The water was not able to quench the thirst of anyone of the three. In the words of the Qur'an, each of them offered self-sacrifice:

﴿ وَيُؤْثِرُونَ عَلَى أَنفُسِهِمْ وَلَوْ كَانَ بِهِمْ خَصَاصَةٌ ﴾

> But they prefer [the Immigrants] to themselves, though poverty be their own lot. (59:9)

That is, while almost in utmost need, they prefer others over themselves.

Now, what will you call this? Whatever you want to call it – morality or whatever – it is an appreciable act. No one can afford not to appreciate it, acknowledge it, or in the words of the Noble Messenger (S), honour it. It is honouring and giving it high regard.

Philosophy Behind Servanthood

As you can see, someone has a slave; on the basis of outward economic relationship, the former is the master while the latter is the servant. Yet, the behaviour of the former toward the latter is far better than that of the person toward his close friend. The latter, on the other hand, would prefer his being servant over emancipation. He would go to the market along with his master and they would buy clothes together. The master would give the new garment to the servant who was a young man while taking himself the old one. He would say, "I am an old man and you are young. The new and more elegant garment is more suitable for you than me who is old." He would give him a better food. He would provide him more comfort. Practically, he would not think of any difference between himself and his servant. The servant, in turn, would feel that for being a servant, he was actually student in the school of this person. This servanthood is only a period of studies in a school in which he is acquiring knowledge and perfection.

Basically, this is exactly the philosophy behind servanthood (*'ubūdiyyah*) in Islam; it is not economic slavery. Servanthood means a compulsory learning; it is an unintentional training. 'Alī ibn Abī Ṭālib (A.S.)[1] would go to the market along with Qanbar, his boy attendant. He would buy two sets of shirts and give the new one to him and keep the old one for himself. What do you call this act?

Fāṭimah al-Zahrā' (S.A.) behaved with his lady attendant Fiḍḍah in such a way that up to the last moments of her life in which she lived in emancipation, the glorious days of this lady were the few years of her service to Fāṭimah al-Zahrā' (S.A.) who considered her a sister in her own house. She divided the house chores between them. One day, she would work herself while her attendant would take a rest while the next day, she would take a rest while her attendant would do the house chores. Who prevented her from having no work every day while the attendant having all the works? Yet, she could not accept this arrangement. What was acceptable to her was that "I am a human and so are you. I can never accept that you work all days while I am idle; hardship is for you while comfort is for me. If ever there were hardship, it must be shouldered by both of us equally. If ever there were comfort, it must also be shared by both of us equally.

---

1. The abbreviation, "'*a*" stands for the Arabic invocative phrase, *'alayhi's-salām*, *'alayhim'us-salām*, or *'alayhā's-salām* (may peace be upon him/them/her), which is mentioned after the names of the prophets, angels, Imāms from the Prophet's progeny, and saints (A.S.). [Trans.]

What can this act be called? Whatever you call it, it is an act which is worthy of appreciation, praise and honour. Can it be reconciled with the logic of self-interest and desire for profit? No. It cannot be compatible with such logic. Even now, humanity is yet to discover the logic behind these acts so much so that the Europeans – of course, their statements are wrong – have said that 'moral' acts are illogical; a person does it while it cannot be reconciled with logic. A moral act is incompatible with logic. What logic demands is the desire for profit. These (moral acts) are acts which are illogical, or if ever there are very respectful, they would say, "These acts are beyond logic. This is a euphemistic equivalent of "These are incompatible with logic." It is not that these are incompatible with logic; rather, these are compatible with higher and loftier logic, and not that these are compatible with logic.

We have heard that in relation to others, there is such a man who would say, "It is unbecoming for me to fill my stomach while there is an empty stomach in Ḥijāz[1] or Yamāmah[2] – and not in the neighbourhood but in far-flung places. Since there is a hungry stomach in those

1. Ḥijāz: the region in Western Arabia bordering the Red Sea that includes Ṭā'if, Mecca and Medina. [Trans.]

2. Yamāmah: an ancient district covering the eastern section of the plateau of Najd in modern-day Saudi Arabia, or sometimes more specifically, the now-extinct ancient village of Jaww al-Yamāmah, near Al-Kharj, after which the rest of the region was named. [Trans.]

places, I cannot afford to fill my stomach here. It behoves me not at all; it is painful; for me it is an affliction that in one corner of the world my stomach is full while there is an empty stomach in another corner of the world."

هَيهاتَ انْ يغْلِبَني هَواي وَ يقودَني جَشَعي الي تَخَيرِ الاطْعِمَةِ وَ لَعَلَّ بِالْحِجازِ اوِ الْيمامَةِ مَنْ لا طَمَعَ لَهُ فِي الْقُرْصِ وَ لا عَهْدَ لَهُ بِالشِّبَعِ! اوْ ابيتَ مِبْطاناً وَ حَوْلي بُطونٌ غَرْثي وَ اكبادٌ حَرّي، اوْ اكونَ كَما قالَ الْقائِلُ:

وَحَسْبُكَ داءً أنْ تَبيتَ بِبِطْنَةٍ وَحَوْلَكَ اكبادٌ تَحِنُّ الَي الْقِدِّ

"It cannot be that my passions lead me and greed take me to choosing good meals while in the Ḥijāz or in Yamāmah there may be people who have no hope of getting bread or who do not have a full meal. Shall I lie with a satiated belly while around me there may be hungry bellies and thirsty livers? Or shall I be as the poet has said? 'It is enough for you to have a disease that you lie with your belly full while around you people may be badly yearning for dried leather.'"[1]

He was sitting in Kūfah. It was reported to him that his representative and governor in Baṣrah attended a party of one of the young noble men of Baṣrah. Was there unlawful (*ḥarām*) food out of unlawful wealth in that party? There was none. Was there any wine served in that

1. Imām 'Alī, *Nahj al-Balāghah*, Fayḍ al-Islām Arrangement, Letter 45, p. 970. This letter was addressed to 'Uthmān ibn Ḥunayf al-Anṣārī who was Imām 'Alī's (A.S.) Governor of Baṣrah. [Trans.]

party? There was none. Was there any gambling involved there? There was none. Was there any playing and amusement there? There was none. Was there any singing and dancing there? There was none. Then, what was wrong with that party? It is a party exclusively intended for the rich and noble, and had nothing to do with the poor and indigent. When he received the report [about the party], he got furious in Kūfah. He wrote a letter which is a source of pride of humanity and not only of us Muslims. It is one of the sources of pride of humanity [that] a person could speak so noble, lofty and elegant and reach the zenith of humanity!

> يَابْنَ حُنَيْف، فَقَدْ بَلَغَنِي أَنَّ رَجُلاً مِنْ فِتْيَةِ أَهْلِ الْبَصْرَةِ دَعَاكَ إِلى مَأْدُبَة، فَأَسْرَعْتَ إِلَيْهَا، تُسْتَطَابُ لَكَ الأَلْوَانُ، وَتُنْقَلُ إِلَيْكَ الْجِفَانُ، وَمَا ظَنَنْتُ أَنَّكَ تُجِيبُ إِلى طَعَامِ قَوْم، عَائِلُهُمْ مَجْفُوٌّ وَغَنِيُّهُمْ مَدْعُوٌّ.
>
> "O Ibn Ḥunayf, I have come to know that a young man of Basrah invited you to a feast and you leapt towards it. Foods of different colours were being chosen for you and big bowls were being given to you. I never thought that you would accept the feast of a people who turn out the beggars and invite the rich."[1]

It is here that he expressed the pain in his heart. Part of it is what I have read to you. He then said:

---

1. *Ibid.*

أَأَقْنَعُ مِنْ نَفْسِي بِأَنْ يُقَالَ: أَمِيرُالْمُؤْمِنِينَ، وَلاَ أُشَارِكُهُمْ فِي مَكَارِهِ الدَّهْرِ

> "Shall I be content with being called *Amīr al-Mu'minīn* (the Commander of the Faithful), although I do not share with the people the hardships of the world?"

Now, let me ask, did and does such a thing exist in the world. Well, [let us assume] not to this extent but a degree lower. What kind of act is this concern, sympathy and empathy to those who are suffering in the world? Can this be called a 'natural' act? Can this desire be called a 'natural' desire? Can this thought be called a 'natural' thought? Or, it is an act which is a degree higher. All people – even those who have never done such an act in their lives – their conscience would appreciate it. They would say, "We are not like that and we do not have such deeds but we do appreciate and praise the one who does it." The loftier the act, the higher will be the appreciation, praise and acknowledgment it deserves. Then it will reach a point when all people would appreciate him:

﴿ إِنَّ الَّذِينَ آمَنُوا وَ عَمِلُوا الصَّالِحَاتِ سَيَجْعَلُ لَهُمُ الرَّحْمَٰنُ وُدًّا ﴾

> Indeed those who have faith and do righteous deeds—the All-beneficent will endear them [to His creation]. (19:96)

The Qur'an states that God endears those who have faith and do righteous deeds to the people. God's act is not without wisdom. The reward He gives for doing an act has nothing to do with [this endearment] in the hearts of the people; rather, these are those who are so good and noble.

God has also created the human hearts with such nature that they cannot afford not to acknowledge, honour and love virtues, nobilities and good deeds.

When Prophet Ibrāhīm (Abraham) (A.S.) reconstructed the *Ka'bah* and left there for the first time [his wife] Ḥājar and their infant Ismā'īl (A.S.), his supplication is the following:

﴿ رَبَّنَا إِنِّي أَسْكَنْتُ مِنْ ذُرِّيَّتِي بِوَادٍ غَيْرِ ذِي زَرْعٍ عِنْدَ بَيْتِكَ الْمُحَرَّمِ رَبَّنَا لِيُقِيمُوا الصَّلَاةَ فَاجْعَلْ أَفْئِدَةً مِنَ النَّاسِ تَهْوِي إِلَيْهِمْ ﴾

> O Lord! I have settled part of my descendants in a barren valley, by Your sacred House, our Lord, that they may maintain the prayer. So make the hearts of a part of the people fond of them. (14:37)

The Imām (A.S.) also said:

نَحْنُ دَعْوَةُ ابراهيم.

> "We are the [accepted] supplication of Ibrāhīm."

Prophet Ibrāhīm (A.S.) wanted the hearts to be the locus of monotheism (*tawḥīd*) and sense of humanity (*insāniyyah*). Even those whose sense of humanity is imperfect, flawed or low cannot afford not to appreciate and pay respect to a noble, perfect and good-mannered person; so are his enemy. Sometimes, a person compels himself; that is, he compels his conscience to conceal his enemy's merits, but his conscience, discernment and intellect remain; he would always conceal [the enemy's merits]. Then, we can hear or see that suddenly his conscience takes this stern enemy out of the veils of all these pretensions and verbally expresses the truth.

Mu'āwiyah's Confession about Imām 'Alī (A.S.)

'Adī ibn Ḥātam – the son of the famous Ḥātam al-Ṭā'ī[1] – became a Muslim during the later part of the life of the Holy Prophet (S). The story of his conversion to Islam is also an interesting story and I have included it in the book *Dāstān-e Rāstān* (*The Narrative of the Veracious*).[2] He was one of those who joined Imām 'Alī (A.S.) and one of the extremely pious and devoted followers of the Imām (A.S.), and he participates in battles on the side of the Imām (A.S.). In the Battle of Ṣiffīn three of his sons, viz. Ṭarīf, Ṭurfah and Ṭārif, attained martyrdom on the side of the Imām (A.S.). He lived for some years after the martyrdom of the Commander of the Faithful (A.S.). One day, he happened to meet Mu'āwiyah. Mu'āwiyah who was one of the most notorious tricksters in the world, as well as hypocrite, wicked and archenemy of the Imām (A.S.), wanted to see what words could upset 'Adī. He wanted to get a word of recantation – even an outward

---

1. Ḥātam al-Ṭā'ī: traditionally the towering example of the pre-Islamic knight who was also a poet and proverbial for his generosity and hospitality. [Trans.]
2. See Murtaḍā Muṭahharī, *The Narrative of the Veracious*, trans. Riḍā Ḥamīdī (Tehran: Department of Translation and Publications, Islamic of Culture and Relations Organization, 1997), vol. 2, "Story 76: Son of Ḥātam," pp. 1-7. [Trans.]

one – from 'Adī against 'Alī. He was thinking that a father whose son was killed – and much more if three sons were killed – would be upset for losing his sons. At least, he would tell himself, "I wished we did not accompany 'Alī; we did not join 'Alī and I would not have lost three sons for the sake of 'Alī." It was this feeling that Mu'āwiyah was thinking that 'Adī had, and through this he hoped he could be able to bring 'Adī to his side. He said, "O 'Adī! "What happened to your three sons, Ṭurayf, Ṭarfah and Ṭarīf?" 'Adī said, "They were martyred in the Battle of Ṣiffīn under the banner of 'Alī." He said, "O 'Adī! 'Alī did not do justice to you. He threw your sons in the mouth of death by sending them to the battlefront and preserved his own sons, Ḥasan and Ḥusayn, in safety." 'Adī replied, "No, it is the opposite. It was me who did not do justice to 'Alī. It is not fair that 'Alī is now buried underground while 'Adī is alive walking on the surface of the earth. I ought to have sacrificed myself for him in his lifetime. Mu'āwiyah saw that he was not getting what he had aimed at. On the other side, he also wanted to hear about the character and life of 'Alī from those who had been nearer to 'Alī and had lived with him day in and day out. He, therefore, asked 'Adī to narrate to him the character of 'Alī as he had seen it. 'Adī asked to be excused, but Mu'āwiyah insisted and then 'Adī said, "By God, 'Alī was the most farsighted and strong man. He talked with righteousness and decided the cases with clarity. He was an ocean of knowledge and wisdom. He hated the worldly pomp and show, and liked the solitude of the night. He wept more (in love of Allah) and thought more (about Allah). In solitude, he scrutinized his own self and pitied about the past. He preferred short clothes and simple life. Among us he was like one of us. If we requested him for anything he granted our request. When we visited him he made us sit near him without keeping any distance. In spite of all this humbleness, his presence was so awe-inspiring that we did not dare utter any words before him. He was so majestic that we could not look at him. When he smiled his teeth appeared like a string of pearls. He respected the honest and pious people and was kind to the indigent. Neither a strong man had any fear of injustice from him, nor did a weak person ever lose hope of his justice. By God, one night I saw him standing in his place of worship when the dark night had engulfed everything; tears were rolling down on his face and beard; he was restless like a snake-bitten person and was weeping like a bereaved man. It seems as if even now I am hearing his voice as he was addressing the world: 'O world! Why do you present yourself toward me and want to lure me? Go and deceive someone else. You will never get a chance with me. I have divorced you thrice after which there is no return. Your pleasure is valueless and your importance insignificant. Alas! The provision is too little; the journey too long and there is no companion'." Hearing these worlds of 'Adī, Mu'āwiyah started crying, then wiping off the tears, he said: "By God, the world is now barren it does not produce the like of 'Alī ibn Abī Ṭālib; he was one of a kind and he passed away."

What is this? This is an appreciation of the world's bitterest enemy to a certain man. What level does this act belong to? It is higher than the common deed of all people and whatever the animals do. This is what they call human act, moral deed, moral action, and moral trait. 'Alī's act is called moral act. 'Alī's inclinations and feelings are called moral inclinations and feelings. 'Alī's thinking is called moral thinking. Can the humanity be able [to negate] these?

There is a story of Imām 'Alī (A.S.), among many others, which you might have heard a lot and which I have included in *Dāstān-e Rāstān*.[1] One of our friends told me that he lent a copy of the book *Dāstān-e Rāstān* to a certain leftist and communist. According to him, when the borrower returned the book, he said, "The truth is that the last story [of the first volume] made me shed tears." This is what a communist says. The story is more or less as follows:

Imām 'Alī (A.S.) would take a walk in the streets and alleys. He would not completely rely on the guards on duty. He himself would occasionally come to the scene and directly witness [the state of affairs]. He would observe things which would sometimes upset him – why is it so? One day he saw a lady carrying water bouget on

1. See *The Narrative of the Veracious*, vol. 1, "Story 75: The Unknown," pp. 176-178. [Trans.]

her shoulder. He told himself, "Why is it that a lady would carry a water bouget herself? There must be something unusual." He would not tell any guard to follow her and know the matter. He would rather go himself but he wanted to know the truth of the matter. He would not come to inquest or cross-question her while carrying a heavy load. He would come forward first and then greet her, "Lady, will you allow me to help you and bring this water bouget to your house?" She replied, "Very good." He was the caliph of the time. He would carry water bouget on his shoulder but nobody was aware of his feeling at that moment. (Now, if anyone like us does it, he will continuously praise himself; the opposite is true to him.) He would carry it until the lady returns home. He would know her residence. He would put the water bouget on the ground and then with utmost respect, he would say, "O woman! It is obvious that there is no man in the house; otherwise, at least you would not have done it yourself." She replied, "Yes, my husband, so-and-so, was killed on the side of 'Alī ibn Abī Ṭālib in the Battle of Ṣiffīn. After him, it is me and some orphans [that remain here]. I have no option but to do the works both inside and outside the house, and no one else attends to us."

It is written that Imām 'Alī (A.S.) left and he returned home. But he remained sleepless that night. He would lie on this side and that side like someone who has a 41 degrees [centigrade] fever. He was waiting for the morning. The following day, again he did not delegate to anybody else but he himself did it. He would get a basket and put some money, meat, date fruits and flour on it, and he would hurriedly bring it to that house. He knocked the door. The woman asked, “Who is this?” He answered, “It is me, the same Muslim who was here yesterday. I bring presents to these orphans. I would like to come in if you allow me.” When the woman felt that a stranger man was attending to her while ‘Alī who was the responsible was supposed to do so, she said, “May God take ‘Alī from our hearts! Why ‘Alī is not attending to us?” Imām ‘Alī (A.S.) did not introduce himself. He sensed that the children were hungry. He immediately roasted the meat and served it to them. He also fed them with the date fruits. He then told the lady, “O woman! Either you attend to the children while I am kneading the flour and baking it, or I attend to the children while you do it yourself.” She replied, “I could make bread better. You attend to the children.” He said, “I will light the oven myself.” He lighted the oven himself. Then he started feeding the children and playing with them, while always saying: “O children! Forgive ‘Alī. Forgive his shortcomings. ‘Alī fell short in attending to you.” The poor woman also did not know who he was. While Imām ‘Alī (A.S.) was lighting the oven, a lady neighbour would pay a visit and see that there was a man there and she knew him. She exclaimed! “O woman! Who is this man that you have brought here?!” She said, “He is a good man. He saw me in the alley and carried himself the water bouget up here.

Today, he has also brought some money and foods for us." The neighbour said, "Do you know who this man is that you brought to serve you? He is 'Alī ibn Abī Ṭālib, the caliph." This woman apologized to him but the Imām (A.S.) said, "It is me that should ask apology and forgiveness from you."

A moral and humane action is this. That is, it is an act which is above that of the natural actions of a person.

The movement of Ḥusayn ibn 'Alī ibn Abī Ṭālib (A.S.) is a moral and humane movement. That is, it is for the salvation of humanity. (We say that it is for the sake of Islam. Islam is for the sake of what? It is for the sake of saving humanity.) It is for this reason that it is sacred, noble and extremely worthy of appreciation.

There was a man who, upon seeing the enemies, felt that they were thirsty and he immediately said [to his companions], "Open the water skins and give water to their horses and also give water to the men." And he would do similar things there...

Sending Off the Ahl al-Bayt (A.S.) to Kūfah

It is the twelfth day of Muḥarram and it is the second night of mourning of the *Ahl al-Bayt* (A.S.). It is the second night that they are mourning. According to the narrations (*riwāyāt*) on the tragedy (*maqātil*), on the night similar to this night, they (surviving members of the *Ahl al-Bayt* (A.S.)) were immediately sent off by these headsmen toward Kūfah by letting them ride on unsaddled camels. These [headsmen] were not concerned with their sleep, food or comfort, for they have to arrive on time in Kūfah where there was an organize program and the city was embellished in celebration of the victory of the Muslim caliph over a foreign enemy which staged an insurrection. On one hand, they had separately sent off the decapitated heads [to Kūfah]. Now, their only concern was to let the captives arrive on time [in Kūfah]. God knows what transpired to the members of the Household of the Prophet (S).

On the afternoon of *'Āshūrā'* (10th day of Muḥarram) when the scourge came to an end and Imām al-Ḥusayn (A.S.) was the last person to attain martyrdom, ['Umar] ibn Sa'd committed certain acts. His first act was this – I do not want at all to mention this hideous and filthy act of theirs – that act of that perpetually and eternally accursed was that he said, "I know that there is no suffering for a person after death, but I swore beforehand to do it anyway." The other one is that he ordered the tents of Imām al-Ḥusayn (A.S.) to be set on fire. Of course, beforehand they had rushed to the tents to loot.

Another thing which we regarded as extremely necessary to do was the burial of their dead ones. Their dead ones were many. It was the afternoon of *'Āshūrā'* and they stayed there on the evening and the following morning until noon of that day – that is, until noontime of the 11th day like today – and they buried their dead ones and they left unburied the pure bodies of the martyrs, and it was better that they just left these unburied lest their filthy hands could have touched on these bodies. As they finished doing these things, he ordered the decapitation of the holy heads and sent off [to Kūfah] another set of heads. He also ordered the captives to mount the camels. They came forward to let them ride on. Since a number of these captives were women and children, Zaynab (A.S.) who was then the caravan leader ordered that no one has the right to come forward to let them ride on: "If we are supposed to mount [the camels], we will do so by ourselves. The non-*maḥram*[1] men must go ahead." When the caravan was about to set off, said Sayyīd ibn Ṭāwūs in his *Al-Luhūf*, thus:

وَ قُلْنَ

"And they (feminine plural) said..."

He does not say, "Only Zaynab or Sakīnah said; rather, the women said..." It was like a collective request:

وَقُلْنَ بِحَقِّ اللّهِ الّا ما مَرَرْتُمْ بِنا عَلي مَصْرَعِ الْحُسَيْنِ.

That is to say, "By Allah, as you are now sending us off to Kūfah, we ask you to bring us to the battlefield so that we could see our [fallen] loved ones for the last time."[2] They granted the request. When they passed by the battlefield and the captives saw the pure corpses, they dismounted and threw themselves on the ground, shouting, with the exception of [Imām] Zayn al-'Ābidīn

---

1. *Maḥram*: one with whom marriage is prohibited (usually because of close kinship). [Trans.]
2. Ibn Ṭāwūs , *Al-Luhūf*, 55.

(A.S.) who was sick and whose feet were enchained. Each of them tightly embraced the corpse of their loved ones. Each of them was near the corpse of their loved ones. Zaynab who had lost seven brothers and a son in Karbalā' had only one beloved and dear one. Now, in the midst of the swords of those who were killed, the stones and clods, God knows why she felt! It is said:

گلي گم كرده‌ام مي‌جويم او را   به هر گل مي‌رسم مي‌بويم او را

I have lost a flower [and] I search for it.
I kiss it whenever I come across a flower.

She searched here and there until she found the corpse of [Imām] al-Ḥusayn (A.S.) and she threw herself on this body... It is here that it is narrated that Zaynab (A.S.) began reciting a monody. She recited a monody that brought tears to friends and foes alike. Even those headsmen wept. She raised her voice saying, thus:

بِأبِي الْمَهْمومُ حَتّي قَضي بِأبِي الْعَطْشانُ حَتّي مَضي

May I be your ransom, O father! We grieve for you passed away!
May I be your ransom, O father! We are thirsty for you left us!

ولا حول ولا قوة الّا باللّه العلي العظيم وصلّي اللّه علي محمد وآله الطاهرين باسمک العظيم الاعظم الاعز الاجلّ الاكرم يا اللّه....

"And there is neither power nor might except that of Allah, the Exalted and Mighty, and may Allah's benediction be upon Muḥammad and his pure progeny. By Your Greatest,

> Paramount, Most Cherished, Glorified, and Honourable Name, O Allah..."

O God! Bestow our hearts with the radiant light of faith. Let us know the truths of Islam. Make us real followers of the lofty teachings of Islam. Endow us with sublime morality and noble traits. Make pure our intentions. Shower our deceased one with Your mercy.

O God! Make us be grateful of Islam and the Qur'an. Make us be appreciative of the Prophet and [his] progeny. Grant our legitimate wishes.

وعجّل في فرج مولانا صاحب الزمان.

> And may He expedite the advent of our chief, the Master of the Time.

Chapter 2: Natural Action and Moral Action

﴿ خُذِ الْعَفْوَ وَأْمُرْ بِالْعُرْفِ وَأَعْرِضْ عَنِ الْجَاهِلِينَ ﴾

> Adopt [a policy of] excusing [the faults of people], bid what is right, and turn away from the ignorant. (7:199)

We have said earlier that some human actions are called 'moral' in contrast to the usual and natural actions. This question comes to the fore: what is morality and what does it mean by an act to be called 'moral'? How could a human action be called 'moral'? And we have said that although initially it seems that this question is very simple and has an easy answer, when we deeply deal with the subject, we will see that the answer to this question on the secret behind 'moralness' is not that simple; rather, it is one of the most problematic intellectual questions and most complex philosophical issues, and for the past thousands of years up to now, the philosophers throughout the world have not yet arrived at a consensus on it. Instead of stating first the criteria for morality in the schools of ethics and say, for example, what Plato has said about the criterion for morality; what Aristotle has said about the criterion for morality; what Ghazālī has said about the criterion for morality; what each of the European philosophers in the modern world has said [about the criterion for morality]; instead of these, first we shall mention very clear simple cases and then attempt to interpret them, for prior to clarification of the cases of a moral action, engaging in interpretation is not that helpful. Earlier, we have mentioned indisputable cases of a moral action such as examples of self-sacrifice (that is, giving preference to others over oneself and prioritizing others' comfort over one's comfort) both in the Muslim and non-Muslim histories and biographies, as well as examples of another case of morality; that is, sympathy to those who are suffering. Now, we still want to deal with other similar examples. All these we are doing so that the subject could be completely clarified. Before mentioning these examples, in order for you to understand the importance of the subject, it is necessary for me to mention one point.

The Value of Moral Action

We can see that the difference between the actions which we call 'moral' and the common actions is that the former is worthy of appreciation, praise and acknowledgment. In other words, human beings give value to such actions. The difference between a moral action and a natural action is that the former has a value in the conscience of every person. It is a valuable and precious action, and a person believes in a sort of cost for this action. The cost for which he believes in is not like the cost or value for a labourer's work he believes in, which it is said to be creating a 'material value' and acquiring right of an equivalent monetary amount or goods for the work being done. It is rather a kind of value which is above these values and cannot be exchanged with money and material goods. The action of the combatant who sacrificed himself for the sake of others is valuable, but its value is unlike material values in that we could say, for example, that the value of every hour of work of so-and-so is 25 *tūmāns*,[1] that of an architect is 80 *tūmāns*, that of an engineer is 150 *tūmāns*, and that of another person is 500 *tūmāns* and even much higher. It is said, for instance, that so-and-so came and shut down the oil well, and every hour of his work is valued at 5,000 *tūmāns*. After all, these are convertible to material values.

Moral actions have values and costs in the human mind or conscience. They are valuable but their kind of value is different from those material values in whatever amount of value. It is a value which is above material values. The examples of Imām 'Alī (A.S.) we have mentioned are

1. *Tūmān*: every *tūmān* is equivalent to ten Iranian *rials*. Although this monetary unit is unofficial, this is widely used in practice due to the continuing devaluation of Iranian rials in the foreign exchange market. [Trans.]

things which we cannot say that if we evaluate them, they are worth such millions of *tūmāns* or such milliards of dollar. These cannot be converted into *tūmān* or dollar. Of course, they have value or cost but their type of value is different from those values.

After proving that there are human actions which have certain value or cost whose type is different from that of material values, inevitably this question comes to the fore: how can these values be justified? That is, on the basis of which philosophy or school of thought that we can justify these values and costs for moral actions of a person? In other words, which school of thought could be able to interpret, justify and confirm the moral value of a human action? Are all schools of thought capable of explaining such actions? Is the school of thought capable? All schools of thought are not capable. For the meantime, I do not want to elaborate on this subject. I have pointed this out so as to prepare your mind to the issue of which school of thought is capable of explaining and which school of thought is incapable. Some of the schools of thought that are incapable of explaining are frank enough. They openly acknowledge it. Neither are they shamed of [this confession of inability]. They deny [morality] and say, "Morality is nonsensical at all. Doing a moral action is a product of naivety. An intelligent person does not pursue any moral action; he is in pursuit of happiness and enjoyment. With the exception of profit and pleasure, nothing is logical in this world. Again, this is good. At least it says, "I have a school of thought whose outcome is this." The worldview, philosophy and intellectual foundation of some schools of thought, however, give such an outcome; that is, it reaches such a point, but they do not openly acknowledge it, but instead say, "We also believe in moral values and value sense of humanity." But with which school of thought [they have such a belief]?! These are not compatible with the foundation to which you rely. At any rate, we will discuss this subject later.

Now, we shall deal with other examples of the moralness of some actions.

Forgiveness and clemency

This is a separate issue. It is thus stated in a Prophetic tradition (*ḥadīth*):

> ثَلاثٌ مِنْ مَكارِمِ الْأخْلاقِ: تَصِلُ مَنْ قَطَعَك وَتُعْطي مَنْ حَرَمَك وَتَعْفو عَمَّنْ ظَلَمَك.
>
> "Three of the noble traits are the following: (1) to establish relation with whomever severs relationship with you, (2) to be kind to whoever deprives you, and (3) to forgive whoever oppresses you."[1]

There is someone who always commits offenses, misdemeanours or mistakes against you. Of course, some of the actions here are related to your person while

1. Ḥusayn ibn 'Alī ibn Shu'ba Ḥarrānī, *Tuḥaf al-'Uqūl 'an Āl al-Rasūl*.

others are related to the society. For example, someone kills another person. This act has criminal as well as societal dimension. The argument there is that the said action has no connection to the society and it does not create any right for the society. Someone falsely accuses you [of something], lies to you, backbites you, and does similar things, but he does so from his personal and individual capacity and not his societal capacity. You excuse and forgive him. He asks forgiveness and you forgive him; you exonerate him. This act [of yours] is also regarded as a moral act; it is above common acts, and it is a kind of heroic act.

Gratitude and Loyalty

Someone is kind and does something good to you. You reaction to him may be one of the two. One is that after knowing that he got over his own difficulties, you would disregard him, forget him and not pay attention to him. Another one is that he would be grateful to him the rest of your life, never forgetting his goodness and thus you will always to indebted and loyal to him. Even after twenty years when you happen to meet him in need of help, you would immediately extend your hand on the basis of this passage:

﴿ هَلْ جَزَاءُ الإِحْسَانِ إِلا الإِحْسَانُ ﴾

> Is the requital of goodness anything but goodness? (55:60)

This in itself is an intrinsic moral principle mentioned

by the Qur'an – that is, one's natural urge to pay goodness with goodness. This is a moral act.

Kindness to Animals

Even the uncleanness of the animals which are unclean in one aspect is not contradictory with being kind to them. For example, due to the microbes in its saliva or in its entire body, we regard the dog as unclean. That is, we treat it the way we behave toward anything with dangerous microbes. This does not contradict the fact that this animal is worthy of our kindness as it is. When a person sees a hungry or thirsty animal, he may be indifferent toward it; another person may attend to it. It is mentioned in a *ḥadīth* that a man was passing by a road. He saw a dog which was almost licking the ground due to extreme thirst. There was a well there. He took a pair of his shoes to use for fetching water and then apparently gave water to the dog with his own hands, thereby quenching its thirst and saving its life. A Divine revelation came to the prophet of his time that God showed gratitude for the act of this man; that is, He acknowledged this act (in the sense that it is accepted by Him):

شَكَرَ اللّٰهُ لَهُ وَ اَدْخَلَهُ الْجَنَّةَ.

> "Allah thanked him and admitted him to paradise."

In other words, God recognized the value of his act; that is, He recognized him in the sense that He rewarded him and admitted him to paradise. It is the same tradition which Sa'dī[1] thus mentions in *Bustān*:

یکي در بیابان سگي تشنه یافت برون از رمق در حیاتش نیافت

A certain one found, in the desert, a thirsty dog;
He found not beyond a spark of life in him.[2]

Sa'dī say, "He made a cap-bucket" but the *ḥadīth* mentions that he made a shoe-bucket.

کله دلو کرد آن پسندیده کیش
چو حبل اندر آن بست دستار خویش
به خدمت میان بست و بازو گشاد
سگ ناتوان را دمي آب داد
خبر داد پیغمبر از حال مرد
که داور گناهان از او عفو کرد

He of approved religion made a cap-bucket;

---

1. Shaykh Muṣlīḥ al-Dīn Sa'dī (1184-1283) was one of the greatest Persian poets. Born in Shīrāz, he studied Sufi mysticism at the Niẓāmiyyah madrasah at Baghdad, with Shaykh 'Abd al-Qādir al-Jīlānī and with Shahāb al-Dīn Suhrawardī. He made the pilgrimage to Mecca many times and traveled to Central Asia, India, the Seljuq territories in Anatolia, Syria, Egypt, Arabia, Yemen, Abyssinia, and Morocco. His best known works are *Būstān* [Garden] and *Gulistān* [Rose-Garden], also known as *Sa'dī-Nāmeh*. The former is a collection of poems on ethical subjects while the latter is a collection of moral stories in prose. He also wrote a number of odes, and collections of poems known as *Pleasantries*, *Jests* and *Obscenities*. His influence on Persian, Turkish and Indian literatures has been very considerable, and his works were often translated into European languages from the 17th century onward. [Trans.]
2. *Būstān*, Chapter 2 on Beneficence. [Trans.]

Bound to it his own turban, rope-like.
Bound his loins in service; and stretched forth his arm;
Gave a little water to the powerless dog.
The Prophet gave intelligence of the man's state,
Saying: "The Ruler (God) pardoned his sins."[1]

What is the secret here that this act is valuable in the sight of God and His creation?

Statement of Sarī al-Saqaṭī

It is said that one of the mystics named Sarī al-Saqaṭī[2] used to say:

انّي اسْتَغْفِرُ اللّهَ مُنْذُ ثَلاثِينَ سَنَةً لِقَوْلي الْحَمْدُ لِلّهِ.

"Indeed I seek Allah's forgiveness (*istighfār*) for thirty years due to uttering *Al-ḥamdu lillāh* (All praise is due to Allah) [once]."

He was asked, "Why?" He said, "I was a shopkeeper in Baghdad.[3] One day there was news that a certain bazaar in Baghdad caught fire and it was burned. My shop was also located in the said bazaar. I immediately went there to see

---

1. *Ibid.*
2. Shaykh Abū'l-Ḥasan Sarī (al-Sirrī) ibn al-Maghallis al-Saqaṭī (867 C.E.) was one of the famous earlier Sufis of Baghdad, who was a student of Mar'ūf Karkhī, a friend of Bashīr Hāfī and uncle and spiritual master of Junayd of Baghdad. [Trans.]
3. Shaykh Muṣlīḥ al-Dīn Sa'dī has also mentioned this story in his poetry.

whether my shop was burned or not. Someone told me, 'The fire did not spread toward your shop.' I uttered, 'All praise is due to Allah (*al-ḥamdu lillāh*).' Later on, I realized and told myself, 'Are you the only person in the world? After all, forty shops got burned. Your shop was not burned while those of others were burned. *Al-ḥamdu lillāh* means that all praise is due to Allah because my shop was not burned while those of others were burned. I was therefore pleased that their shops caught fire while mine did not.' I told myself:

اوَ لاتَهْتَمُّ لِلْمُسْلِمينَ؟

> '[O Sarī!] Don't you have the Muslims' grief in your heart?'

(It alludes to the Prophet's saying:

مَنْ اصْبَحَ لايهْتَمُّ بِامورِ الْمُسْلِمينَ فَلَيسَ بِمُسْلِمٍ.

> "Whoever wakes up without concern about the Muslims' affairs is not a Muslim.")[1]

"And it has been thirty years now that I seek Allah's forgiveness for that utterance of *Al-ḥamdu lillāh*." What is this?

Du'ā' Makārim al-Akhlāq

Ṣaḥīfah al-Sajjādiyyah[2] is [a collection of] of very reliable

1. Abū Ja'far Muḥammad ibn Ya'qūb al-Kulaynī , *Uṣūl al-Kāfī*, vol. 3, section (*bāb*) 258, 239, *ḥadīth* 5; Shaykh 'Abbās Qummī, *Safīnat al-Biḥār*, vol. 2, 723.
2. The book of fifty-seven prayers known as *Al-Ṣaḥīfah (al-Kāmilah) al-Sajjādiyyah*, which is one of the major Islamic manuals of

(*mu'tabar*) supplications – both in terms of the chain of transmission (*sanad*) and content (*maḍmūn*) – from Zayn al-'Ābidīn 'Alī ibn al-Ḥusayn (A.S.), to which the Shī'ah scholars (*'ulamā'*) from the early period of Islam have given importance. And next to the Qur'an, it is the collection which has been extant in a book form from the later part of the first century and early part of the second century A.H. *Nahj al-Balāghah*[1] is also in book form but it is [a collection of] sermons [as well as letters and sayings] of Imām 'Alī (A.S.) which were scattered in the hands of people. Sayyīd al-Raḍī[2] collected them during the fourth century AH and compiled them in the form of a book. *Uṣūl*

←

supplications, was transmitted from Imām Zayn al-'Ābidīn as-Sajjād (A.S.), the fourth of the Twelve Imāms and the only son of Imām Ḥusayn to survive the massacre at Karbalā. [Trans.]

1. Imām 'Alī, *Nahj al-Balāghah* (The Peak of Eloquence) is a collection of speeches, sayings and letters of the Commander of the Faithful, Imām 'Alī ibn Abī Ṭālib (A.S.) compiled by Sharīf al-Raḍī Muḥammad ibn al-Ḥusayn (d. 406 A.H./1016). Its contents concern the three essential topics of God, man and the universe, and include comments on scientific, literary, social, ethical, and political issues. With the exception of the words of the Glorious Qur'an and of the Holy Prophet (ṣ), no words of man can equal it in eloquence. So far, over a hundred commentaries have been written on the *Nahj al-Balāghah*, indicating the importance of this treatise to scholars and learned men of research and investigation. [Trans.]
2. Abū'l-Ḥasan Muḥammad ibn al-Ḥusayn al-Mūsawī, better known as Sharīf al-Raḍī or Sayyid Raḍī (circa 970 - 1015 C.E.) was a Muslim scholar and poet of Baghdad, who wrote several books on Islamic subjects and exegesis of the Qur'an, and whose most famous work is *Nahj al-Balāghah* which is a collection of Imām 'Alī's sermons, letters and sayings. [Trans.]

al-Kāfi[1] was compiled in book form during the fourth century AH and there were also others books prior to *Uṣūl al-Kāfi*. The books such as *Muṣḥaf Fāṭimah* (S.A.) and *Kitāb 'Alī* (A.S.) - which were occasionally mentioned by the Imāms (A.S.) - are no longer extant. Next to the Qur'an, therefore, the oldest Shī'ah book which has been compiled in book form from the beginning and is still extant today is *Ṣaḥīfah al-Sajjādiyyah*. When Zayd ibn 'Alī ibn al-Ḥusayn attained martyrdom in his uprising against the Umayyads, a copy of the same book was with him and he gave it to a certain person. That was one of the two copies which were first written. *Ṣaḥīfah al-Sajjādiyyah* contains many supplications. Now, I do not want to talk about its significance as it will digress us from the main topic. One of its supplications is called *Du'ā' Makārim al-Akhlāq* which means supplication for noble traits.

I have read this *ḥadīth* before that the Holy Prophet (S) - as narrated in the Sunnī corpus of *ḥadīth* - said:

بُعِثْتُ لِاُتَمِّمَ مَكارِمَ الْاَخلاق.

> "I was sent so as to perfect excellent pattern of morality."[2]

1. *Al-Kāfi*: more fully, *Al-Kāfi fī 'l-Ḥadīth*: one of the most important Shī'ah collections of *hadīth*, compiled by Shaykh Abū Ja'far Muḥammad ibn Ya'qūb al-Kulaynī (d. 329 A.H./941 C.E.) and divided into three sections: *Uṣūl al-Kāfi*, *Furū' al-Kāfi* and *Rawḍah al-Kāfi* consisting of 34 books, 326 sections, and over 16,000 *aḥādīth* that can be traced back to the Prophet and his family by an unbroken chain of transmission. [Trans.]
2. Shaykh 'Abbās Qummī, *Safīnat al-Biḥār*, vol. 1, 411; Mullā Muḥsin al-Fayḍ al-Kāshānī, *al-Maḥajjat al-Bayḍā'*, vol. 4, 121; Mullā Muḥsin Fayḍ Kāshānī, *'Ilm al-Yaqīn fī Uṣūl al-Dīn*, 439.

And in the Shī'ah corpus of *ḥadīth*, the Prophet (S) said:

عَلَيكُمْ بِمَكارِمِ الْاخْلاقِ فَانَّ رَبِّي بَعَثَني بِها.

> "May you have the excellent pattern of behaviour as I have sent for it."

And we have said that the Prophet had made both statements on two separate occasions, but the content is one.

The name of this supplication is *Dū'ā' Makārim al-Akhlāq*. Perhaps, this is because one line of supplication is as follows:

وَهَبْ لي مَعالِي الْاخْلاقِ.

> "And endow me with the most excellent moral traits."

If ever we will have opportunity these nights, I shall read some parts of this noble supplication. [It is so fitting because for] introducing the ethical school of Islam, one of the best pieces is *Du'ā' Makārim al-Akhlāq*. One of my wishes for the past many years is for me to find an opportunity to translate this supplication into Fārsī (Persian), to specifically give commentary on it, to elucidate the philosophies and subtle points contained in this supplication, and to present it to our Fārsī-speaking audience. This is one of my wishes. I hope that God, the Exalted, will grant me that opportunity and may the holy existence of 'Alī ibn al-Ḥusayn (A.S.) himself would ask God, the Exalted, to grant me that opportunity. Now, I shall read a portion of this supplication as an example [of the intended commentary work]. Anyone who could hear these lines and take someone whose wish is to be like that – and of course, he is such and he is teaching everyone that every follower of Islam must be like that – would tell himself, "How could such acts acquire such value and worth?"

Each section of this supplication begins with *ṣalawāt* (benediction) upon the Prophet and his progeny. Every after some lines of the supplication, there is another *ṣalawāt*. Meanwhile, [yet another] part of this supplication is as follows:

The supplicant implores God, thus:

> أَللّٰهُمَّ صَلِّ عَلَى مُحَمَّد وَآلِهِ، وَسَدِّدْنِي لِأَنْ أُعَارِضَ مَنْ غَشَّنِي بِالنُّصْحِ.
>
> "O Allah, bless Muḥammad and his Household, and point me straight to resist him who is dishonest toward me[1] with good counsel."
>
> وَأَجْزِيَ مَنْ هَجَرَنِي بِالْبِرِّ.
>
> "And repay him who separates from me with gentle devotion."

How? For his or her abandoning me and stopping doing good to me, I remain good to him or her.

> وَأُثِيبَ مَنْ حَرَمَنِي بِالْبَذْلِ.
>
> "And reward him who deprives me with free giving."
>
> وَأُكَافِيَ مَنْ قَطَعَنِي بِالصِّلَةِ.
>
> "And recompense him who cuts off with joining."

That is to say, "Give me chance to re-establish relations

1. It refers to the one who is outwardly a friend but actually nurses a grudge against you.

with my relatives and friends that severed relationship with me. I shall reconnect whatever they cut off. They severed this relationship; the 'punishment' for me is to re-establish it. Theirs is disjoining while mine is joining."

وأُخَالِفَ مَنِ اغْتَابَنِي إِلَى حُسْنِ الذِّكْرِ.

> "And oppose him who slanders me with excellent mention."

That is to say, "Let me oppose him or her who speaks ill against me by mentioning his good traits and merits instead."

وَأَنْ أَشْكُرَ الْحَسَنَةَ وَأُغْضِيَ عَنِ السَّيِّئَةِ.

> "And given thanks for good, and shut my eyes to evil!"

That is to say, "Let me be grateful to the good deeds of people toward me, and let me overlook their evil acts toward me." What desire is this for a person? Now, whether we have these wishes or not, whether we do these acts ourselves or not, are these things worthy of the highest appreciation or not? Are these things valuable or not? Are these things worthwhile or not? What kind of value do these things have? In our opinion, is such a person (the supplicant) a hero or not? He is a hero. What does this heroism mean? What is the secret behind this heroism? This is the reason behind our continuous questions which we will answer one by one later: what is the secret behind the 'moralness' of these actions, these ideas, these intentions, these desires, and these wishes?

Statement of Khwājah 'Abd Allāh al-Anṣārī

Khwājah 'Abd Allāh al-Anṣārī[1] has an expression which is perhaps a description of himself. Anyway, he was a pious and mystic man. He says, "Doing evil with evil is dog-imitation." Someone does something bad to another person. The other person retaliates in kind. This is a dog's behaviour because if dog bites another dog, it will retaliate in kind. "And doing goodness with goodness is donkey-imitation." Someone does something good to another person. The other person also reciprocates his goodness. This act is not that valuable. I do not know if you have seen or not. Anyone like me, a villager, knows. If a donkey lets another donkey lick its shoulder, the other donkey will also instantly let the first donkey lick its shoulder. If it sees that the fellow donkey enjoys licking its shoulder, it will also quickly let the other one lick the shoulder of a third donkey. "Doing goodness with evil is Khwājah 'Abd Allāh al-Anṣāri's work." Now, there is the fourth part, and that is, "Doing evil with goodness and that is our work, we, common people!"

There is a poem in Dīwān Mansūb beh Amīr al-Mu'minīn (Collection of Poems Attributed to the Commander of the Faithful), which states, thus:

---

1. Shaykh Abū Ismā'īl 'Abd Allāh al-Hirawī al-Anṣārī or Khwājah 'Abd Allāh al-Anṣārī (1006–1088) was a famous Persian exegete (*mufassir*) of the Qur'an, traditionist (*muḥaddith*), polemicist (*mutakallim*), and Sufi spiritual master, known for his oratory and poetic talents in Arabic and Persian. [Trans.]

وَ ذي سَفَهٍ يواجِهُني بِجَهْلٍ وَ اكرَهُ انْ اكونَ لَهُ مُجيباً

Safiyah does not mean 'insane'. It rather means anyone who is mentally immature. In the poem, if, instead of a *safiyah* (mentally immature), it is someone who is mentally mature and has a specific motive, his action acquires a social implication and it is no longer excusable.

﴿ وَإِذَا خَاطَبَهُمُ الْجَاهِلُونَ قَالُوا سَلَامًا ﴾

> And when the ignorant address them, they say, 'Peace!' (25:63)

The Commander of the Faithful (A.S.) wants to drive this point.

That is to say, "Many times people who are mentally immature deal with me out of their ignorance and lack of knowledge. They speak ill against me; they verbally abuse me. And I abhor retaliating to them in kind."

يزيدُ سَفاهَةً وَ ازيدُ حِلْماً كعودٍ زادَ فِي الْاحْراقِ طيباً

> He increases foolishness and I increase fortitude.
> I'm like an aloes wood whose good [smell] is enhanced in burning.[1]

That is to say, "Oftentimes, he increases his foolishness, ignorance and verbal abuse while I increase my patience and fortitude (*ḥilm*). My similitude is that of an aloes wood which is burned in fire. The more it is burned, the more it emits its natural fragrance." The point is that fortitude is also a moral value. This poem can be found in *Al-Muṭawwal:*[2]

---

1. *Dīwān Mansūb beh Amīr al-Mu'minīn*, 11.

2. *Al-Muṭawwal* (747 A.H.) is the classical work on Arabic rhetoric (*balāghah*) by Sa'd al-Dīn Mas'ūd ibn 'Umar ibn 'Abd Allāh al-

وَ لَقَدْ امُرُّ عَلَي اللَّئيمِ يسُبُّني فَمَضَيتُ ثَمَّةَ قُلْتُ لايعْنيني

That is to say, "I pass by some mean and ignoble people, and one of them abuses me and I tell myself, 'He is not dealing with me'."

Mālik al-Ashtar and a Merchant

You have all heard the story of Mālik al-Ashtar.[1] He, who was possessing handsome personality with broad shoulders, big bones, tall, having sunburnt face with a scar on the corner of his eye - which witnessed his presence in the battlefields - passed through the market of Kūfah with firm and assured steps. On the other side, as it is written, a young merchant sitting in his shop, in order to entertain his friends and make them happy, threw a handful of garbage Mālik's head and face. Without having a wrinkle on his eyebrows or paying any attention, Mālik continued walking with the assured and

←

Taftāzānī, better known as 'Allāmah al-Taftāzānī (1322-1390), a Persian Muslim polymath, which is a commentary on *Talkhīṣ al-Miftāḥ* by Khaṭīb al-Qazwīnī (died 1338), which itself is a commentary on *Miftāḥ al-'Ulūm*, an earlier book on Arabic rhetoric by Abū Ya'qūb al-Sikākī (died 1228). [Trans.]

1. Mālik al-Ashtar: more fully, Mālik ibn Ḥārith from Nakha' and famous as al-Ashtar, was among the prominent commanders of Imām 'Alī's army and the governor appointed to Egypt by the Imām, but on his way to Egypt, he was killed through the conspiracy of Mu'āwiyah. For the text of the Imām's famous instructions to him before setting forth to Egypt, see *Nahj al-Balāghah*, Letter 53. [Trans.]

firm steps. As he went a few steps ahead, one of his friends in the market said to him, “Did you recognize the passerby, the person whom you have insulted?” He said, “No, I did not recognize him!” “It is strange! You did not recognize him?! He was Mālik al-Ashtar, the chief of staff and military general of ‘Alī ibn Abī Ṭālib.” His whole body trembled and he said, “Before he is going to issue an order to punish and chastise me severely, I will run and throw myself on his feet and beg him so that he may excuse me about my blunder.” He began to run after Mālik al-Ashtar, and started following him, observing him to turn toward the mosque. He also entered and mosque and saw him performing prayers. He waited till Mālik completed his prayers. Then, introducing himself in a pleading and supplicating tone, he said, “I am the one who made a blunder and impudence against you,” and words like that. Mālik said in reply, “As for me, I swear to God, I had no intention of coming to the mosque; I was supposed to go somewhere else. I swear to God, I did not come to the mosque except in order to perform two *rak‘ahs* of prayers and then to pray to God to forgive you sins and guide you.”

What is the name of this act? It is a very lofty moral value. Regarding the pure Imāms, we have so many such stories, anecdotes and accounts.

Imām al-Ḥusayn (A.S.) and a Man from Shām

There is a story which is attributed to both Imām al-Ḥasan and Imām al-Ḥusayn (A.S.), and this narration I am going to narrate pertains to Imām al-Ḥusayn (A.S.). A man from Shām[1] with the name of ‘Iṣām ibn al-Muṣṭalaq arrived in the Mosque of Madīnah. His eyes were casted over a man with appalling presence.[2] Paying attention to him, he asked, “Who is this man? Obviously, he must be somebody.” Someone said, “He is Ḥusayn, son of ‘Alī ibn Abī Ṭālib.”[3] The amazing propaganda penetrated on his

---

1. Shām or Shāmāt: the capital of the Umayyad dynasty. Up until five centuries ago, it included Syria of today, Lebanon and parts of Jordan and Palestine. [Trans.]
2. That we say, “ with appalling presence,” it is not that we are supposed to say it, but it is what history states. During the time of Mu‘āwiyah, somebody wanted to go to Shām. Mu‘āwiyah wanted to tell him how he should behave with Ḥusayn ibn ‘Alī if ever he will meet him in Madīnah. He said, “If ever you go to the Mosque of the Prophet and see a man *with appalling presence* sits in a particular manner, surrounded by people who are obviously captivated by his appalling presence, as well as this and that signs, he is Ḥusayn ibn ‘Alī.”
3. For thirty years, Mu‘āwiyah used to stage a sinister campaign against Imām ‘Alī (A.S.) in Shām and what a false propaganda it was! For this reason, the people of Shām basically used to regard the Imām (A.S.) as the archenemy of Islam and a person who had nothing to do with Islam at all.

   One day a man from Shām and another man from Kūfah was debating on an issue pertaining to the ritual prayers (*ṣalāh*) in a coffee shop along the way – in today’s jargon – and the one from Kūfah wanted to prove that he is correct, saying: “Well, I saw ‘Alī praying like that.” [In astonishment], the one from Shām said, “Does ‘Alī know how to pray?!” What a misfortunate! The people of Shām were unaware and misguided up to such extent.

soul made him boil with anger. And to please God, he insulted and defamed Ḥusayn ibn ʻAlī and his father (A.S.) as much as he could. In order to relieve his heart, he said, "You destroyed Islam and you are hypocrites" and other things he wanted to say. Without losing his temper or expressing anger, Imām al-Ḥusayn (A.S.) made a glance full of affection and kindness at him. As he finished his talk, the Imām (A.S.) asked, "Are you from Shām?" He replied, "Yes." The Imām (A.S.) said not more than this sentence:

شِنْشِنَةٌ اعْرِفُها مِنْ اخْزَم.

It is a proverb which is like saying, "I have the experience of this disposition and character. I know the origin of this."[1] Then he added, "You are a stranger in our city. If you are in need, we are ready to render you help, and we are also ready to welcome you and give you a good hospitality at home, clothing you and providing you money." Expecting a violent reaction and never supposing to face with such leniency and tolerance, the man from Shām was so touched by Ḥusayn's (A.S.) words that he said, "I wished the earth had split and swallowed me at that moment."

يزيدُ سَفاهَةً وَ ازيدُ حِلْماً   كعودٍ زادَ فِي الْاحْراقِ طيباً

He increases foolishness and I increase fortitude.
I'm like an aloes wood whose good [smell] is enhanced in burning.

1. *Muntahā'l-Āmāl*, vol. 1, 209.

Another Highlight of *Du'ā' Makārim al-Akhlāq*

Again, we can see that the parts of *Ṣaḥīfah al-Sajjādiyyah* which I have read are full of lofty moral values. I shall hereby read to you another part of *Ṣaḥīfah al-Sajjādiyyah.*

After the said portion, the supplicant gives *ṣalawāt* again to the Prophet and his Household, and beseeches God, the Exalted, thus:

وَحَلِّنِي بِحِلْيَةِ الصَّالِحِينَ وَأَلْبِسْنِي زِينَةَ الْمُتَّقِينَ.

> "And adorn me with the adornment of the righteous and clothe me in the ornaments of the God-wary."

This line [of the supplication] itself does not identify this 'adornment of the righteous' and the 'ornaments of the God-wary' and what things constitute adornment for the righteous (*ṣāliḥun*) and what things serve as ornaments for the God-wary (*muttaqūn*). The righteous and the God-wary whom we know are so different from this one described by Imām al-Sajjād (A.S.) here:

وَحَلِّنِي بِحِلْيَةِ الصَّالِحِينَ وَأَلْبِسْنِي زِينَةَ الْمُتَّقِينَ فِي بَسْطِ الْعَدْلِ وَكَظْمِ الْغَيْظِ وَإِطْفَاءِ النَّائِرَةِ وَضَمِّ أَهْلِ الْفُرْقَةِ وَإِصْلَاحِ ذَاتِ الْبَيْنِ وَإِفْشَاءِ الْعَارِفَةِ، وَسَتْرِ الْعَائِبَةِ، وَلِينِ الْعَرِيكَةِ، وَخَفْضِ الْجَنَاحِ.

> "Adorn me with the adornment of the righteous, and clothe me in the ornaments of the God-wary, through spreading justice, restraining rage, quenching the flame of hate, bringing together the people of separation, correcting discord, spreading about good behaviour, covering faults, mildness of temper, and lowering the wing."

Then, in order for the people to know the things that constitute "adornment of the righteous and ornaments of the God-wary," the supplicant says, "...through spreading justice." One thing that constitutes "adornment of the righteous and ornaments of the God-wary" is the spreading of justice. And when I am angry, I have to control my anger and restrain (*kaẓm*) my rage. What does it mean by *kaẓm*? The rage (*ghayẓ*) which a person feels is exactly like an impediment (problem) which he feels. Solving this problem is what we call *kaẓm*. It is like a cancerous tumour that turns into liquid when laser treatment is undertaken. Spiritually, *kaẓmu ghayẓ* is for a person to do something so that the rage would not take effect and the impediment – the hatred which is in his heart – will be solved and like an ice cube, it will turn into water. The adornment of the righteous and ornaments of the God-wary is that they could be able contain the rage within themselves. And it is "to quench the flame of hate." (It is clear that what is meant here is that there is a conflict, dispute or flame of sedition between two believers.) Now, in that case, like most of us people, shall I kindle the flame of fire so as to intensify it?! No. whenever there is a flame of conflict between two believing brothers, I shall serve as the fireman that puts off the flame. And it is "to bring together the people of separation." And it is "to correct discord" and the faithful and Muslims. And it is "to spread about [their] good behaviour." And on the contrary, it is "to cover [their] faults [and lapses]."[1] Everyone must be such that in order to promote the people's integrity and foster the Muslims' favourable opinion on each other, he is supposed to the good merits of people here and there and cover their faults and defects - even their real faults and defects. This in itself is an Islamic duty - to spread people's merits and to conceal their demerits. When a person has some merits and then the people know him with such merits, this in itself can be a factor for his demerits to lessen. On the contrary, if a person has some merits as well as some demerits, and then the people know him only with such demerits, he will be upset and gradually he will turn into a bad person.

The Qur'an's Strong Prohibition of Exposing a Believer's Faults

As such, the Qur'an strongly prohibits the faults (*fāḥishah* in the language of the Qur'an) of fellow Muslims - even their real faults:

﴿ إِنَّ الَّذِينَ يُحِبُّونَ أَن تَشِيعَ الْفَاحِشَةُ فِي الَّذِينَ آمَنُوا لَهُمْ عَذَابٌ أَلِيمٌ فِي الدُّنْيَا وَالآخِرَةِ ﴾

> Indeed those who want indecency to spread among the faithful—there is a painful punishment for them in the world and the Hereafter. (24:19)

---

1. All these can be found in moral subjects. They do not include social subjects which bestow collective rights, because in those subjects, there are other precepts involved which are also mentioned in this *Du'ā' Makārim al-Akhlāq*.

According to one of two exegeses of this verse, "Those who want the indecencies of the faithful and Muslims to spread..." God forbid that a time will come when it is announced that a fault is found on so-and-so. By the way, what I mean are real [faults]; it is worse if these are lies. There is a tradition (*ḥadīth*) that if a Muslim slanders a fellow Muslim, faith (*īmān*) in his soul begins to melt in the same way that salt is dissolved in water. No faith will be left in him. If it is true, one person tells it to another person who, in turn, will tell it to a third person [and it will gradually spread in that way]. And if it is a lie, God knows it. This is something that the Qur'an definitely abhors. Why is it that backbiting (*ghībah*) is prohibited (*ḥarām*)? It is because it fosters pessimism; backbiting means exposition of faults – that is, real faults.

Instances Where Backbiting Is Permitted

The prohibition of backbiting is there except in exceptional cases which have all social repercussions. One example is in giving a professional opinion: One person wants another person to be his partner in putting up a company. The former comes to you who knows very well the latter and asks your opinion, "Sir! This person who has been with you for some time, what kind of person is he? I want to put up a company in partnership with him." Or, "He gives a marriage proposal to my daughter." Or, "My son wants to marry his daughter," or cases like that. Here, consultation is involved and it is permissible, nay necessary, for you to say whatever you know for you are now being consulted. "That person is such-and-such." Or, in case where you are oppressed by a certain person in the sense that you right has been violated by him, either you close your mouth and not tell anybody that your right has been violated by that person and his right will also be violated by that person, or you expose his violation of your right, thereby backbiting him. This backbiting is permissible:

﴿ لا يُحِبُّ اللّهُ الْجَهْرَ بِالسُّوءِ مِنَ الْقَوْلِ إِلا مَنْ ظُلِمَ ﴾

> Allah does not like the disclosure of [anyone's] evil [conduct] in speech except by someone who has been wronged.(4:148)

This is especially so if I do it while avoiding going to extremes, and our shortcoming - we Muslim community (shortcoming which history testifies) - is that we - especially we Iranians - go either this extreme or that extreme; we do not stand in the middle. Either we are a people that continuously backbite, or we reach a point in which we do not consider permissible to backbite even a person like Ḥajjāj.[1]

---

1. It refers to Ḥajjāj ibn Yūsuf al-Thaqafī (d. 714 C.E.), the notorious lieutenant appointed by the 'Umayyad caliph, 'Abd al-Malik (r. 685-705 C.E.), who was known for his reign of terror, ordering the bombardment of the Sacred Mosque in order to suppress dissent in Makkah, and for his bloody persecution of the Shī'ah, particularly for having killed Sa'īd ibn Zubayr (d. 713 C.E.), who was one of the early exegetes (*mufassirūn*) of the Qur'an. [Trans.]

The Incorrect Statement of Ibn Sīrīn and the Mistake of Ghazālī

Ibn Sīrīn was one of the Muslim scholars of Persia in the second century AH. After the death of Ḥajjāj, the Bloodthirsty and Terrible – who was an embodiment of atrocity – a person was in the presence of Ibn Sīrīn, reviling Ḥajjāj. The holier-than-thou Ibn Sīrīn said, "Do not backbite. Now, your sin of backbiting is heavier than the sins of Ḥajjāj. I am not willing to listen to any backbite against Ḥajjāj." This is nonsense. It is mindboggling that Ghazālī, with such greatness and high station, would narrate and affirm such a story. This is a mistake. Although we do recognize Ghazālī as a great man (in the sense that he was highly intellectual), great men may also have some big mistakes. One of the serious mistakes of Ghazālī – according to Ibn al-Jawzī [1] – is that in many instances, he would give Sufi colour to the Islamic Law (*sharī'ah*). Ghazālī's Sufi tendencies would sometimes make him digress from the Islamic jurisprudence (*fiqh*), such as when he said, "Ibn Sīrīn was correct in saying that that person had no right to backbite Ḥajjāj. [After all,] Ḥajjāj was a Muslim." If one cannot backbite Ḥajjāj, then who can be backbite in the world?! It follows that since we expose his acts of oppression, we are backbiting Yazīd

1. Most probably, it refers to Abū'l-Faraj ibn al-Jawzī (508-597 A.H.), the famous prolific Ḥanbalī Muslim scholar from Baghdad. [Trans.]

ibn Mu'āwiyah on top of the pulpit every day. [It also follows that] God 'backbit' the Pharaoh; He 'backbit' Nimrūd (Nimrod); He 'backbit' Qārūn (Korah); He 'backbit' Bal'am al-Bā'ūrā[1] and hundreds of other people; He also 'backbit' communities; one time He 'backbit' all the Children of Israel. It is not so. These are not backbiting. Let us not also go to the other extreme [of prohibiting backbiting *in all circumstances*].

These are the words of the Imām (A.S.):

> وَإِفْشَاءِ الْعَارِفَةِ، وَسَتْرِ الْعَائِبَةِ
>
> "...spreading about good behaviour, and covering faults..."

I am mentioning all these things so that when a person reaches a point when his wish is such a wish, it is worthy of admiration; when his idea is such an idea, it is worthy of admiration; when his action is such an action; when his habits are such habits, these are heroic habits; these are valuable, adorable and admirable habits. From where do these valuable things emanate? From where and how these [ideas or acts] become valuable? We must delve into the root of these precious things.

It is here that the different schools of thought have emerged to show the secret behind the 'moralness' of

---

1. Bal'am ibn Bā'ūr (or Bal'am al-Bā'ūrā) refers to the man at the time of Pharaoh who knew the Greatest Name of God (*Ism al-A'ẓam*), through which anything and everything sought for is immediately granted by God but later on, he became an infidel and died as such. See Mīr Aḥmad 'Alī's commentary of *Sūrah al-A'rāf* (7:175). [Trans.]

actions and have expressed their respective views. Starting tomorrow night, we will begin stating the views of these schools of thought – such-and-such school of thought says that the secret behind morality lies in such-and-such while another school of thought maintains that it lies in such-and-such. In the end, we would like to state the secret behind morality in the Islamic school of thought. Let us see what and from where does Islam regard the secret behind this value, loftiness and worth. In addition, we will also see how Islam justifies [moral actions] and how these actions are compatible with the Islamic school of thought. Of course, these are most compatible with this school of thought. We will also see how other schools of thought, especially the materialist philosophies, can be able to explain and affirm the moral values.

> وصلّي اللّه علي محمّد وآله الطاهرين. باسمک العظيم الاعظم الاعزّ الاجلّ الاكرم يا اللّه...
>
> "And may Allah's benediction be upon Muḥammad and his pure Household. By Your Exalted, Great, Glorious, Majestic, and Honourable Name, O Allah..."

O God! Illuminate our hearts with the light of faith and the light of the Qur'an.

O God! Take gloominess and darkness out of our souls by Your grace and munificence.

O God! Let us correctly know Islam.

O God! Let us all know our duties and responsibilities. Help all Muslims in all fronts.

O God! Grant victory and triumph to all Muslims – whether in the spiritual front, moral front, or outward front – by Your grace.

O God! Shower our deceased ones with Your favour and forgiveness.

رحم اللّه من قرأ الفاتحة مع الصّلوات.

> "May Allah's mercy be upon him who recites *[Sūrat] al-Fātiḥah* with *ṣalāwāt*."

Chapter 3: Theory of Emotionalism and the Muslim Philosophers' Theory

﴿ خُذِ الْعَفْوَ وَأْمُرْ بِالْعُرْفِ وَأَعْرِضْ عَنِ الْجَاهِلِينَ ﴾

> Adopt [a policy of] excusing [the faults of people], bid what is right, and turn away from the ignorant. (7:199)

Generally, we have mentioned that human actions are of two types. One type refers to those natural, common and usual actions which are not worthy of appreciation, admiration and heroism. The other type refers to those actions which are regarded by people as worthy of appreciation and the doers as admirable and a sort of heroes. We call these as moral actions. We have reached this point: what is the secret behind being moral? How could an action acquire a moral 'colour' that distinguishes it from natural actions? In other words, what is the basis or criterion for being 'moral'? There are many theories in this regard. Initially, we shall mention these theories and then scrutinize and criticize. Which of these theories are/is correct and which are/is not correct? Or, it is possible that part of a theory is correct while another part is not.

Theory of Emotionalism

One of the theories about the criterion for morality – which is one of the most ancient theories – is the theory of emotionalism. A group identifies the secret behind morality in human emotion, saying that a common or usual action is the action which is rooted in selfish motives and natural desires and the purpose behind that action is to gain or to be happy. Any action which springs from such desires and for such purposes is a common or usual action, and it is not moral. Examples of it are most of the actions that the people do. A labourer is engrossed in work since morning so as to have an income and with that income he could pay for his living expenses. His work is something common and usual. In the same manner, the work of an employee who works in an office or a company, or that of a merchant who engages in trading and gaining profits is a natural action so long as it is related to himself and his life, originating from a desire which is related to himself, and whose purpose is happiness that he will feel or prevention of any harm that he might experience (just like one's consultation with a doctor with the purpose of removing any harm or danger that threatens him). Moral action is that which emanates from an emotion which is higher than personal inclinations – that is, feeling of love of others. Moral actions of a person are actions which are done because he loves others as well. That is, he does not love himself along. He is also concerned with the plight of others as he does for his own, and he will be glad that others would gain or be happy in the same degree if he himself gains something or be happy. Of course, these have many levels. Sometimes, the feeling of love for others is such in some individuals that they will be more glad if they could make others gain something or become happy than if they themselves gain something or become happy. That is, they are happier to provide clothes to others than to themselves. They are happier to give food to others than to themselves. They are happier to give comfort to others than to themselves.

Origin and Goal in Human Action

Every human action has an origin and a goal. That is, human being has a feeling, a desire or an emotion which stimulates him to do something, and without this, it is impossible for him to do that action. It is impossible for a person to do anything without having a motivation, a desire or a feeling of fear. Every action has a purpose. For every action, one has a goal which he wants to achieve. Moral action is an action which in terms of origin emanates from a desire which does not pertain to the doer himself. It pertains to others, and we call it feeling for others. In terms of the goal, one's intention is to get something good for himself; it is getting something good for others. According to this theory, natural action does not go beyond the domain of the 'self' and 'I'. The desire which is related to the 'self' and 'I' wants to address others through this 'self' and 'I'. Animals are also like that. Moral action, however, goes beyond the domain of the 'self' in terms of desire (in the sense that the desire is basically not related to the 'self' but to others) as well as in terms of the goal, because the goal is to address others and not one's self. As such, the moral person is someone who steps beyond the domain of the 'self' and reaches out to others.

This is the same path that in ethics, love is promoted as the foundation of morality and that morality is identical with love. The teacher of morality whose morality is based on this regards himself as a messenger of love. Part of this theory common at least among all religions and most philosophical schools of thought in the world. Perhaps, we do not have any religion in the world which does not enjoin love. There is this sentence recoded in our traditions (*aḥādīth*) and narrations:

احْبِبْ لِغَيرِک ما تُحِبُّ لِنَفْسِک وَ اکرَهْ لَهُ ما تَکرَهُ لَها

> "Love others as you love yourself and hate [something] for his sake what you hate for yourself."

(We have many such sayings.) I have read in one history book that this advice exists in all major religions of the world, as it is supposed to exist. The fact is that some creeds or religions focus on love; that is, the pivot of their code of morality is love and nothing else. Others, however, take love as just one element of their respective codes of morality; there are other elements apart from love.

Hindu Morality

Hindu morality is a morality of emotion; that is, the foundation of Hindu morality is the emotion. In the same manner, perhaps it can be said that in Christian morality the sole foundation is love. Gandhi, in his published book entitled *This is My Religion* and whose comprehensive preface which summarizes the whole book is written by a certain European, says: "By studying *Upanishads,*[1] I have arrived at these three principles."

One principle is that in the entire world, there is one knowledge or gnosis and that is knowledge of the essence.[2] In the world, there is only one knowledge, and that is knowledge of the self; that is to know the self. In epistemology, the foundation of Hindu culture is knowledge of the self; that is, one must know himself; one must discover himself. All Hindu mortifications are also

1. *Upanishad* is a collection of millennia-old ancient Hindu religious books and considered among the important books in the world. Our esteemed teacher, 'Allāmah Ṭabāṭabā'ī who had studied the book many years ago was so amazed, saying that there are profoundly extraordinary meanings in it. Now, Europe gives particular importance to this book.
2. What is written in the translation is 'essence'. My guess is that most probably the correct translation is 'self' instead of 'essence'.

meant to achieve it. He says, "I have understood that one principle is that in the entire world, there is one knowledge or gnosis and that is knowledge and discovery of the self."

The second principle is that anyone who knows himself knows God and the universe.[1] This is also a correct proposition.

Both these principles he mentions can be found in the sayings of the Holy Prophet (S) and the Commander of the Faithful (A.S.). They cannot be found in the sayings of the Commander of the Faithful (A.S.) in *Nahj al-Balāghah*, but in *Ghurar al-Ḥikam wa Durar al-Kalim*. The Imām (A.S.) says,

مَعْرِفَةُ النَّفْسِ انْفَعُ الْمَعارِفِ

> "Knowledge of the self is the most beneficial of all pieces of knowledge."

Regarding the saying that anyone who knows himself knows God and the universe, there are sayings of the Holy Prophet and the Commander of the Faithful (A.S.) with this meaning: "He who knows himself knows God."

The third principle is that in the entire world, there is only one force and one good. That force is control over the self. Anyone who controls himself – in his words – has control over the universe, and in the entire world, there is only one good and that is to love others just like loving oneself. Let everyone be witness to what I say in quoting Gandhi's statement. That is, we say that the Hindu morality is founded on love. In Christianity we can also

---

1. Āmadī, *Ghurar al-Ḥikam wa Durar al-Kalim*, chap, 80, 768, *ḥadīth* 151.

see that - at least based on the claim - love is emphasized.[1] Christian missionaries and propagators always say that they are harbingers of love and that Christ is the Messenger of Love - "Show love!" "Express love!" - such much so that they say, "On the contrary, whoever slaps you on the right cheek, turn the other to him as well."[2]

According to this theory, morality means to do good which in turn means to love and care for others. Is this theory correct or not?

Criticism of this Theory

1. Not Every Love Is Morality

Fifty percent of this theory is correct while the other fifty percent is not. There are certain flaws of this theory. One is that not every act of love can be considered morality. Although it may be worthy of praise and admiration, it is not necessarily moral. Every act which is admirable cannot be called 'moral'. The work of an athletic champion who has strong physique is admirable and praiseworthy but it is not considered 'moral'. In morality, there is an embedded element of freewill and acquisition which is not instinctive. If doing an act is instinctive for a person in the sense that it is natural, inherent and innate,

---

1. The Hindus who are Orientals have less lies and hypocrisy. The Christians who are Occidentals, most of them tend to misrepresent facts. That is why regarding them, we say, "based on the claim."
2. Matthew 9:39 (New International Version). [Trans.]

and he does not acquire it or does it out of his own will, that act may be fantastic, magnificent and admirable and yet it is not 'moral'. One example is the love of parents to their child, especially the motherly love. The feelings of a mother toward her child are so great, fantastic and magnificent; they are admirable and praiseworthy, but just because a mother has extremely tender feelings toward her child, we cannot say that her feelings are 'moral' because she does not have exactly the same feelings toward her neighbour's child. These feelings are feelings toward others but these 'others' are exclusive to her children. Moreover, she has not externally acquired or obtained these feelings; she has not obtained them out of her will; rather, the wise law of creation has endowed these strong feelings so as to conduct properly the state of affairs, because without such feelings, no mother would take care of her child. The mother's feelings, therefore, are not feelings for others; they originate from an emotion outside the domain of the 'self' or 'individual' but these feelings and the mother's act cannot be called 'moral'. Paternal feelings, familial feelings, patriotism, and nationalism are also like that. Feelings which are not acquired by a person cannot be regarded as morality.

2. Morality as not Limited to Loving Others

Another objection is that the domain of morality transcends beyond the confines of loving others. All morals – that is, not all sacred and glorious acts of a person are a kind of loving others. There is another kind – that is, there is a set of magnificent, glorious, admirable, sacred, appreciable, and praiseworthy actions of a person – without necessarily having to do with loving others. Just as a person sanctifies self-sacrifice and kindness, he also does the same for this set of actions. One example is what the Arabs describe as *ibā' al-ḍaym* (اباءُ الضَّيم); that is, not to yield to humiliation. At a time when individuals are in danger and their option is either to endure harm so as to preserve their dignity, or to compromise their dignity so as to avoid loss to their property or lives, their reactions may differ from person to person. In history, we can see individuals who would lose their lives but did not yield to humiliation. It is thus said:

الْمَوْتُ اوْلي مِنْ رُكوبِ الْعارِ

> "Death is better than yielding to humiliation."[1]

The Commander of the Faithful (A.S.) said:

وَ الْحَيوةُ فِي مَوْتِكُمْ قاهِرينَ

> "Real life is in dying as subjugators."

Gandhi says, "There is only one goodness in the universe and that is to love others." It is not so; there are other acts of goodness apart from loving others. One example is I have mentioned.

3. The Concept of Humanitarianism

Thirdly, [the concept of] loving fellow human needs an

---

1. Ibn Ṭāwūs , *Al-Luhūf* (with translation), 119; Shaykh 'Abbās Qummī, *Nafs al-Mahmūm*, 187.

explanation. It is mostly interpreted as loving others. And those who have gone higher said that [it is humanitarianism].[1] First of all, the objection is: why humanitarianism? It is better to say 'love for the living.' If a person really expresses his emotion toward an animal (like the story of the one mentioned in a *ḥadīth* who gave water to a dog by making a shoe-bucket to get water from a nearby well), does it mean that his action is not 'moral' simply because this is not humanitarianism? Should a person love fellow human beings only and not express the same to other living beings? One must rather love all. In the words of Sa'dī,

به جهان خرم از آنم که جهان خرم ازوست
عاشقم بر همه عالم که همه عالم ازوست
به غنیمت شمر اي دوست دم عيسي صبح
تا دل مرده مگر زنده كني كاين دم ازوست

> I belong to the pleasant world as the pleasant world is from Him.
> I am in love with the entire world as the entire world is from Him.[2]

Why should we only say, 'humanitarianism'? At least we say, 'love for the living.' In addition, 'humanitarianism' necessitates interpretation. In these cases when if there is only a bit of extremism, under the garb of 'humanitarianism,' anti-humanism could be done. How?

---

1. [This part was missed in the audio cassette recording.]
2. Shaykh Muṣliḥ al-Dīn Sa'dī, *Mawā'iẓ, ghazal* 13.

What does it mean by 'human'? Whenever we see an animal having a head and two ears, could we say that it is 'human' and a descendant of Adam? Should be love anyone that descended from Adam whether he is Lumumba[1] or Moïse Tshombe[2] for they are both the same in this respect? Or, what is meant by 'human' is not every human – not any potentially human and inhuman human. It is rather a human with sense of humanity, and humanitarianism for the sake of humanity means for the sake of love for human values. Every human deserves love commensurate to the degree of his human values or lack of the same. Although the latter may be apparently like other human beings, [he is worthy of our animosity. Outwardly,] Genghis Khan, Yazīd ibn Mu'āwiyah and Ḥajjāj ibn Yūsuf are also human beings, but they are human being who are bereft of human values. They are humans who are anti-human. Humanitarianism, therefore, necessitates interpretation. Humanitarianism means every person who possesses human values in varying degrees deserves love, and anyone who is also actually bereft of human values still deserves love so as for his to possess human values. A perfect man also loves a person

1. Patrice É. Lumumba (1925-1961): a Congolese independence leader and the first legally elected Prime Minister of the Republic of the Congo after helping it win its independence from Belgium in June 1960. Few months after, he was imprisoned and murdered through a reported support and complicity of Belgium and the US. [Trans.]

2. Moïse K. Tshombe (1919-1969): a pro-Western Congolese politician who reportedly had a hand in the murder of Patrice Lumumba. [Trans.]

who is devoid of human values, but not in the sense that since he loves him, he will just feed him. He wants to save him and lets him possess human values. It is for this reason that the Holy Prophet (S) is 'a mercy of the worlds' (*raḥmatun li'l-'ālamīn*); [among others,] it is meant for all people whether believing or non-believing.

This is, therefore, one criterion for the systems of morality mentioned and we saw that this criterion is not complete. We do not reject it totally but it is not a complete criterion. There is some truth in this criterion but not the whole truth.

Muslim Philosophers' Theory on Willpower

There is another theory on the criteria for morality, and that is the theory of willpower (*irādah*). This theory requires a bit of elucidation. If it is a bit complicated, I will try to explain further. It is known that every animal that moves has willpower. That is, every animal that has willpower moves. It wills to go a particular place and it moves accordingly. Like every animal that moves, the human being has also willpower. Yet, this is wrong. What exists in the animals is desire (*meyl*) and urge (*shawq*). There is also a set of desires and urges in the human being, but there is something called 'willpower' which exists in him and does not exist in the animals. Willpower is the partner of the intellect (*'aql*). Wherever there is intellect, willpower is also there. Wherever there is no intellect, willpower is also not there. A person can be moving and has willpower but sometimes he is not so; he is sometimes moving with desires and urges. The animal is always moving with desires and urges.

The Difference between Desire and Willpower

What is the difference between desire and willpower? Desire in the human being is an inducement toward something external. A person is hungry and places foods on the table. He feels within him a desire for food. That is, there is a force within a person that draws him toward food. Or, desire is the power in food which draws a person toward it. Desire is an attraction and inducement for the human being and it is an external factor which draws a person toward that external object. A human being or an animal gets hungry; a desire for something to eat will exist in him or it. He or it gets thirsty; a desire for something to drink will exist in him or it. Sexual instinct is the desire for the opposite sex. To take a rest is also a desire. Desire is an inducement; it is like a magnet. Once it comes out, it will draw a person toward an external object. A mother's emotion is also a desire. Even lofty human emotions are also a desire. For example, in dealing with a needy, he will have a feeling to help the needy; that is, a desire will emerge in him to help the needy.

Willpower, meanwhile, is related to the inside and not to the outside; that is, it is not a relationship between man and the outside world. On the contrary, after thinking about the actions, calculating, evaluating, weighing up, and prioritizing which one should be done first, or the least to be done, he will have the willpower to do what his intellect dictates, and not what his desire wants. In many cases or perhaps in most cases, what the intellect considers expedient and a person wills to do on the basis of what the intellect dictates is against the desire which he feels within. Let us assume that someone is in food diet. She sits in front of a dining table in which there is an exquisite food. The desire would urge her to eat that exquisite food. But she generally evaluates the arbitrary consequence of eating that food. Contrary to her desire, she would decide not to eat it. Or, someone does not like medicine at all. It is not only that she has no desire for medicine; in fact, she has dislike for it. Yet, when she makes an overall evaluation, she will realize that it is expedient for her to take a medicine. She will make a decision and notwithstanding her abhorrence or dislike for medicine, she will take it. Willpower means to control all selfish desires, and selfish dislikes mean abhorrence, fear and dread. Contrary to desire, fear keeps a person aloof. Sometimes, however, willpower fights against fear; it is as if saying, "You resist!" This is called 'courage'.

Willpower, therefore, is the power in the human being that takes control of all desires and dislikes, attractions and repulsions, fear and apprehension, and it does not allow a desire or dislike draws a person to a particular direction. It is as if saying to the intellect, "O intellect!

Take a pause and evaluate very well what happiness and wellbeing necessitate. Tell me whatever is good. Acting upon it is mine."

According to this theory, moral action is that action which originates neither from the dominance of one desire even if it is the feeling of love [nor from the dominance of a dislike]. That is, if you compel the desire of a person under the influence of the feeling of love, this is not moral. For instance, you suddenly feel sorry [for someone]; you become impulsive and did something. You are asked, "Why did you do it?" You replied, "I felt sorry [for him]." This is human being's weakness. If the feeling of love is under the control of the intellect and willpower, at one time the intellect tells the willpower to follow a certain individual desire and at another time not to follow it. The same is true with respect to other desires: "I am hungry; I need food; eating food is expedient." Willpower allows the desire to act upon. I eat food out of desire and continue doing so up to a certain extent. After some morsels of food, willpower will say, "It is enough; if you eat more than this, it will bring discomfort to you; stop eating although your desire is to eat more." Then you stop eating. The same is true with humanitarian feelings. In some cases, oftentimes, the feeling dictates something which the intellect and willpower dictate otherwise. Emotion is to sympathize; one feels sorry for another person, but the intellect and willpower is to be forethoughtful.

We have a verse in the Qur'an and Sa'dī has a poem [relevant to this]. The Qur'anic verse is about the fornicator and fornicatress:

> ﴿ ٱلزَّانِيَةُ وَالزَّانِي فَاجْلِدُوا كُلَّ وَاحِدٍ مِّنْهُمَا مِئَةَ جَلْدَةٍ وَلاَ تَأْخُذْكُم بِهِمَا رَأْفَةٌ فِي دِينِ اللَّهِ إِن كُنتُمْ تُؤْمِنُونَ بِاللَّهِ وَالْيَوْمِ الآخِرِ وَلْيَشْهَدْ عَذَابَهُمَا طَائِفَةٌ مِّنَ الْمُؤْمِنِينَ ﴾
>
> As for the fornicatress and the fornicator, strike each of them a hundred lashes, and let not pity for them overcome you in Allah's law, if you believe in Allah and the Last Day, and let their punishment be witnessed by a group of the faithful. (24:2)

The Qur'an is aware that when a fornicator is to be punished, some people will feel sorry for him, saying that it is better not to implement the punishment. This is a momentary feeling. It is not considered that if every person is supposed to be excused from punishment, he will commit one crime after another. The emotion dictates, "Do not execute the punishment." The intellect and expediency dictate, "Execute the punishment" although what is involved here is humanitarian feeling and not individual feeling. But emotion is not necessarily logical. It is to sympathize. The offending person says, "Do not execute it." The intellect and expediency resort to violence here saying, "You do not understand; you are shortsighted; you are not forethoughtful. If you were only forethoughtful and not shortsighted, you would not have such opinion." The Qur'an states, *"Let not pity for them overcome you in Allah's law.*" Whenever the Divine penal law which is for the general welfare of humanity is at stake, do not let the feeling of pity momentarily deceive you. Sa'dī says,

ترحم با پلنگ تیزدندان ستمکاري بود بر گوسفندان

To have mercy on sharp-toothed tigers
Is to be tyrannical toward sheep.[1]

It is so elegantly said. To have mercy on a tiger – independent of logic, welfare, intellect, and willpower – is an emotional matter. Let us assume that a tiger devours our sheep. We shall deal with it or release it? If we tend to be short-sighted and consider only the tiger, we will show mercy to it and release it. If we tend to be forethoughtful, however, we will deal with it. There are no other beings in this world apart from this tiger, this feeling might be correct. If we open our eyes and look forward in advance, however, we will see that our show of mercy to this tiger is tantamount to atrocity to hundreds of sheep. There should be no room for emotion when showing mercy to one is tantamount to atrocity to others. The intellect and expediency dictate that everything must be taken into consideration. Behind this emotion lie many atrocities.

Similar to this is what is said about the punishment for theft – that cutting the fingers of a thief is atrocious and repugnant to the sense of humanity and humanitarianism. If a thief commits theft, let us not cut his fingers; let us

1. *Gulistān*, chapter 8 "On Rules for Conduct in Life," Maxim 33. [Trans.]

release him and then morally nurture him! We have always seen the outcome of moral training and upbringing. It is not so. The outcome is what we currently see. If a law is announced that after this, the fingers of a thief shall be cut off and then the fingers of a thief are indeed cut off, none would dare to commit theft anymore. This is while we can see now that because of theft, what other crimes and killings are being committed! That is, theft tends to necessitate killings and very heinous crimes.

This theory maintains that the criterion or standard for morality is not the emotion but rather the intellect and willpower. The emotion must also function under the command of the intellect and willpower; otherwise, if we let the emotion function in the name of morality, it may do something immoral. In morality which has been much emphasized in Islamic philosophy, there is this issue that complete morality is that morality which is based upon the power of the intellect and willpower and in which kinds of desires and urges must be under the control of the intellect and willpower. According to this theory, the real champion of morality is the one in whose being the intellect and willpower reign. Of course, many non-individualist emotions also exist in a person but they are springs in his being which shall be open in their rightful places under the control of the intellect and willpower. As such, such perfect men sometimes do certain things with utmost subtlety of emotions and when one looks at their spirits in such a scene, he will see that they are tenderer than the flower and subtler than the breeze. But you can also see the same personages in another instance with such severity that even the mountain could not surpass. In a certain instance, you would see them slaughtering a hundred people like sheep or even below than sheep while not being emotionally touched. In another place, by seeing a very small scenario, they would be so emotionally touched beyond control and restraint. Was 'Alī ibn Abī Ṭālib not like that? If a person is supposed to be solely influenced by his emotion in which emotion is blind and knows no logic, he must be like that in all circumstances. When the source of emotion in his being is under the control of the intellect and willpower, however, his spirit would display such tenderness, subtlety and magnificence in one occasion, and in another occasion, you will see him in extreme severity that none could shake him.

According to this theory, morality means the rule of the intellect and willpower over a person's being such that all desires (both individual and collective desires) are under the control of the intellect and willpower. Ethics in this school of thought, therefore, is rooted in the rule of the intellect and the dominance of willpower. The reason why I say it is the theory of Muslim philosophers and not the theory of Islam per se is that the theory of Islam is one thing while that of the Muslim philosophers is another thing. It does not necessarily follow that in their explanations the Muslim philosophers have been able to explain perfectly all the Islamic issues. At least, they might have said part of the truth, and I do not talk in the name of Islam.

I shall also concisely mention a third view.

Conscience Theory

The conscience theory does not regard morality as a matter of emotion just as Hindu morality and Christian morality consider it, or as a matter of the intellect and willpower just as the Muslim philosopher claim. Instead, they regard morality as a matter of conscience inspirations. You have heard the word 'conscience' (*wijdān*) a lot. A group believes that God, the Exalted, has set a power within a person which is distinct from the intellect and emotion. It is the power which instils duty to a person; that is, within him, he is being commanded to do or not to do a certain thing. This power has nothing to do with the intellect. The intellect is more an acquired (*iktisābī*) matter while this one is intrinsic (*fiṭrī*). God, the Exalted, has created every person with a conscience and that conscience inspires him on many issues – and not everything. Conscience inspires a person in matters which we call 'moral' – inspiring him to do or not do a certain thing. Moral action is that action which is inspired by the conscience. Natural action is an action which has nothing to do with conscience. It has to do with nature; such as eating food, drinking water and the like. Moral action, on the other hand, has nothing to do with man's nature; it has to do with his conscience; it has to do with the command post which originates within him.

The Qur'anic View on Conscience

The Qur'an has not been silent about the fact that the human being is endowed with a set of intrinsic inspirations. In the bless *Sūrat al-Shams*, we thus read:

﴿ وَالشَّمْسِ وَضُحَاهَا * وَالْقَمَرِ إِذَا تَلَاهَا * وَالنَّهَارِ إِذَا جَلَّاهَا * وَاللَّيْلِ إِذَا يَغْشَاهَا * وَالسَّمَاءِ وَمَا بَنَاهَا * وَالْأَرْضِ وَمَا طَحَاهَا * وَنَفْسٍ وَمَا سَوَّاهَا * فَأَلْهَمَهَا فُجُورَهَا وَتَقْوَاهَا ﴾

> By the sun and her forenoon splendor, by the moon when he follows her, by the day when it reveals her, by the night when it covers her, by the sky and Him who built it, by the earth and Him who spread it, by the soul and Him who fashioned it, and inspired it with [discernment between] its virtues and vices. (91:1-8)

The last oath is this: "By the soul and Him who fashioned it, and inspired it with [discernment between] its virtues [which must be acted upon] and vices [which must be shunned]."

﴿ وَتَعَاوَنُوا عَلَى الْبِرِّ وَالتَّقْوَى وَلَا تَعَاوَنُوا عَلَى الْإِثْمِ وَالْعُدْوَانِ ﴾

> Cooperate in piety and God-wariness, but do not cooperate in sin and aggression. (5:2)

When this Qur'anic verse was revealed, a man named Wābiṣah came to the Noble Messenger and said, "O Messenger of Allah! I have a question." The Prophet (S) replied, "Shall I tell you what your question is?" "Please tell," he said. The Prophet (S) said, "You came so that I could explain 'piety' (*birr*) and 'God-wariness' (*taqwā*) as well as 'sin' (*ithm*) and 'aggression' (*'udwān*) to you." He said, "Yes, O Messenger of Allah. I came here for that purpose." It is written that the Prophet (S) placed his three fingers on the chest of Wābiṣah, saying:

يا وابِصَةُ! اسْتَفْتِ قَلْبَک، اسْتَفْتِ قَلْبَک، اسْتَفْتِ قَلْبَک.

> "O Wābiṣah! You ask your heart. You ask your heart. You ask your heart."[1]

That is, "You pose this question to your heart. Get the answer from your heart." God has inspired this knowledge in the form of an inspiration to the heart of every person. This poem of Mawlawī (Rūmī) "Said the Prophet, 'Ask the hearts...'' refers to this tradition (*ḥadīth*).

Or, another verse of the Qur'an states, thus:

﴿ وَأَوْحَيْنَا إِلَيْهِمْ فِعْلَ الْخَيْرَاتِ ﴾

> And We revealed to them the performance of good deeds. (21:73)

There is a very elegant inference in the exegesis *Al-Mīzān*. It is thus said, "It is not stated, 'And We revealed to them *to perform* good deeds'." If it is so, then this revelation would just be common. That is, "We commanded them." It is rather stated, "*And We revealed to them the performance of good deeds.*" That is, "We revealed the act; We revealed to them the act itself."

---

1. Mullā Muḥsin al-Fayḍ al-Kāshānī, *Al-Maḥajjat al-Bayḍā'*, vol. 1, 58.

Kant's View

In the world, there are those in the East and the West (there are many in our Muslim East and some in the non-Muslim West) who believe and have faith in such an independent conscience in the human being; that God has indeed endowed the human being with such conscience. One of them is Kant,[1] the famous German philosopher, who is regarded in the world as one of the greatest philosophers and of the same category with Aristotle and Plato in ingenuity. He is indeed an extraordinary philosopher. He has a book on theoretical reason and another book on practical reason. And in practical reason, he has dealt with ethics, the root of ethics and the philosophy of ethics, and he pays more importance to the issues of practical wisdom and practical ethics. In his philosophy, this man believes that moral action - that is, an action which a person does as a duty - emanates from his conscience. Moral action means an action which must be done according to the dictate of conscience and which a person unconditionally does, not for the sake of any

---

1. Immanuel Kant (1724-1804): the German philosopher regarded by many as the most influential thinker of modern times. Describing in the *Metaphysics of Ethics* (1797) his ethical system which is anchored in a notion that the reason is the final authority for morality, actions of any sort, Kant believed, must be undertaken from a sense of duty dictated by reason, and no action performed for expediency or solely in obedience to law or custom can be regarded as moral. [Trans.]

purpose or motive, but merely in obedience to the command or dictate of the conscience. Moral action, therefore, is an action which comes out of the dictate of conscience. He has many discussions about conscience and man's essence. There is a statement - which may be part of his last will and testament, or something composed by others for him - which is inscribed on his grave. It is a very elegant statement. It is as follows:

> "Two things fill my mind with ever-increasing wonder and awe, the more often and the more intensely the reflection dwells on them: the starry heavens above me and the moral law within me."

In this school of thought, basically, ethics is the intrinsic human conscience which is endowed by God, the Exalted, on every person.

In psychology, there is a lengthy discussion about human conscience or consciences - and in the language conducive to our jargon - about intrinsic matters in the human being or the things in his natural disposition. These are discussed in four subjects. One is the truth-seeking conscience or conscience of knowledge. Does the human being love knowledge just for the sake of knowledge? That is, is he created a seeker on the basis of his natural disposition and instinct? Another is this moral conscience. Is the human being created as a doer of good on the basis of his natural disposition? Is he endowed with conscience to invite him to do good deeds and urge him to be good? The third is aesthetic conscience. Is everyone created to be inclined and attracted to beauty and beautiful on the basis of his conscience and natural disposition? The fourth is the conscience of worship; that is, the religious or spiritual conscience. Is every person created to be a worshipper, seeker, conscious and lover of God on the basis of his nature and disposition, or not? Kant has given emphasis on the issue of moral conscience.

According to this theory, therefore, morality refers to the explicit and definitive orders that the human conscience inspires into a person. If you ask, "Why do some people sacrifice themselves?" It replies, "This is a matter of the conscience; there is no question about it; there is no specific reason; the conscience orders so." Why are people grateful? The reply is: "Gratefulness is inspired by the conscience." Why are some people more pleased with forgiveness than revenge, and instead of taking revenge, they would pardon [others]? It replies, "It is the dictate of conscience." Why is it more difficult for a person to submit to humiliation than to give is life? The reply is: "It is the dictate of conscience, and there is nothing else other than the dictate of conscience."

Let me give a few words about the tragedy. You have heard many times and you know that in the event of Karbalā', one of the moral elements that manifested in the holy personalities of the Doyen of the Martyrs, his companions and members of his household is this moral state that we do not submit to humiliation. We may be captives; our hands may be enchained; our necks may be enchained; our feet may be enchained; we may be wounded with blood gushing forth from our bodies. Yet, our spirits would never allow to submit to humiliation even if we were women captives.

The captives were brought to the court of ['Ubayd Allāh] ibn Ziyād. The womenfolk of the *Ahl al-Bayt* (A.S.) and womenfolk of some of the companions, attendants, and servants were all gathered around Ḥaḍrat[1] Zaynab. Zaynab entered the court of Ibn Ziyād in such a condition. She was a dignified lady. She was a towering figure in the assembly. She entered without giving any salutation. Ibn Ziyād was expecting that after this event - in which he thought they were totally shattered and in which all their energy was spent - they must have to surrender; he thought it was the time for begging and imploring; he thought at least Zaynab would greet him as a bribery to him, but even such a bribery was not given by Zaynab. He was upset; he did not know that their spirits were unshakeable. He arrogantly and compellingly asked:

مَنْ هذِهِ الْمُتَكَبِّرَةُ؟

"Who is this proud [lady]?"

Or,

مَنْ هذِهِ الْمُتَنَكِّرَةُ؟

"Who is this disguised [lady]?"

(She took a seat in two ways - proudly and in disguise.)

1. *Ḥaḍrat*: The Arabic word *Ḥaḍrat* is used as a respectful form of address. [Trans.]

That is, "Who is this arrogant lady? Why did she not greet us?" Or, "Who is this unknown lady?" Nobody answered him. He repeated his question. Again, nobody dared to answer him. As he repeated his question for the third or fourth time, one of the ladies said:

هذِهِ زَيْنَبُ بِنْتُ عَلي بْنِ ابي طالِبٍ

> "This is Zaynab, daughter of 'Alī ibn Abī Ṭālib."[1]

Ibn Ziyād started showing rascality and meanness by saying:

الْحَمْدُ لِلَّهِ الَّذي فَضَحَكُمْ وَ اكذَبَ احدوثَتَكمْ

That is to say, "All praise is due to Allah who exposed your ignominy and lies, and all praise is due to Allah who healed our hatred and difficulty with your brother,"[2] and similar words of mockery. Zaynab said in reply: "All praise is due to Allah who has granted us the honour of martyrdom; all praise is due to Allah who has placed prophethood upon our Household." [She continued:]

انّما يفْتَضِحُ الْفاسِقُ وَ يكذِبُ الْفاجِرُ وَ هُوَ غَيرُنا، ثَكلَتْک امُّک يا ابْنَ مَرْجانَةَ

> "Indeed ignominy belongs to the transgressor while lying belongs to the debauchee and he is none of us. May your mother bereave for you, O son of Marjānah!"[3]

---

1. Muḥammad Bāqir Majlisī, *Biḥār al-Anwār*, vol. 45, section (*bāb*) 39, 115.
2. Ibn Ṭāwūs ,*Al-Luhūf* (with translation),160.
3. Muḥammad Bāqir Majlisī, *Biḥār al-Anwār*, vol. 45, section (*bāb*) 39, 117.

The phrase "son of Marjānah" speaks about a whole book because Marjānah was an ill-reputed woman. By saying "You are a son of Marjānah," she made Ibn Yizād and all those who were present be reminded of a whole book subject. Ibn Yizād said, "Do you still have tongues [with which to speak]?! Do you still something to say?! Do you still stand on your place?!" It reached a point when he threatened, "Jalād! Strike the neck of this woman." He then talked with Imām Zayn al-'Ābidīn (A.S.) who was replying to him in the same tone. Ibn Ziyād said, "Jalād! Strike the neck of this young man." All of a sudden, Zaynab moved from her place and threw herself on Zayn al-'Ābidīn, saying: "By Allah, you cannot strike his neck without striking my neck first. Ibn Ziyād was observing and exclaimed:

عَجَباً لِلرَّحِمِ، سُبْحانَ اللّٰهِ!

That is to say, "I can now see that if I order the beheading of this young man, first I have to order the beheading of this woman."[1]

> ولا حول ولا قوة الّا باللّه العلي العظيم وصلّي اللّه علي محمّد وآله الطاهرين. بإسمک العظيم الاعظم الاعزّ الاجلّ الاکرم يا اللّه
>
> "And there is neither power nor might except that of Allah, the Exalted and Mighty, and may Allah's benediction be upon Muḥammad and his pure Household. By Your Exalted, Great, Glorious, Majestic, and Honourable Name, O Allah..."

1. *Ibid.*

O God! Illuminate our hearts with the light of faith. Make our morality a Qur'anic morality. Purge our hearts of moral impurities. Grant all the Muslims honour and perfect understanding of the teachings of the Qur'an. Shower our deceased parents with Your mercy.

Chapter 4: Conscience Theory

﴿ وَنَفْسٍ وَمَا سَوَّاهَا * فَأَلْهَمَهَا فُجُورَهَا وَتَقْوَاهَا ﴾

> By the soul and Him who fashioned it, and inspired it with [discernment between] its virtues and vices. (91:7-8)

The lecture ended in conscience theory of morality, the theory of those who regards the origin of moral actions, thoughts and decisions of a person as something called 'conscience' (*wijdān*). In view of the fact that this theory has been expressed by one of the greatest philosophers in the world, apart from the fact that the theory itself is explainable and that if a theory is supposed to take into all these, one must lay down the theory in full and then examine and criticize it. As such, with the permission of the esteemed audience, I will elaborate on this theory, and I think the audience's mode is they do not oppose the presentation of such issues, but rather agree on it.

Are all Contents of the Human Mind Derived from Experiences?

First of all, this theory is based upon another theory

which Kant himself and other philosophers in the world have held and do hold. To elaborate, this question is presented in the world: are all contents of the human mind, mental resources and conscience derived from sensory perceptions and experiences of a person? That is, are all thoughts, ideas and feelings which exist in the human being did not initially have any form when he was born and that he acquires whatever he acquires through the sensory perceptions (sight, hearing, taste, smell, and touch)? Or, is there a set of laws alongside the human mind from the beginning? Some have believed and do believe that there is nothing in the human mind that had not existed before in his sensory perceptions. All the contents of the human mind have entered the mind through the same windows, and there is nothing other than this. According to these individuals, the human mind is like a stockroom which was totally empty in the beginning. Through five or more doors (depending of the number of sensory perceptions) things are stored in this stockroom until it is filled. But this filled up stockroom had nothing stored there before except from one of those windows, and in this stockroom there is nothing which does not from these windows.

Another theory is the theory of those who claim that the things in the stockroom of the human mind are of two types. Some of them are placed there through the windows of the sensory perceptions (eyes, ears, tongue, nose, and skin) while some have been already there in the mind prior to the sensory perceptions. Mr. Kant has held the second view, believing in truths prior to experience. This is but an introduction.

Theoretical Intellect and Practical Intellect

Another subject - which our predecessors had also frequently discussed - is that the human intellect is of two types, viz. theoretical and practical. Or, the rules of the human intellect are of two types, viz. theoretical and practical. One segment of the functions of the human intellect is to perceive the things that exist. This is called 'theoretical intellect'. Another segment is to perceive the things which we *must* do. It is to perceive the 'must' and ought-to-be'. This is called 'practical intellect'. Kant's entire philosophy is a critical examination of the theoretical and practical intellect - what functions can be expected from the theoretical intellect and what functions can be expected from the practical intellect. In the end, he reaches the conclusion that only a few functions can be expected from the theoretical intellect; the main function is that of the practical intellect, and it is here that he ends up in the issue of conscience. This is but a second introduction.

The Rules of Conscience According to Kant

What follows is the third introduction. Kant holds that the conscience or practical intellect is a set of prior rules. That is, it is not acquired by the person through the means of sensory perceptions and experience; it is an integral part of the human nature and disposition. For example, the command to be honest and not to tell a lie is a command that precedes human experience about honesty and dishonesty and seeing the consequences of honesty and dishonesty. Conscience tells the person to be truthful and not to tell a lie. The commands that the conscience gives, therefore, are all intrinsic and *a priori* commands – and in the laity's jargon, they are in-born; they have nothing to do with the human experience and sensory perceptions. For this reason, moral command is not concerned with the outcomes of actions; it is the very basis. For example, we say, "Be honest." Then we justifying it by saying, "If a person tells the truth, the people will trust him; the people will not be misguided; he will earn good reputation." We enumerate the merits of honesty. Similarly, we say, "Do not tell a lie." Then we mention the negative outcomes of telling a lie. The moral conscience has nothing to do these outcomes; it is an absolute command. In other words, it is the intellect which has to do with what is expedient. It is wrong for us to come forward and reason about moral issues, saying: "O people! Be trustworthy because of this and that reason..." and then we mention the benefit, goodness and effects of trustworthiness. "O people! Do not commit treachery..." and then we mention the dire consequences of treachery. "O people! Be just..." and then we mention that goodness and beneficial effects of being just and fair. "Do not be unjust and iniquitous..." and then we mention that ill effects of injustice and inequity. [According to this theory,] this is wrong. It is the function of the intellect to look for what is good and expedient. Since the intellect is looking for what is good and expedient, its rules are always conditional; that is, it always commands something due a particular expediency. There is a time when the intellect does not see anything expedient in something. As such, it gives a command accordingly. For example, the intellect commands, thus: "Be trustworthy due to a particular expediency." At another time, such expediency does not exist; so, its command is not to be trustworthy this time. Or, it commands, thus: "Tell the truth due a particular expediency." At another instance, such expediency does not exist. So, its command is this: "Here, do not tell the truth; it is a time for telling a lie." Kant says that sometimes moralists allow themselves to behave contrary to moral principles. The reason for this is that they have decided not to get inspiration for their conscience; instead, they have decided to receive command from the intellect. It is this intellect which looks for what is expedient. The conscience is not concerned with such things. It thus dictates, "Tell the truth." It gives an absolute, unconditional and unqualified rule without having concern with the outcome and consequence [of the action to the person]. It thus commands, "Tell the truth even if it entails harmful effects to you and do not tell a lie even if telling a lie brings amble benefits to you." Basically, it has nothing to do with these things (expediencies). It says, "Be honest at all times and never tell a lie." It is thus said,

در اندرون من خسته دل ندانم کیست
که من خموشم و او در فغان و در غوغاست

Within this shattered heart, I know not who is.
For, I am silent, and in clamour and tumult, it
(my heart, in which is the true beloved) is.[1]

God has endowed such power with a set of commands and duties within us that gives moral command to us. In other words, man has come to this world with inherent duties. (You can see that some overcoats are said to have raglan sleeves.)[2] Some say that man has come to this world disposed with duties; that is, he is born fit to discharge duties afterward. Kant says, "In essence, man has come to this world duty-bound. His duties have been with him.[3] Man has come to this world duty-bound. That is, some duties are embedded within him; there is a power within him that constantly gives him those commands.

Conscience-prick

He then says, "Have you ever tasted the bitterness of regret?" There is nobody who has done something immoral and then he has not tasted the bitterness of that

---

1. *Dīwān-e Ḥāfiẓ, ghazaliyāt*, couplet 22. [Trans.]
2. As raglan sleeve refers to a type of sleeve whose distinguishing characteristic is to extend in one piece fully to the collar, the author seems to point out that there are also overcoats which are said to have 'integral' or 'inherent' sleeves. [Trans.]
3. Of course, it does not refer to non-conscience duties; it just refers to some duties. He only refers to moral duties.

action. A person backbites and while backbiting he is ardent; he is like someone who is injected with anaesthesia and so long as it has effect, he will not feel any pain, but once this effect is no more and his sense of touch returns to normal, he will start to feel the pain. While a person feels passionate in backbiting, he feels a kind of enjoyment just like the one felt by someone hungry – which in the language of the Qur'an – who eats the flesh of his brother. But once this feeling subsides, he will feel an inner hatred of himself; he feels that he abhors himself. It is as if he wants to separate from his self, condemning and reproaching himself. Nowadays, this feeling is called 'conscience-prick' and this is indeed real. Most criminals in the world – even for a few moments – feel conscience-prick.[1] Most criminals in the world are addicted to a set of very strong amusements; they are addicted to a set of narcotics such as opium and heroin, as well as intoxicants and gambling, or other very powerful pastimes and diversions. These are meant to divert their attention from themselves. They themselves feel that if they are left with themselves, they will suffer and it is as if there are snakes and scorpions within themselves, constantly stinging them. Just as a person who suffers from extreme pain is injected with morphine so as for him not to feel the pain, these amusements,

---

1. We do not say all criminals because I do not have such statistical data [to support it], nor is there anything otherwise to disprove.

narcotics, intoxicants, and gambling which are commonly found in corrupt and criminal individuals are meant to escape from themselves. They want to escape from themselves and what a misfortune it is! Why should a person mould himself in such a way that he could be alone with himself?! On the contrary, why do the people of prayer, God-wariness and morality who always listen to and obey the voice of their conscience keep aloof from anything that would misguide themselves, always desiring to be themselves in action and thought? It is because their inward world is indeed more wholesome than their outward world. The former whose inward world is like a wild forest full of predators, marauders and ferocious animals escape from themselves and take refuge in narcotics. The latter, however, do the opposite. Mawlānā Rūmī thus says,

> یک زمان تنها بماني تو ز خلق　　در غم و اندیشه ماني تا به حلق
>
> You are left alone by people for a single moment;
>
> You remain up to the throat in grief and anxiety.[1]

In sum, it is said that man cannot be left with himself because he has lost his real self, and in their words, even for a single moment, he cannot be left alone with his conscience. Conscience would ask, "Why did you do it?! You were not supposed to do it."

---

1. Mawlānā Jalāl al-Dīn Rūmī, *Mathnawī-ye Ma'nawī*, Book 4, line 805. [Trans.]

Kant asks, "Where do these bitterness of regrets and conscience-pricks come from?" If such commands did not come from within a person, he would be pleased with his actions, or at least he will not feel any disquietude within; his discomfort will be outward. But he always experiences disquietude within. It is said that the reason for this is that this power is a kind of *a priori* power; that is, it is not derived from experience. It is absolute and it is like the rule of intellect which is not dependent on expediency. It is general and it is applicable in all circumstances. It is applicable to me in the same manner that it is applicable to you, and it is applicable to you in the same degree that it is applicable to other persons. In the same manner, it is necessary and determinist in the sense that it is irreversible. A person may yield to a tyrant or a wicked act, but the conscience is such that it will never yield. The conscience of even the most notorious criminals in the world will not yield to the concerned person; that is, it will not tell him, "Well done. You have done something good." It will stand on its rule. It is like Abū Dharr's enjoining of good and forbidding of bad which no power could make him compromise. It (conscience) enjoins a person within himself to do good and forbid evil. This is the secret behind the insanity of many criminals who committed heinous crimes; when they are left alone, they are so mentally disturbed that they become mad, and we have many such instances in history. The bitterness of regret, therefore, is the very proof that indeed the human being has conscience.

Moral Conscience and Felicity

He says, "This conscience (that is, moral conscience) invites man toward perfection and not felicity. Felicity is one thing and perfection is another thing." He recognizes only one goodness, saying that in the entire world, there is one goodness and that is goodwill. Goodwill also means absolute obedience to the dictates of conscience. Now, since a person should absolutely obey the dictates of [his] conscience, it follows that he must unconditionally obey and submit to them. And since moral conscience is not concerned with the outcomes of an action and just urges a person to do certain thing whether it is beneficial to him or not, brings pleasure or not, or results in prosperity or affliction to him or not, it follows that it has nothing to do with man's felicity (*sa'ādah*) because felicity basically means pleasure although not every enjoyment brings pleasure. Enjoyment which is to be followed by suffering is not pleasant. Felicity means maximum pleasure which is devoid of any kind of suffering and sorrow (spiritual or physical, worldly or otherworldly) while adversity (*shiqāwah*) means pain and suffering. The totality of pain and suffering as well as that of pleasures (spiritual or physical, worldly or otherworldly) must be taken into account. That which brings the maximum pleasure is felicity. The foundation of felicity, therefore, is pleasure. Yet, this conscience is not concerned with pleasure; its concern is perfection (*kamāl*). It says, "You do this action because it essentially brings about perfection. It is your perfection and it does not matter whether it bring pleasure to others or not." It is here that Mr. Kant gives distinction between perfection and felicity, and this notion has been prevalent since his time up to the present time. The Europeans says, "Perfection is one thing and felicity is another thing."

Is Perfection Other than Felicity?

The issue of perfection and felicity is discussed in Islamic philosophy. Abū 'Alī Sīnā[1] in *Al-Ishārāt* and others have discussed this issue. They believe that felicity and perfection are inseparable as they are inextricably interwoven with each other. Every perfection is a kind of felicity and we shall explain it to you later. Kant, however, differentiates the two and then says, "It is so problematic that we separate duty from beauty and ethics from felicity, and now all philosophers in the world regard

1. Abū 'Alī al-Ḥusayn ibn 'Abd Allāh ibn Sīnā Balkhī, known as Abū 'Alī Sīnā Balkhī or Ibn Sīnā and commonly known in English by his Latinized name "Avicenna" (c. 980-1037) and the title "Prince of Physicians" was a Persian polymath and the foremost physician and philosopher of his time. He was also an astronomer, chemist, geologist, logician, paleontologist, mathematician, physicist, poet, psychologist, scientist, and teacher. His important works include *Al-Qānūn fi'ṭ- Ṭibb* (The Canon in Medicine) which is the most famous single book in the history of medicine in both the East and West, *Al-Shifā'* (an encyclopedic work covering, among other things, logic, physics and metaphysics), *Al-Najāt* (a summary of *Al-Shifā'*), and *Al-Ishārāt* or in full, *Al-Ishārāt wa 't-Tanbīhāt* (a latter work consisting of four parts, viz. logic, physics, metaphysics, and mysticism). [Trans.]

ethics as inseparable with felicity." For instance, Fārābī,[1] who had discussed felicity a lot and wrote some books about it and one of which is entitled, *Taḥṣīl al-Sa'ādah* (*The Attainment of Felicity*), regarded ethics and felicity as essentially intertwined. Or, according to scholars of ethics such as the author[2] of *Jāmi' al-Sa'ādāt* (*The Collector of Felicitesi*) and the author[3] of *Mi'rāj al-Sa'ādah* (*The Ascension to Felicity*) which are books on ethics, the concept of felicity is essentially a pillar of ethics. However, Kant says, "The main concern of ethics is not felicity; its main concern is perfection." He then complains that if ethics is supposed to be separate from felicity, then any moral action is very difficult. With certainty that he is about to be kept away from felicity, a moral person must obey the dictate of his moral sense, and to do this is very difficult. He says, "I admit that it is difficult but the only way to ascend to heaven is for a person to choose the path of perfection and not that of felicity.

There is a serious objection here to Mr. Kant for mentioning 'heaven' as the end point. When a person

---

1. Abū Naṣr al-Fārābī (known in the West as Alpharabius) (c. 872 - 950/951 C.E.): a Muslim polymath (in the fields of cosmology, logic, music, psychology, and sociology) and one of the greatest scientists and philosophers of the world during his time. [Trans.]
2. It refers to Muḥammad Mahdī al-Narāqī (died 1268 A.H.) who belonged to a family of celebrated Muslim scholars of their times. [Trans.]
3. It refers to Mullāh Aḥmad al-Narāqī (1185 - 1249 A.H.), the elder brother of Muḥammad Mahdī al-Narāqī and also a celebrated Muslim scholar of his time. [Trans.]

ascends to heaven, is he wretched or felicitous? Does the perfection which makes a person ascend to heaven make him felicitous or wretched? He has no option but to say, "Felicitous." It becomes clear here that the felicity he refers to is sensory felicity; that is, material and worldly pleasure, otherwise it is basically impossible to separate felicity from perfection. And as what Abū 'Alī Sīnā and his likes have said, felicity and perfection are inseparable. In the end, Kant was also not able to separate the two. In order to explain his statement, we have to say that what he means by 'felicity' is what is called 'sensory felicity' by our predecessors who believe in two types of felicity, viz. sensory and non-sensory felicity.

Conscience and Proof of Man's Freedom of Will

As we have said, the pivot of Kant's philosophy revolves around [the notion of] moral conscience. In the framework of theoretical intellect or what we call 'philosophy and theosophy,' in spite of his efforts he ended up in doubt; that is, he has reached nowhere. When it comes to the realm of ethics, however, in his opinion he has reached the point of discovering the keys to everything. He has discovered the key to religion; he has unearthed the explanation of freedom and freedom of will; he has unravelled the secret behind the immorality and perpetuity of the soul; he has uncovered the veil of the Resurrection; he has brought to light the proof of God's existence. He says, "If we want to prove through theoretical intellect (which we have just identified today as 'philosophy') that the human being is free and independent, we cannot succeed. Theoretical intellect will reach the point in which a person would say that the human being has no freedom and he is a compelled being. Through the path of moral sense, however, which is something inward, conscience-related and discoverable by anyone through his intuitive knowledge (*'ilm al-ḥuḍūrī*), we will reach the point that the human being is free and independent.[1] He says, "If we pursue it through philosophy, in the end we will reach the point that the human being is a compelled being, but if we refer to our moral sense and conscience, we can perceive in our conscience that he is a free and independent being." He proves freedom and freedom of will through inward sense and innate nature.

This is not a new opinion. Many others also prove [man's] freedom of will through the path of inward sense. Mawlānā [Rūmī] says,

این که گویي این کنم یا آن کنم　　خود دلیل اختیار استاي صنم

> That you say, "I will do this or I will do that"[2]
> Is a proof of the power to choose, O worshipful one.[3]

---

1. Intuitive or presential knowledge (*'ilm al-ḥuḍūrī*) means that a person could directly perceive his inward being.
2. That is a dictate of the conscience.
3. Mawlānā Jalāl al-Dīn Rūmī, *Mathnawī-ye Ma'nawī*, Book 5, line 3024, with a slight variation. [Trans.]

[According to Kant,] therefore, on the basis of his conscience - and not on the basis of philosophical proofs - is a free and independent being.

Conscience and Proof of the Soul's Perpetuation and Immortality

Right here, the issue of the soul's perpetuation and immortality shall be proved. You know that one of the even important questions of mankind is this: After death, does the human soul or spirit endure and is immortal, and is felicitous or wretched in the other world? Does the human soul or spirit cease to exist and become extinct after death? This is one of the most significant intellectual and philosophical questions in the world. Even today, if you go this so-called industrialized world of Europe, you can still see that some great European philosophers are materialists while others are metaphysical. Kant believes that the soul's immortality and everlastingness cannot be proved through philosophical proofs but the human conscience says that the soul is immortal and everlasting; it will be there always; it will receive reward or punishment in the other world. He says that its proof is as follows:

The conscience always tells the person to observe honesty, trustworthiness, truthfulness, and justice. In practice, one can always observe that honesty, trustworthiness, truthfulness, justice, and the like do not necessarily bring about reward in this world, and in terms of achieving material rewards, these [moral values] pose as hindrance or restriction for a person. If a person gets rid of these hindrances and restrictions, viz. honesty, trustworthiness, justice, and the like [that stand in his way],[1] he will be relieved.

I shall mention the following example. 'Alī ibn Abī Ṭālib (A.S.) and Mu'āwiyah were at logger heads with each others. 'Alī was a person who would observe justice and oppose discrimination, dishonesty and deception. His entire policy is based on this. Meanwhile, Mu'āwiyah was a person who would not observe any of these [moral values]. His desire was to achieve his goal and fulfil his ambition. If he could achieve his goal through justice, he would observe justice, and if not, he would resort to discrimination, bribery, embezzlement, plunder, deception, treachery, and dishonesty. Naturally, he would succeed and 'Alī (A.S.) would fail.

All human beings can feel that these [moral values] pose as limitation and restriction for them. Yet, man's innermost being commands him to be honest, trustworthy, just, and the like. He does not turn his back from his innermost being's command. What is the reason? He (Kant) says that it is impossible for a person within his innermost being to be unconsciously uncertain of the good outcome of these things that can never be lost or wasted. In the depth of man's conscience and being, unconsciously there is this faith or belief. Perhaps, he

1. [Missing part in the audio cassette recording.]

would deny, saying that "We do not know if there is really Day of Judgment; if there is the Resurrection; if there is something after death, or not. Yet, unconsciously, he believes in these realities in his innermost being. As such, even if a hundred times he would be honest and become a victim of dishonesty, and observe justice and become a victim of injustice, for a hundred and one times more, he will not relinquish honesty and justice. This is because in his innermost being, conscience and intuitive knowledge, he discerns the reality that life is not limited here [in this world and that] the period of life in this world is like that of a foetus in womb which is expecting to come to this world.[1] Thus, sense of duty involves faith in reward; that is, it involves faith in the soul's immortality and everlastingness. Faith in the soul's immortality means that the feeling that "I shall endure and get my reward in the next world, and it shall never be lost." This, in turn, involves faith in the Creator. Faith in the immorality of the 'self' necessitates faith in the Originator [of the self or soul].

As such, on the basis of this moral conscience, Mr. Kant not only infers moral injunctions but rather, it is the foundation of his philosophy in everything metaphysical; it is on this basis that he proves freedom and freedom of will; it is on this basis that he proves the hereafter and the soul's immortality and endlessness; it is on this basis that he proves the existence of God. As such, he says,

---

1. It is Kant's own expression.

> "Two things fill my mind with ever-increasing wonder and awe, the more often and the more intensely the reflection dwells on them: the starry heavens above me and the moral law within me."

The reason for this is that Kant believes in so many things in man's innermost being, discovering many principles from man's innermost being and constitution. Sometimes, our scholars and mystics or their scholars use the word 'heart' (*qalb* or *fu'ād*) instead of 'intellect' or 'reason' (*'aql*). In these cases, the 'heart' refers to the conscience (*wijdān*). Kant has said that Rousseau (that is, the famous Jean-Jacques Rousseau, author of the books *Emile*, *Confessions* and *The Social Contract*) has this statement about God: "The heart has logic which the head cannot understand." That is, sometimes a person feels certain things through his conscience which his mind cannot fathom. Kant then says, "Rousseau has rightly said." He also says, "Pascal[1] has rightly said that the heart has its proofs that the head (that is, the intellect) is basically not aware of. Their statements are correct." He means that in order to prove the existence of God, one must not always look for intellectual evidence. They are a set of proofs, but the heart has its own proofs other than those proofs of the intellect. The path of the heart and disposition is one path leading to God while the path of

1. Blaise Pascal (1623-1662) is one of the European mathematical geniuses and it is said that he is an extraordinary genius.

the intellect is another path leading to God. One wants to tread the former path while another person wants to tread the other path.

A Tradition from Imām al-Ṣādiq (A.S.)

Someone came to Imām al-Ṣādiq (A.S.) and said, "On what basis should I believe in the existence of God?" The Imām (A.S.) replied through the path of conscience, saying: "Have you ever experienced travelling by boat?" The man said, "Yes." The Imām (A.S.) continued, "Have you ever been caught in a fierce storm in middle of nowhere, your rudder gone, your sails torn away, trying desperately to keep your boat afloat? The answer was "Yes." Then the Imām (A.S.) asked, "And sometimes perhaps even that leaking boat went down leaving you exhausted and helpless on the mercy of raging waves?" The answer was again "Yes." Then the Imām (A.S.) asked, "Was not there, in all that black despair, a glimmer of hope in your heart that some unnamed and unknown power could still save you?" When he agreed, the Imām (A.S.) said, "That power is God." [That is to say,] "When we are cut off from all means and factors [to be saved], it is this conscience of yours that wittingly or unwittingly does not allow you to be hopeless, because there is really such thing in your conscience; it dictates that there is such..."[1] When his willpower to do something is set in, any set of factors that stands along his way will be nothing.

1. [Missing part in the audio cassette recording.].

This theory which is the theory of conscience is a specific theory which does not depend on the emotion, willpower or intellect. It is solely concerned with the conscience. Does this theory deserve criticism or not?

A Criticism of this Theory

1. Contempt on Philosophy

Although there are excellent points and many subtleties in this theory, it [still] deserves criticism and there is an array of criticisms against it – criticisms which are also justifiable. Now, I shall concisely mention them and then we may possibly elaborate later on.

First and foremost, in this theory the output of theoretical intellect or what we call 'philosophy' has been extremely held in contempt. Kant's theory is wrong is maintaining that through the path of theoretical intellect, we cannot prove any of these issues. Incidentally, through the path of theoretical intellect – without necessarily denying the path of conscience and practical intellect – we can also prove the human being's freedom and freedom of will, as well as the soul's immortality and perpetuity, the existence of God, and moral commands. Even these commands that one must get inspiration from the conscience, the intellect – at least as a confirmation of the conscience – affirm these commands. Of course, since this discussion is a broad one, we will not delve into it.

2. Distinction between Perfection and Happiness

The other problem is that perfection and felicity are

distinguished from one another. This is a gross error. Perfection cannot be separated from felicity. Every perfection is a kind of felicity, but felicity is pleasure which is not only limited to physical pleasure. Mr. Kant must be told, "You say that when a person goes against the dictate of his conscience, he experiences a kind of bitter feeling. This is true. Yet, how comes that when he disobeys the dictate of his conscience he feels bitted but when he obeys it he does not feel a kind of higher, more profound, more innate, subtler, more enduring, and more lasting joy and mirth?!"

According to Mr. Kant, therefore, if a person obeys the dictate of his conscience, he will also feel bitter because as he said, we have to separate it from felicity, and thus, it is something hard and difficult. If we follow the dictate of our conscience, we feel a sense of duty equated with burden and hardship; if we go against [its dictate], we suffer more mentally. As such, whether we obey or not obey [its dictate], we suffer mentally. This is meaningless and such a thing is impossible because as a person disobeys the dictate of the conscience, he suffers and feels pain. For this reason, when he listens to the voice of the conscience, he is overwhelmed by a distinct kind of mirth and joy. It is a kind of mirth and joy which is beyond description. After a person performs an act of self-sacrifice, he is inwardly filled with joy. The one who gives preference to the comfort of other over his own suffering feels a kind of inner joy and pleasure which is beyond any comparison with other sources of joy.

In this connection, at the conclusion of his *Al-Ishārāt* Abū 'Alī Sīnā has opened a discussion with the title, "It is Wrong to Limit Joy with Sensory Joy." He then gives examples of spiritual and non-sensory joys. In psychology nowadays, it is very clear that a person's joy is not limited to sensory joy. Sensory joy is a kind of joy which is usually related to the sensory organs and an external stimulant. One instance is when food is placed someone's lips, his sense of taste gets stimulated and he feels good. Other joys are experienced through the senses of touch, hearing, sight, and smell. There is a set of joys, however, which is not related to the sensory perceptions. One example is the pleasure of heroism. After having the feeling of being a hero and standing among the crowd, a person feels a kind of joy but this joy has no external factor; that is, it is externally motivated. When a person is loved by people, he feels happy. The one who feels happy for being loved and appreciated by the crowd, he feels a kind of pleasure for being loved. In the same manner, a scientist feels a kind of joy for discovering a scientific fact. Regarding Khwājah Naṣīr al-Dīn al-Ṭūsī,[1] it is written that whenever he would encounter a [intellectual or scientific] problem, he would start profoundly thinking

1. Muḥammad ibn Muḥammad ibn Ḥasan al-Ṭūsī, better known as Khwājah Naṣir al-Dīn al-Ṭūsī (597-672 A.H./1200-73): a Persian polymath and prolific writer—an astronomer, biologist, chemist, mathematician, philosopher, physician, physicist, scientist, theologian, and *marja' al-taqlīd* (religious authority). [Trans.]

about it until he would arrive at the solution. Sometimes, even at midnight when he would find the solution to a problem, he would jump in ecstasy and say,

اينَ الْمُلوک وَ ابْناءُ الْمُلوک مِنْ هذِهِ اللَّذَّةِ؟!

> "Where are the kings and princes from this joy?!"

That is to say, "Where are the kings and princes so that they could come and see which joy is greater, the one I experience now the one they experience for sensory matters?!"

It was the wedding night of Sayyid Muḥammad Bāqir Ḥujjat al-Islam.[1] It was not yet the supposed time for him to proceed to the bridal chamber. He spent his time studying. He was so engrossed in his studies that he totally forgot that it was his wedding night

He told himself, "Now is an opportunity which I am going to utilize to study." He began his reading. The ladies already went out [of the bridal chamber]. The poor bride was left alone. No matter how long she waited for the groom but he did not come. At once the late Sayyid realized that it was already dawn; that is, this man was so engrossed in learning that he totally forgot that it was his wedding night. Then he heard the call to prayer (*adhān*) [for the dawn prayer]. The bride was also upset, thinking that the groom did not really like her. She [went to the other room and] saw [him] and she was upset. He

---

1. It refers to Ḥujjat al-Islam Sayyid Muḥammad Bāqir Shaftī Iṣfahānī (died 1844). [Trans.]

approached her and swore, thus: "By Allah! I was so engrossed in studying that I forgot last night was our wedding night!" This joy is the joy of learning. It is not a sensory joy.

The issue of joy, therefore, cannot be separated from matters pertaining to the conscience. Of course, its scientific and philosophical explanation as Abū 'Alī Sīnā and others have done is something else. At any rate, when a person is happy for something, it is because his inner being wants something which he obtains. Joy is experienced by a person when something is obtained while pain and suffering are felt when perfection which he supposed to achieve is not achieved. It is wrong, therefore, to distinguish perfection from joy or pleasure which is gradually becoming prevalent in European philosophy – should a person seek perfection, or seek pleasure and joy? Wittingly or unwittingly, every perfection beings about a kind of joy even if the seeker of perfection is not after the joy while seeking perfection, and in fact, he is not after the joy. He seeks perfection for the sake of perfection, but achieving perfection inevitable brings joy to a person. As such, this part of his theory is extremely confusing.

3. Not all Rules of Conscience as Absolute

The question of the absoluteness of the rules of conscience which he (Kant) mentions is also criticized by Europeans themselves – "The rules of conscience that you frequently say are not absolute." This discussion is so close to that of our scholastic theologians (*mutakallimūn*) and *Uṣūlīs*[1] about the rules of intellect, and rational goodness and evil! They believe that some rules are absolute, and their view is correct. For example, they say that justice is an absolute rule that it is good while injustice is an absolute rule that it is bad. Honesty, however, is not an absolute rule; rather, it depends on the reason behind doing so, and sometimes it loses the very reason behind doing it. This criticism is given by them to Kant: "You are so subservient to absolute rule and you say, for example, that honesty is an absolute dictate of the conscience and it must be observed under all circumstances. Let us assume that a violent insane is holding a knife and looking for someone to slit his throat, and he asks you, "Do you know where is he?" Here you have to answer. If you do not answer, he will stab you. What will you answer? Will you say that you know where the person he is looking for is, or not? If you say that you do not know, then he will be telling a lie and your conscience will dictate you to be honest. If you say that you know, he will ask further, "Where?" Will you pin point his location or not? If you pin point his location, he will go there and slit his throat. Is the human conscience so absolutist and would say that "You must absolutely tell the truth and not mind the consequences"?!

---

1. In contrast to the *Akhbārīs*, the *Uṣūlī* scholars favour the use of *ijtihād*, i.e. juristic derivation of laws applicable to new conditions, the assessment of *ḥadīth* to exclude traditions they believe unreliable, and obedience a *mujtahid* as obligatory when seeking to determine Islamically correct behaviour. [Trans.]

White Lies

The issue of white lies is mentioned by very own Sa'dī and also discussed in our jurisprudence (*fiqh*). Is white lie better than a sedition-mongering truth, or not? Sa'dī says,

دروغ مصلحت آمیز به از راست فتنه‌انگیز است

> "A falsehood resulting in conciliation is better than a truth producing trouble."[1]

And the story which he narrates [in this context] shows that Sa'dī has a good grasp of the issue. He narrates that someone was brought to the presence of a king. The king gave order for him to be executed. As he was hopeless of remaining alive, he began to insult the king but the king did not understand what he was saying. The king asked, "What is he saying?" The vizier said, "He is saying,

﴿وَالْكَاظِمِينَ الْغَيْظَ وَالْعَافِينَ عَنِ النَّاسِ وَاللَّهُ يُحِبُّ الْمُحْسِنِينَ﴾

> Those who suppress their anger, and excuse [the faults of] the people, and Allah loves the virtuous. (3:134)

Someone who was looking for the vizier's fault so as to replacement him as the vizier said, "Men of our rank ought to speak nothing but the truth in the presence of kings. This fellow has insulted the king and spoken unbecomingly, and you are claiming that he has read a verse of the Qur'an?!" The king said, "That lie was more acceptable to me than this truth you have uttered.[2] A

1. Shaykh Muṣliḥ al-Dīn Sa'dī, *Gulistān*, chap. 1 (The Manners of Kings). [Trans.]

2. Of course, this is a fictitious story which Sa'dī has constructed in order to convey a truth.

falsehood resulting in conciliation is better than a truth producing trouble. That is, by telling a lie he has saved a life and you, by telling the truth, you would put in danger someone's life."

Basically, is it true that a falsehood resulting in conciliation is better than a truth producing trouble? Here I have to tell you something and that is, there is a difference between a white lie and self-motivated lie. So many people confuse, or they want to confuse, white lie with self-motivated lie. White lie is a kind of lie that removes the nature of lying; that is, it is a lie through which a person could protect a truth. Self-motivated lie, on the other hand, is a lie which a person commits for his own interest. The issue of expediency should not be confused with that of self-interest. Expediency revolves around the axis of truth. Expediency and truth are two brothers that are inseparable from each other. Expediency is to preserve the truth and not to protect one's self-interest. Individuals tell a lie which advances their own interests. If you ask, "Why did you tell a lie?" They would say, "It was a white lie." In order to gain an insignificant amount, one would tell a lie and say, "It was a white lie." This is not expediency. It is lie just like any other lies. So, we should not make mistake about it. White lie is different from self-motivated lie.

Another issue is that just as Kant has made his point in such a way that the truth must be said without paying attention to its consequences and a lie must not be told no matter what its consequences might be (because according to him, the dictate of conscience is absolute and it is the dictate of intellect which is conditional; the dictate of conscience does not recognize but-ifs, expedience and the like), some individuals (Zoroastrians in particular) have found fault with Sa'dī for his alleged promotion of evil (dishonesty). It is mentioned in an article written by one[1] of our own scholars that after England (Great Britain) occupied (that is, colonized) India, they subjected the schools under their control. They (British) ordered that Sa'dī must not be taught for the reason of his alleged promotion of evil (dishonesty) – "A falsehood resulting in conciliation is better than a truth producing trouble" – and this will undermine the children's spirit of honesty. You see, how good people they are! They are so concerned with the people of India that they do not want the Indian children to be brought up in such a way; rather, they want them to be honest and not tell even a white lie! But the libertines knew that this action has another cause and that is a different thing which Sa'dī mentioned in the initial part of his *Gulistān*:

اي كريمي كه از خزانه غيب　　گبر و ترسا وظيفه خورداري

دوستان را كجا كني محروم　　تو كه با دشمنان نظر داري

O merciful God who, out of Thine hidden treasures,

---

1. It alludes to Sayyid Muḥammad Ṭabāṭabā'ī, known as Muḥīṭ Ṭabāṭabā'ī (born 1902) who was a prominent intellectual, historian and literary man of contemporary Iran. [Trans.]

Affordest daily sustenance to the Zoroastrian
and the infidel (Christian),
How canst Thou exclude Thy friends,
Thou who designest this favorably to regard
Thine enemies![1]

From the beginning, it was ingrained in children's minds that Zoroastrians and Christians are enemies of God. They were not saying that because of this poetry of him, Sa'dī should not be taught to the Persian-speaking children of India. They were saying, "Do not teach Sa'dī for his moral corruption in saying that 'A falsehood resulting in conciliation is better than a truth producing trouble,' and this will corrupt your children. Sa'dī's teachings are of no use at all!" For this statement of Sa'dī, Zoroastrians are also saying that his statements are not beneficial.

Sa'dī who is purely Iranian and a pride of Iran categorically says that Zoroastrians and Christians are enemies of God. For this reason, Pūrdāwūd[2] used to say, "Sa'dī is of no use because he teaches something evil by saying that a falsehood resulting in conciliation is better than a truth producing trouble." Here, the libertines quickly understood that this was not the flaw of Sa'dī. His

1. Gladwin, *Gulistan or Rose Garden*, preface, p. 9. [Trans.]

2. It refers to Ibrāhīm PūrDāwūd (Ebrahim Pourdavoud) (1885 – 1968), a multi-lingual Iranian intellectual who translated Avesta into Fārsī (6 volumes) and a scholar of Zoroastrian history and teachings. [Trans.]

flaw is in saying, "Affordest daily sustenance to the Zoroastrian and the infidel (Christian)," and that Christians are enemies of God. But they do not point it out; there they want to give vent to their wrath on Sa'dī's head.

Moreover, it is essentially surprisingly this thing to have been said by Kant and his likes. How is it possible for a person to believe that the truth must be said even if its essence would be lost?! A truth will give way to crimes in the world must be said while a lie which may put a stop to crimes in the world and save lives and other truths must not be told! Does conscience give such a dictate?! If a person has an experience about telling the truth and lying, he would not make such a statement. Sometimes, some persons make an utterance of certain things which they do not have any experience. For example, there is a person who has not been honest throughout his life as he is a chronic liar. If he would be asked, "Can one tell a lie if expediency calls for it?" He will say, "One should never tell a lie. One should not lie at all." This is because he has not been honest throughout his life and then he realizes that in some cases telling the truth really brings about trouble. Since he is not like that, what he says is not compatible with the reality. A person with actual experience – that is, one who has been honest throughout his life – really understands that in some cases telling the truth loses its real importance [as it becomes counterproductive]. In Islamic jurisprudence, backbiting and lying have exceptions, and this is the fact.

A Parable

There is a parable of someone who bought a roaster from a chicken shop for two *qirāns*[1] - in old pricing. It was a very good roaster such that its value was actually more than that. He went back home. As he came home, his wife told him, "What have you brought?" "It is a roaster," he replied. She said, "How could an honourable man bring a roaster in his house while his wife is there?!" She immediately covered her face and hid herself. She then said, "I am not willing to live inside a house in which there is a [non-*maḥram*] male. Either this will remain or I will go out. I will not go out of the corner of this house." The husband said, "There is no problem for a roaster; it is not a human male." She said, "No. An honourable man would not bring even a roaster in his house." He was so glad hearing this and then said, "Thanks God, my wife is so modest and chaste." He brought back the roaster to the chicken shop and said, "If it is possible, please take back this roaster and give me back my two *qirāns*. The shop owner asked, "Why? Actually this roaster costs more than that; it costs two *qirāns* and 10 *shāhīs*;[2] I had given you a discount of 10 *shāhīs*." He said, "In any case, I do not like it." The shop owner said, "If you think I am not telling you the truth, know that it really costs more than that."

1. *Qirān*: Iranian monetary unit which is not replaced by the Iranian rial. [Trans.]
2. *Shāhī*: now obsolete, formerly the smallest unit of Iranian currency, worth one-twentieth of a rial. [Trans.]

He said, “That is not the reason. I know that it values more than that, but I do not like it anymore.” The shop owner asked, “Why you do not like it [anymore]?” He retorted, “Why does it matter to you why I do not like it anymore?” The shop owner showed obstinacy and said, “Unless you tell me the reason, I will not take again the roaster from you.” He said, “Well, instead of two *qirāns*, just give me thirty *shāhīs*.” The shop owner insisted, “Even then, I will not give you unless you tell the truth.” He said, “So, just give one *qirān*.” The shop owner said, “Unless you tell the truth, I will not give you even 10 *shāhīs*. You have to tell the truth.” He thus disclosed, “The fact is that my wife is so modest and chaste in that she is now willing to give way to even a roaster in our house.” The shop owner immediately took the roaster, gave him two *qirāns* and said, “Take these two *qirāns* but be sure that your wife is a profligate and wicked woman. If she were really a modest and chaste woman, she would not have said that. This utterance is that of a woman who knows no modesty and chastity for making such vain and vulgar utterance.

Dissimulation

At a time when the real importance of honesty is lost and by telling the truth a person would open the floodgate of a mass murder, if one would say that even in these circumstances truth must be said, it is like [that woman's act of] covering [herself] so as not to be seen by the roaster. In this regard, Islam has a decree which is very important. It says that in order for your soul not to be accustomed with telling a lie, whenever you receive news, [entertain something in your mind and tell something else]. And unless there is news, you are not supposed to do so. As I have said [earlier], you should not confuse self-motivated lie with white lie. Islamic jurisprudence maintains that whenever it is really expedient and telling a truth will bring about many troubles to the community and whenever you are compelled, you have to tell a lie due to certain expediency and not because of selfish interests. (For example, the enemy's spies are undertaking house-to-house search for innocent people. They ask you; you say [to yourself], "I am an honest person; I have to tell them their whereabouts." [In this case,] you are not an honest person; you are a criminal.) In order that you will not to be mentally disturbed and be accustomed to corruption (telling a lie), entertain something in your mind and tell something else. For instance, when they ask you, "Have you seen them?" You say, "No," but what you mean by "no" [is something else]; entertain something else in your mind. Do not directly burden your mind with the lie so that you will not be accustomed to telling a lie. This is called *tawriyah* (dissimulation). The Commander of the Faithful (A.S.) reported that the Prophet (S) said:

لايستقيمُ ايمانُ عَبْدٍ حَتّي يستقيمَ قَلْبُهُ وَ لا يستقيمُ قَلْبُهُ حَتّي يستقيمَ لِسانُهُ

"*The servant's faith shall not be straightened*

unless his heart is straightened and his heart shall not be straightened unless his tongue is straightened."[1]

Now, some continuously tell lies and they call it 'dissimulation', and I know such individuals. I have nothing to do with them. What I am telling is the truth.

These are a set of criticisms against the theory of Mr. Kant, although there are also many correct elements in his theory.

Tomorrow night, God willing, we shall discuss about the theory of beauty – the theory of those who view ethics from the framework of beauty.

ولا حول ولا قوة الّا باللّه العلي العظيم. بإسمک العظيم الاعظم الاجلّ الاکرم يا اللّه...

"And there is neither power nor might except that of Allah, the Exalted and Mighty. By Your Exalted, Great, Majestic, and Honourable Name, O Allah..."

O God! Illuminate our hearts with the light of faith. Familiarize us with the truths of the sacred religion of Islam. Make us be appreciative of Islam and the Qur'an. Make us be grateful to the Prophet and his progeny. Shower our deceased ones with Your mercy.

وعجّل في فرج مولانا صاحب الزمان.

"And expedite the advent of our chief, the Master of the Time."

---

1. Shaykh 'Abbās Qummī, *Safīnat al-Biḥār*, vol. 2, 510; Imām 'Alī, *Nahj al-Balāghah*, Sermon 174.

Chapter 5: Theory of Beauty

﴿ إِنَّ اللَّهَ يَأْمُرُ بِالْعَدْلِ وَالإِحْسَانِ وَإِيتَاءِ ذِي الْقُرْبَى وَيَنْهَى عَنِ
الْفَحْشَاءِ وَالْمُنْكَرِ وَالْبَغْيِ يَعِظُكُمْ لَعَلَّكُمْ تَذَكَّرُونَ ﴾

> Indeed Allah enjoins justice and kindness and generosity toward relatives, and He forbids indecency, wrong, and aggression. He advises you, so that you may take admonition. (16:90)

We have promised to discuss the theory which regards ethics as pertinent to beauty. Let me raise a minor point at the beginning of my remarks and that is, it is possible for some people to think that knowing these theories – Is ethics pertinent to emotion and love? Is it pertinent to knowledge and knowing? Is it pertinent to willpower? Is it pertinent to the conscience? Is it pertinent to beauty? – has no benefit in terms of knowledge and societal upbringing. Accordingly, that which is necessary and useful is that the people practically possess virtuous morality whether we know that ethics is pertinent to which subject or not. These are just part of an array of intellectual discussions which have no scientific output.

What then is the benefit of these discussions? It is like the one who is being asked, "Is *qurmeh* (preserved or potted meat) with [letter] *ghayn* or [letter] *qāf*?"[1] He answered, "It is neither with *ghayn* nor *qāf*. It is with meat and oil." Now, the discussion is: Which subject does ethics pertains to? Some may possible think that it is purely a non-scientific theoretical discussion, but it is not so. To know which subject or category ethics pertains to and that it pertains to one or how many subjects has ample effects in knowing where we should begin in completing or perfecting morality in society, and incidentally, there is such astonishment. Individuals whose way of thinking is that of the Hindu and Christian say, "Morality is to love, not to have an enemy and not to have hatred. If you want to promote morality in society, impart the spirit of love in society and do something to extinguish hatred, antagonism and enmity. Uproot enmity in society and plant the seeds of love in the hearts. This is morality."

One who regards ethics as pertaining to knowledge such as Socrates, however, says something else. He says, "Teach the people; let them learn; make them knowledgeable. When the people become knowledgeable, that is the same morality for them." According to this belief, anyone who is morally corrupt is such because he is not learned. The origin of moral corruption is ignorance. "So, teach them and that is sufficient. Teach

1. That is to say, "Does the word *qurmeh* begin with letter *ghayn* (غ) or letter *qāf* (ق)?" [Trans.]

because education is also training. Training is inseparable with training while training is indivisible with education." He does not say, "Eliminate hatreds and promote love." He says, "Spread knowledge."

As such, for the training of society, we should know whether we must improve the level of education or we must strive hard to eliminate animosities in our midst; whether education can do something [or not].

One who is like Aristotle says, "Mere knowledge can do nothing; one must strengthen his willpower." He recommends another way. One who regards the intrinsic human conscience as the foundation of ethics says, "There is a sacred voice within every person who commands him to do good deeds and forbids him from doing evil. This voice which enjoins honesty and discourages dishonesty; this voice which encourages trustworthiness and campaigns against treachery; this voice which promotes self-sacrifice; this voice which advocates justice with others exists within every person. It is only when other voices and hullabaloos are loud that a person cannot hear the voice of his conscience. For example, in the place where are in now, if a preacher wants to impart the word of God to us, the prevailing silence in the environment is such that we could hear and understand him very well. But if another voice is loud as that of the microphone or an automobile or someone sitting at our back is also talking loudly, we can no longer hear the preacher's voice. In order for one voice to be heard very well, other voices must be silenced. The same is true with respect to seeing. One condition for us to be able to see very well is the absence of smoke, dust or fog [in front of us]; otherwise, we cannot see very well no matter how clear our eyesight is. In reality, we can see but the smoke or dust does not allow. In order to see very well, the dust or smoke must subside. In the words of Sa'dī,

حقیقت، سرايي است آراسته
هوا و هوس گرد برخاسته
نبيني كه هرجا كه برخاست گرد
نبيند نظر گرچه بيناست مرد
تو را تا دهن باشد از حرص، باز
نيايد به گوش دل از غيب، راز

Truths are a decorated house;
Lust and concupiscence are dust up-raised.
Seest thou not, that wherever the dust has risen,
The sight beholds not, though man be possessed of vision.
So long as thy mouth is open, through avarice;
The secret (of God) from the hidden comes not to the ear of the heart.[1]

As such, if we ask the one who holds that morality means the voice of conscience, "If we want to lead the society toward morality, what should we do?" he will say, "Do something so that each person listens to the voice of

1. Shaykh Muṣliḥ al-Dīn Sa'dī, *Būstān*, chap. 3 on love, "Story of Sulṭān Maḥmūd and Ayyāz." [Trans.]

his conscience." "What should we do?" "You must minimize the volume of other sounds and voices." That voice is always there and it cannot be muted. Contrary sounds and voices do not allow it to be heard by you. He says, "Morality means to listen to the voice of your heart."

The one who believes that ethics pertains to beauty says, "Promote the sense of beauty among the people (in a way which we shall explain later). If a person senses the excellent and noble moral traits, he will not commit any wicked act. The reason why individuals tell a lie is that they do not comprehend the beauty of honesty. The reason why they commit treachery is that they do not perceive the beauty of trustworthiness. So, nurture the zeal of every individual. Zeal is related to beauty. Do something so that he would not limit beauty to the tangible manifestations of beauty; that he should also pay attention to rational beauties; that he should also enter into the realm of rational beauties.

Each of those who have other theories recommends a particular way to perfect morality in society.

This discussion, therefore, is not merely a theoretical and philosophical discussion which has no scientific bearing at all. It is a discussion which has considerable scientific bearing. In addition, unless we accurately, elaborately and comprehensively present them, we cannot correctly know our own moral school of Islam. Let us see on which foundation or foundations Islam has based morality.

Is Beauty Definable?

We have said that one theory on ethics is that ethics pertains to the subject of beauty. Many questions are raised here. At the outset, we have to answer the questions so that we could later arrive at the main point that ethics pertains to the subject of beauty. The first question is this: What is beauty (*jamāl*)? That is, how can we define beauty, and in the logicians' parlance, what is the genus (*jins*) and differentia (*faṣl*) of beauty? Beauty is within which category (*maqūlah*)? Is it within the category of quantity (*kammiyyah*) or quantities (*kammiyyāt*)? Is it part of [the category of] qualities (*kayfiyyāt*)? Is it within the category of relation (*iḍāfah*) and is it a relation? Is it a passio (*infi'āl*)? Is it an essence (*jawhar*). Or, without considering its analytic composition, what are the components of beauty in terms of formula and property? Can one obtain a formula of beauty? Just as in chemistry there is a definite formula for every form of matter, and for example, it is said that the formula of water is H_2O, does beauty have also any formula in nature? And after all, what is beauty?

This is a question – what is beauty is – which no one has answered yet. In fact, according to some people, not only that no one knows its answer but also this question has no answer in view of the fact that of all the realities in the universe, the loftiest realities are realities which cannot be quantified.

Given this, can beauty be defined? No, it cannot be

defined. Regarding eloquence (*faṣāḥah*) which belongs to the category of beauty, the scholars say that in reality, eloquence cannot be truly defined:

مِمّا يدْرَکُ وَلایوصَفُ

> "It can be perceived but it cannot be described."

And we have so many things in the world which one can perceive but he cannot describe it. Beauty is one of them.

Plato has attempted to define beauty. First of all, he was not sure if his definition is correct or not, and secondly, it is not a complete definition. He has said, "Beauty means harmony of the parts with the whole." That is, if we have a whole, say, a building, once all its parts (door, wall, foundations, ceiling, and others) have a specific harmony and coordination, the whole is beautiful. The beauty of a building is due to the fact that there is there is a harmony and coordination among its parts. Let us assume for the meantime that this notion is correct and harmony means that there is a specific correlation, but can it is stated what correlation is in the manifestations of beauties? For example, just as with regards to water, the amount of H (hydrogen) and the amount of O (oxygen) can be determined, can we do the same here? No. Is it necessary that we should be able to define it? No. There is no need. It is because in order to acknowledge the existence of a thing, there is no longer essential to define the same at the outset. If we can, we define it; if we cannot, we say that in terms of nature and essence but it does exist.

Beauty does exist although human being could not be able define it. Even this electricity cannot be defined by human being, yet there is no doubt that it does exist.

Is Beauty Absolute or Relative?

The second question which is raised here is this: Is beauty absolute or relative? In other words, is that which is beautiful essentially beautiful in itself whether a person perceives its beauty or not, just like so many things in the world? For example, there is the Damāvand[1] summit and it is the loftiest peak in this region, whether the people of the world know it or not. It does exist by itself. Is 'beauty' truly a reality which exists in [anything] beautiful, or is it just an enigmatic relationship between the perceiver (*mudrik*) and the perceived (*madrūk*)? You can observe that in the eyes of a person a certain object or person (his beloved) is so beautiful but the same object or person is not good-looking for another person. It is clear, therefore, that according to these individuals, beauty is not an absolute reality; that is, it is possible for a person to be so good-looking in the eyes of a certain person while he is not so in the eyes of other persons. The famous story of Majnūn[2] is exactly like this. Since Majnūn did compose all

1. With a height of 5,670 m, Mount Damāvand which is located near Tehran is the loftiest peak of Alborz Mountains, a mountain range in northern Iran, extending along the southern shore of the Caspian Sea. [Trans.]
2. It refers to *Majnūn wa Laylā* which is a classical Arabic story of star-crossed lovers based on the real story of a young man called Qays

these poems and couplets in describing his beloved Laylā, Hārūn al-Rāshīd[1] was thinking that Laylā is a lady whose beauty is unsurpassed in the world. When the rude desert-dwelling Laylā brought to him, he saw that she is a black woman who is not attractive at all.

به مجنون گفت روزي عيب جويي
كه پيدا كن به از ليلي نكويي
كه ليلي گر چه در چشم تو حوريست
به هر جزوي ز حسن او قصوريست
چو مجنون اين سخن بشنيد آشفت
در آن آشفتگي خندان شد و گفت
تو مو بيني و مجنون پيچش مو
تو ابرو، او اشارت‌هاي ابرو

One day a criticizer told Majnūn:
"Look for someone better than Laylā.
Even if Laylā is a ḥūrī (damsel) in your eyes.
But any part of her goodness has deficiency."
When Majnūn heard it, he got angry.
But he laughed and said:
"You see the hair while Majnūn sees its waves.
You [see] the eyebrow while Majnūn sees its gestures."[2]

←

ibn al-Mulawwaḥ al-'Āmirī from the northern Arabian Peninsula in the Umayyad era during the 7th century. [Trans.]

1. Hārūn al-Rashīd: the 'Abbāsid caliph who reigned from 180-193 AH (786-809 CE) and was the contemporary of the seventh and eighth Imāms, Mūsā al-Kāẓim and 'Alī al-Riḍā (A.S.). [Trans.]
2. Waḥshī, *Farhād and Shīrīn*. [Trans.]

It states the same relativity in beauty; that is, she is beautiful for him but not for others. This is an issue in itself. It is said that contrary to what people think that beauty brings about love, the truth is the opposite. Love creates beauty; that is, there is no beauty in the beginning such that due to its effect, love is nurtured. In the beginning there is love and then this love brings about beauty. Of course, this is an extremist view. One cannot totally deny the outward existence of beauty.

Now, is beauty absolute or relative? Once again, for our discussion there is no need for us to definitely investigate this matter – whether beauty is something absolute or relative. It is so clear that there is such thing called 'beauty' in the outside world. It is not true that beauty is purely a product of love and that love is something futile that sprouts just like that; rather, beauty is a reality. Even if we assume that it is something relative, it is still a reality.

The Relationship of Beauty with Love and Action

As an introduction to this discussion, the third issue is that beauty on one hand, and attraction, love, desire, action, and appreciation, on the other hand. That is, they are realities which are joined to each other. That is, whenever there is beauty, there is also a force of attraction. Beautiful is attractive. Wherever there is beauty, there is love and desire in the other person; there is action and motion. That is, beauty itself brings about action and motion. Even according to the belief of theosophers, all motions in this universe - including transubstantial motion (*ḥarikat al-jawhāriyyah*) and the foundation which has brought out the entire world of nature as a single motion or movement is a product of love:

كتحريک الْمَعْشوقِ لِلعاشِقِ و تَحْريک الْمُعَلِّلِ لِلْمُتَعَلِّلِ

> "It is like the beloved's incitement of the lover to act and the cause's inducement of the effect."

They say so. Many things are said in this regard. Wahshī Bāfqī[1] has poems about 'desire,' which maintain that there are desire and attraction in all specks of atom in the universe. He then says that the philosophers call this as 'love' (*'ishq*). At any rate, wherever there is beauty, there is attraction; there are love and desire; there are motion and movement; there are appreciation and glorification. Beauty necessitates appreciation and glorification.

Beauty as not only Limited to Beauty Related to Sexual Instinct

Now, is beauty limited to beauty of a person - beauty to which two persons of opposite sex are attracted to one another, especially man's attraction to a woman? When it is said, "Beautiful!" does it mean, for example, the face or body parts of a beautiful woman? Other than these, is there nothing else beautiful in this world? Individuals who do not correctly discern beauty think in this way. In

1. Kamāl al-Dīn Bāfqī, known by his pen name Waḥshī (1532-83) was a Persian poet of the Safavid period. [Trans.]

nature, however, there are thousand kinds of beauty in the inanimate objects, plants, and animals as well as in the sky, land and seas. Is there anyone who cannot perceive beauty in the flowers?! Perhaps there are many individuals who only know of the flower's fragrant smell while those whose eyes could perceive the beauty could perceive beauty in a flower beyond its fragrant smell; that is, for them it is more important than that. The beauty of flowers; the beauty of trees; the beauty of jungles; the beauty of mountains; the beauty of the sky which is above us; the beauty of the horizon; the beauty of day break; the beauty of the sunrise; the beauty of the sunset; the beauty of the twilight; and thousands of other manifestations of perceptible beauty do exist in the world. All beauties are not limited to that beauty which pertains to man's sexual desire. In reality, anyone who perceives beauty as confined to that which pertains to man's sexual instinct does not perceive beauty at all. Beauty is not only related to man's sexual instinct such that they would say that they immediately perceive the 'beauty' of some individuals in the sense of things pertaining to the sexual instinct. It is not so. There are thousands of manifestations of beauty in nature itself. Moreover, what we talk about are manifestations of beauty in relation of the faculty of sight. Each of the faculties of hearing, touch, smell, and taste also perceives forms of beauty. Basically, that which is 'good' in each of these faculties means 'beautiful'. That which is 'good' in the eyes is 'beautiful' for the eyes. That which is 'good' in the ears is 'beautiful' for the ears. So are the things which are 'good' for the [faculties of] touch, taste and smell. As such, let us make no mistake in this regard such that it would be said that the [sense of] beauty of those whose perception of beauty is so weak is immediately explained away by focusing on sexual issues.

Intangible Beauty

In addition, we do have also intangible beauty? The overwhelming majority of people could perceive absolutely tangible beauties. Do we have not also intangible or spiritual beauty? Yes, there are also many manifestations of it. The least manifestations of it are those that pertain to the human being's faculty of imagination; that is, his ideas. How about the beauty of rhetoric and eloquence? Why could an eloquent and fluent expression attract and draw a person toward it? Why do Sa'dī's works and poems attract a person? Around seven centuries have already passed since the time of Sa'dī. Why those short statements of Sa'dī are still repeated and why a person is attract to them once he hears them? It is a [manifestation of] beauty which does so. What beauty is that? Is it beauty of the terms? No. It is not only related to the terms. It has something to do more with the meanings of those terms. Of course, terms are a contributory factor in eloquence but they are not the only element. The meanings of these terms and mental qualities are so elegantly put together that they could attract and draw the human soul toward them. So are the poems of Ḥāfiẓ and Mawlawī (Rūmī). Those who could perceive mental beauties are sometimes so engrossed with and fascinated by these poems to such an extent that they become oblivious of themselves.

The late Adīb Pishāwarī[1] was one of the preeminent men of letters and products of the old Islamic seminary (*ḥawzah al-'ilmiyyah*). Of course, we have not seen him; what we saw was his picture. He was a *sayyid* (descendant of Prophet Muḥammad (S)) and in sensed he looked so much like one of the Islamic scholars (*'ulamā'*), and in literature he was really extraordinarily learned and unparallel. Sometimes, he would also compose poetry. I read in a book that the late Adīb had said, "Two times in my life when reading a poem made me swoon and be unconscious. The first time I read a *ghazal*[2] of Ḥāfiẓ. I was so enamoured by it that it brought me unconscious." It is a famous *ghazal*:

1. It refers to Sayyid Aḥmad ibn Shiḥāb al-Dīn al-Raḍawī, better known as Adīb Pīshāwarī (1844 – 1930), a prominent poet and religious scholar who attended the classes of Muslim scholars such as Mullā Hādī Sabziwārī, studied literary and philosophical books and compiled a collection of poetry in Fārsī language which is a masterpiece. [Trans.]

2. *Ghazal* is a lyric form of Persian poetry, with rhyme in the first two and in even numbered lines, and allowing various metric forms. With respect to content, it usually does not express the linear development of an idea, but rather its couplets express variations on an idea or mood. [Trans.]

زان يار دلنوازم شكري است با شكايت
گر نكته دان عشقي بشنو تو اين حكايت
بي مزد بود و منت هر خدمتي كه كردم
يارب مباد كس را مخدوم بي‌عنايت
رندان تشنه لب را آبي نمي‌دهد كس
گويي ولي شناسان رفتند از اين ولايت
در اين شب سياهم گم گشت راه مقصود
از گوشه‌اي برون آي‌اي كوكب هدايت
از هر طرف كه رفتم جز وحشتم نيفزود
زنهار از اين بيابان وين راه بي‌نهايت
اين راه را نهايت صورت كجا توان بست
كش صدهزار منزل بيش است در بدايت
در زلف چون كمندش‌اي دل مپيچ كانجا
سرها بريده بيني بي‌جرم و بي‌جنايت
چشمت به غمزه ما را خون خورد و مي‌پسندي
جانا روا نباشد خونريز را حمايت
اي آفتاب خوبان مي‌سوزد اندرونم
يكساعتم بگنجان در سايه عنايت
هرچند بردي آبم روي از درت نتابم
جور از حبيب خوشتر كز مدعي رعايت
عشقت رسد به فريادگر خود به سان حافظ
قرآن ز بر بخواني در چارده روايت

On account of that heart-cherishing beloved, thanks (mixed) with complaint are mine (and, verily, this is wonderful):
If thou be a subtlety-understander of love list well to this tale.
Rewardless was and thankless every service that I rendered:

O Lord! Void of kindness let none be the served one (master).
To profligates, thirsty of lip, none giveth (even) a little water:
Thou mayest say: "Those recognizing holy men have departed from this land."
O heart! In His tress-like noose, twist not; (and from its fancy come out). For, there.
Thou seest severed heads – crimeless, guiltless.
With a glance, Thy eye drank our blood; and Thou approves:
O Soul (of mine)! Lawful is not protection to the blood-shedder.
In this dark night (the world), lost to me became the path of my purpose (knowledge of the true beloved):
O Star of guidance (the Murshid, perfect and excellent)! Come forth from the corner (and help).
From every direction, where I went naught increased to me save terror.
Beware of this desert, and of this endless Path.
O sun of lovely ones! My heart consumeth:
Contain me, a moment, in the shade of thy protection.
Of this Path (of love), the end openeth no form
For, in its beginning, are a hundred thousand stages (and) more.

> Although, thou snatchedest my honour (and madest me despicable), I turn not my face from Thy door:
> More pleasant is violence from the beloved, than from the enemy, courtesy.
> To thy complaint, love reacheth, if like Ḥāfiẓ
> Thou recite (by heart) the Qur'an with the fourteen traditions.[1]

He has said, "There was a time when I read these poems. I was so drawn upon them that I fell unconscious." It is the beauty of poem which attracts a man of letters to this extent. Moreover, this is a man of letters. If a mystic (*'ārif*) would read the poems of Ḥāfiẓ, definitely he will not choose this *ghazal.* He will choose mystical *ghazal*s and only very few people who have mystical inclination would not be extremely touched after reading Ḥāfiẓ's mystical *ghazal*s such as these:

سالها دل طلب جام جم از ما مي كرد
آنچه خود داشت ز بيگانه تمنّا مي كرد
گوهري كز صدف كون و مكان بيرون بود
طلب از گمشدگان لب دريا مي كرد
بيدلي در همه احوال خدا با او بود
او نمي‌ديدش و از دور خدايا مي كرد
مشكل خويش بر پير مغان بردم دوش
كو به تأييد نظر حل معما مي كرد
گفتم اين جام جهان بين به توكي داد حكيم
گفت آن روز كه اين گنبد مينا مي كرد

1. *Dīwān-e Ḥāfiẓ, ghazaliyāt, ghazal* 94. [Trans.]

گفت آن یار کز او گشت سردار بلند
جرمش آن بود که اسرار هویدا مي کرد

Search for the cup of Jamshīd (divine knowledge) from me (*Ẓāhid* and *'Ābid*), years my heart made.
And for what it (the cup) possessed, from a stranger, entreaty made.
A jewel (the true beloved) that is beyond the shell of existence and of time,
From those lost on the shore of the sea, search it (my heart) made.
Last night, I took my difficulty to the Pīr of the Magians (the Murshid),
Who, by strengthening of sight, the solving of subtlety made.
Him, happy, laughing, wine-goblet in hand, I saw:
And in the mirror (of the goblet), a hundred kinds of views (mysteries of divine knowledge) he made.
I said: "When gave the All-wise this cup world-viewing to thee?"
He said: "On that day, when the azure dome (of heaven) he made."
One heart bereft (the lover of God), with him, in all states, is God:
(But) he beheld him not, and from afar (the cry): "For God's sake (be my helper)" made.

All those sorceries that (in the stage of love and of divine knowledge) reason here made;
In the presence of the staff and of the white hand of Mūsā, Samīrī made.
He said: "That friend (Ḥusayn Manṣūr al-Ḥallāj), by whom lofty became the head of the gibbet,
"His crime was this that clear, the mysteries of the sky, he made."[1]

Eloquence of the Qur'an

Why are we going far? What is the source of the Qur'an's extraordinary power? It is its elegance and eloquence. The Qur'an could be able to express in so simple and common expressions the concepts which pertain to the depths of the human soul, whereas in its own expression, the Qur'an is a 'reminder' (*mudhakkir*); that is, it brings these [concepts] our of the human's innermost being. Since this Book is the Prophet's enduring miracle (*mu'jizah*), however, the God of Islam and the Prophet (S) has expressed these truths with unprecedented beauty. In your opinion, how much the Qur'an's eloquence moved people to shed tears?! In the words of the Qur'an itself,

﴿ يَخِرُّونَ لِلأَذْقَانِ سُجَّدًا ﴾

They fall down in prostration on their faces. (17:107)

1. *Ibid., ghazal* 143. [Trans.]

﴿ وَيَخِرُّونَ لِلأَذْقَانِ يَبْكُونَ وَيَزِيدُهُمْ خُشُوعًا ﴾

Weeping, they fall down on their faces, and it increases them in humility. (17:109)

At the middle of the night, how many people the verses of the Qur'an moved to shed tears! It is because those meanings in this so elegant framework [of words] take control of the human being's sense of spiritual beauty and seize him.

﴿ وَإِذَا سَمِعُوا مَا أُنْزِلَ إِلَى الرَّسُولِ تَرَى أَعْيُنَهُمْ تَفِيضُ مِنَ الدَّمْعِ مِمَّا عَرَفُوا مِنَ الْحَقِّ ﴾

When they hear what has been revealed to the Apostle, you see their eyes fill with tears because of the truth that they recognize. (5:83)

Elegance of Imām 'Alī's (A.S.) Words

In the words of Lady Zaynab, [the Umayyads] took control of the earth's regions and the sky's horizons so as to efface 'Alī's name on the surface of the earth and there will be no more mention of him. One fundamental factor why 'Alī (A.S.) did not die in this world – what we call outward natural factors – is that 'Alī has words with utmost elegance. *Nahj al-Balāghah* (*Peak of Eloquence*) is indeed peak of eloquence. Even the enemy wants to preserve and memorize 'Alī's words. We have so many Arab rhetoricians and orators – including those who do not have good opinion about 'Alī – whenever they are asked, "From where did you learn this level of eloquence?" One of them will say, "I have memorized a hundred of 'Alī's sermons, and then my mind was influenced by them." Another will say, "I have committed to memory eighty [of his] sermons." A third person will say,

> "I have memorized the words of the bald one."[1]

'Abd al-Ḥamīd al-Kātib was very famous. He was a Persian scribe in the court of the last Umayyad caliph known as Marwān al-Ḥimār. He was an extraordinary scribe such that it is said:

> "Writing began with 'Abd al-Ḥamīd and ended with Ibn al-'Amīd."

He was either practicing dissimulation (*taqiyyah*) or he had really no good opinion of Imām 'Alī (A.S.). He was asked, "From whom did you learn the art of writing?" He said, "I have memorized the words of the bald one." Even the enemy could not afford to discard preserving and memorizing the words of 'Alī.

Those who say that *Nahj al-Balāghah* is a product of Sayyid al-Raḍī and such vain words [must bear in mind that] Mas'ūdī was exactly a hundred years prior to Sayyid al-Raḍī. He was a historian who is acceptable to all, and it is not clear whether he was a Sunnī or a Shī'ah. If ever he was a Shī'ah, it is obvious he was not like the Shī'ah as we are today. He was somehow inclined to 'Alī (A.S.) or at least, he was not inimical to 'Alī. He cannot be considered a Shī'ah. In his book *Murawwij al-Dhahab* which he had

1."The bald one" alludes to Imām 'Alī ibn Abī Ṭālib (A.S.) who became bald during the later part of his life. [Trans.]

written a hundred years before Sayyid al-Raḍī, in a section called *Dhikr Lam' Min Kalāmuhu wa Akhbāruhu wa Zuhdahu* in which he has quoted statements from 'Alī's (A.S.) speeches, he said, "Now, there are over four hundred and eighty sermons of 'Alī are memorized by the people." This is while what are included in *Nahj al-Balāghah* are only 239 sermons. In other words, Sayyid al-Raḍī has been able to collect less than half of the number mentioned by Mas'ūdī.

Therefore, that extraordinary eloquence of 'Alī (A.S.), that is, that extraordinary beauty of his words about which it is said that

دونَ كلامِ الْخالِقِ وَ فَوْقَ كلامِ الْمَخْلوقِ.

"They are below the Creator's words and above the creature's words," did not allow and still does not allow these words to be relegated to oblivion, it is such an extremely effective factor. All the poems, eloquence, rhetoric and lofty prose pertain to the subject of beauty but these are mental beauty and not sensory beauty; that is, these are not related to the eyes, ears, skin, tongue, and nose; they are related to the human mind only and nothing else.

Rational Beauty

Now, as we reached the point that beauty is not limited to the beauties related to the sexual instinct, it exists in all tangibles of this world, and it is not limited to the tangibles of this world as well; it is also related to concepts in the mind. Let us go further; there is a point higher – rational beauty; that is, a kind of beauty which can only be perceived by the human intellect. It can be perceived neither by the human sensory perceptions nor by his faculty of imagination. It is a higher level or stage and it is called 'rational beauty' or 'rational goodness'. Its opposite is 'rational ugliness' or 'rational wickedness'. It is here that Muslim theologians (*mutakallimūn*) – of course, the Shīʿah and Muʿtazilite theologians and not Ashʿarite theologians) as well as Muslim jurisprudents (*fuqahā*) – again, the Shīʿah jurisprudents and those Sunnī jurisprudents who are Muʿtazilites in terms of theology (*ʿilm al-kalām*) – believe in the rational goodness of some actions and the rational wickedness of some other actions. In other words, they claim that human actions are of two types. Some actions are essentially or by themselves beautiful and elegant; magnificent; attractive and appealing; action-inducing; love- and affection-nurturing; and appreciation-provoking [while other actions are not like that.] Basically, our discussion started here that we can observe that some human actions are different from the natural and common actions of a person. A person's natural and common actions are actions which do not incur appreciations, praises and admirations. There are other actions, however, which are glorious, magnificent and splendid; they are beautiful and elegant; they provoke humility, humbleness and admiration. And they are indeed such. Is there anyone who could not admire a person who sacrifices himself for the sake of the community and endures hardship for the sake of others' comfort?! Regarding the Noble Messenger (S), the Holy Qur'an states:

> ﴿ لَقَدْ جَاءَكُمْ رَسُولٌ مِّنْ أَنفُسِكُمْ عَزِيزٌ عَلَيْهِ مَا عَنِتُّمْ حَرِيصٌ عَلَيْكُم بِالْمُؤْمِنِينَ رَؤُوفٌ رَّحِيمٌ ﴾
>
> There has certainly come to you an apostle from among yourselves. Grievous to him is your distress; he has deep concern for you, and is most kind and merciful to the faithful. (9:128)

That is to say, "There has certainly come to you an apostle from among yourselves. One of his distinctive features is that [grievous to him is] your misfortunes, distress, difficulties, and troubles and because of your ignorance, lack of insight and the like, you could not perceive [these afflictions]. You are in utmost misfortune and you cannot discern it but it is grievous to him; he suffers from this grief and sorrow; the pain of his concern to you." Obviously, this is something venerable, magnificent and glorious.

Therefore, [this theory maintains that] in the school of ethics you have to do something so that one could perceive the spiritual beauties of moral actions – the beauty of self-sacrifice, the beauty of perseverance, the beauty of justice in dealing with others; the beauty of forgiveness, the beauty of fortitude, the beauty of tolerance, the beauty of pardon, [and] the beauty of generosity. Once he perceives these beauties, just as he could perceive sensory beauties, [he will be drawn toward these actions.] For example, once he sees a beautiful carpet, he will be fascinated by and attracted to it and would even buy it higher than its actual price. Why? It is because he can perceive its beauty. Do something so that the people would be able to perceive the beauties of excellent moral traits; speaking of beauties, they should not limit their minds to the issues related to sexual matters. There are thousands of other manifestations of beauty that exist in nature – beauties that the mind can perceive, sense and even beyond that; it can perceive the beauties of righteous deeds or moral actions. On the contrary, it could also sense the evil, wickedness and abomination of bad deeds. You have to do something so that lie would appear as something filthy, stinking and foul-smelling to a person; as something he would definitely shun. Totally change his taste such that he would abhor backbiting. Do you believe that the moralists – that is, those who have trained themselves – really hate backbiting, are disgusted of telling a lie, detest treachery, and are repulsive to injustice and transgression of the rights of others? Of course, their taste dislikes, reject and throw out these actions. Change the taste including the rational, mental and spiritual taste. As the taste is changed, the person will also change accordingly. How to do it? Of course, there is a way of doing it.

Through training, every intrinsic sensory perception can be nurtured very well. In our lives, we have really seen individuals whose tastes were moulded in such a way.

Their taste finds delight in remembering God which cannot be surpassed by any delicious food or any physical pleasure. The taste of such a person is such that it finds delight in acts of worship and enlightening and guiding the people; it abhors backbiting and cheating people. Even if God would tell him, "I shall not punish you for backbiting and I shall not reward you for being honest; your acts shall not be reckoned; you are free and independent; you may backbite or not backbite," still he will not backbite because his taste attains such a state that he has abhorrence to backbiting, slandering, obscenity, and every wicked act. He perceives the beauty of justice; he perceives the beauty of kindness; he perceives the ugliness of obscenity; he perceives the ugliness of rebellion (*baghī*) (in the expression of the Qur'an). The Qur'an has an astonishing expression regarding *ma'rūf* (good) and *munkar* (evil) (literally, 'ugly'):

﴿ إِنَّ اللَّهَ يَأْمُرُ بِالْعَدْلِ وَالإِحْسَانِ وَإِيتَاءِ ذِي الْقُرْبَىٰ وَيَنْهَىٰ عَنِ الْفَحْشَاءِ وَالْمُنْكَرِ وَالْبَغْيِ يَعِظُكُمْ لَعَلَّكُمْ تَذَكَّرُونَ ﴾

> Indeed Allah enjoins justice and kindness and generosity toward relatives, and He forbids indecency, wrong, and aggression. He advises you, so that you may take admonition. (16:90)

This was the subject being mentioned by Muslim theologians (*mutakallimūn*) and subsequently the Muslim jurisprudents (*fuqahā*) on goodness (*ḥasan*) and wickedness (*qabaḥ*).

Plato's View

There is yet another view and that is, ethics is basically related to the spirit of beauty and not that a certain action is essentially beautiful. Ethics means that the human soul attains such a state that the soul itself becomes beautiful. If the action is beautiful, natural the human soul [from which it emanates] is beautiful. In the first view, the action is beautiful in itself and the soul discovers its beauty through its action, but according to this view, the soul is beautiful and the beautiful action discovers itself from the soul. In view is associated with Plato who has set justice as the foundation of morality. In other words, he regards morality as the same with justice and justice as identical with morality. He says, "Although the human beings know justice, beauty and truth, no one of them can be defined." Yet, still he has tried to give an incomplete definition of justice. He says, "Justice means harmony of the parts with the whole." He also defines social justice by saying that "Social justice means that every individual works according to his ability, and he shall be rewarded according to the extent of his work. If the society is composed of such individuals, then the members of this society are all harmonious, and it is not that one works more while another person works less and the product of work of the first shall be given to the second, or one does not work at all and then allocates to himself the product of others' work. In this case, apart from the fact that the individuals are not just, the society is also not just. A society which is not just is not beautiful, and a society which is not just and beautiful will not endure.

As far as justice is concerned, he has such a view, saying that morality is the spiritual apparatus of man which consists of ideas, inclinations and desires, tendencies and decisions. Like the spare parts of an automobile, they must be compatible with each other. We have said, however, that no one could state the formula of this compatibility. He just says that there is perfect proportionality, balance and harmony between the spiritual elements of man. According to him, the man who is highly praised by others (that is, the perfect man or *Insān al-Kāmil*) is the man whose soul is of utmost beauty. As we have said, beauty entails attraction and lure; it breeds love and desire; it incites action; it induces appreciation. As we can see, one of the distinctive features of Imām 'Alī (A.S.) is the perfect balance, equilibrium and harmony which exist in the spirit of this celestial being. He is a man who has been known as the man of excellent traits and full of contradictions. Ṣafī al-Dīn al-Ḥillī says:

جُمِعَتْ في صِفاتِکَ الأضْدادُ   وَلِهذا عَزَّتْ لَکَ الأنْدادُ

That is to say, "In your being are gathered many a contradiction and for this reason, your equals cannot be found."[1] And concerning the speeches of Imām 'Alī (A.S.),

1. Shaykh 'Abbās Qummī, *Muntahā'l-Āmāl*, vol. 1, 256.

Sayyid al-Raḍī says, "His speech is multidimensional and in all dimensions, it is beautiful." In all aspects, 'Alī talks and he does so beautifully because his spirit is an all-dimensional spirit, and in today's parlance, it is called 'multi-faceted.' It is not only multi-faceted; rather, while being multi-faceted, there is a sort of balance and equilibrium between its various facets. This is something which exists in the souls and intellects. This is no longer related to the sight, hearing, smell, or taste; in general, it is not related to the sensory perceptions; it is related to the human soul. People can perceive the beauty of 'Alī without being able to describe it, and since beauty elicits attraction , they are drawn toward 'Alī. Fourteen centuries have already passed, and there is no century in which 'Alī did not have thousands, nay millions, of lovers and admirers. Why is it that loving 'Alī is faith (*īmān*)? It is because loving 'Alī means love for the spirit of balance and equilibrium, for love the perfect man, love for the perfection of humanity, love for that which God and the Prophet invite [the people to]. And this is not idol-worship; it is not also mere loving a person; it is beyond that. The one who really loves 'Alī actually admires himself in that "I can perceive the extraordinary beauty of that noble spirit; I can perceive that perfect balance and equilibrium; I can perceive the meaning of the 'perfect man'. He is a man who has been totally despised, dejected and oppressed by the history of his own time. Yet, we can hear the sound of admiration to him from the depth of fourteen centuries of history not from the tongues of those who call themselves 'Shī'ah' but also from those of the Sunnīs, and not only from the tongues of the Muslims but also from those of non-Muslims, Christians and Jews. Anyone who has conscience will become a real admirer of 'Alī.

While Ibn Shahr Āshūb[1] was writing his *Al-Manāqib*, he claimed that "As I am writing *Al-Manāqib*,[2] there exist a thousand *manāqibs* [of Imām 'Alī (A.S.)]." Now, I do not know if he had those books in his library or he had at least the list of those books. This (writing about someone's feats which were already written about by many others) emanates from man's natural disposition (*fiṭrah*). In the same manner, man's natural disposition will be attracted to a beauty such of that of Prophet Yūsuf (Joseph) (A.S.), and the Noble Qur'an has narrated the story of Yūsuf in utmost beauty, eloquence and rhetoric such that it is astonishing:

﴿ فَلَمَّا رَأَيْنَهُ أَكْبَرْنَهُ وَقَطَّعْنَ أَيْدِيَهُنَّ وَقُلْنَ حَاشَ لِلَّهِ مَا هَٰذَا بَشَرًا إِنْ هَٰذَا إِلَّا مَلَكٌ كَرِيمٌ ﴾

So when they saw him, they marveled at him

1. It refers to Abū 'Abd Allāh Muḥammad ibn 'Alī ibn Shahr Āshūb Sārawī Māzandaranī (488 A.H./1095 - 588 A.H./1192) better known as Ibn Shahr Āshūb, Muslim scholar in jurisprudence *fiqh* and *ḥadīth* of the 5th and early 6th centuries A.H., who wrote many works including *Al-Manāqib* and *Ma'ālim al-'Ulamā'*. [Trans.]
2. *Al-Manāqib*, more fully *Manāqib Āl Abī Ṭālib*, is a treatise about the merits and virtues of Prophet Muḥammad (A.S.), Imāms from the *Ahl al-Bayt* (A.S.) and Companions (*ṣaḥābah*). [Trans.]

> and cut their hands [absent-mindedly], and they said, 'Good heavens! This is not a human being! This is but a noble angel!' (12:31)

Yes, just as the countenance of Yūsuf could attract man's natural disposition, the spiritual countenance of a perfect man could also attract people from the depth of their natural dispositions.

So is Ḥusayn ibn 'Alī (A.S.). The Prophet (S)said:

انَّ لِلْحُسَيْنِ مَحَبَّةً مَكنونَةً في قُلوبِ الْمُؤْمِنينَ

> "Indeed there is a hidden love for Ḥusayn in the hearts of the faithful."[1]

This word *maknūnah* (hidden) is full of meaning. In other words, it exists in the hearts of the faithful (*mu'minūn*) and sometimes, they are not aware of it; unconsciously, the love for Ḥusayn (A.S.) exists in the heart of every believer. Perhaps, some would imagine that this means that God has coercively and compulsorily inserted love into the hearts of the faithful. It is not so. In the depth of being of every believer, there is veneration for every Ḥusayn-like. Even if Ḥusayn (A.S.) did not exist and there were somebody in his stead who would do whatever he did, can the pure hearts of the faithful afford not to admire and love him?! How does a woman who has only one child who dies cry? One should cry like her for

1. Ḥusayn Muḥaddith Nūrī, *Mustadrak al-Wasā'il wa Mustanbaṭ al-Masā'il*, vol. 1, 211; Ḥusayn Muḥaddith Nūrī, *Lu'lu wa Marjān*,38; Muḥammad Bāqir Majlisī, *Biḥār al-Anwār*, vol. 43, 272, with a slight variation.

Ḥusayn.

ولا حول ولا قوة الّا باللّه العلي العظيم وصلّي اللّه علي محمّد وآله الطاهرين.

"And there is neither power nor might except that of Allah, the Exalted and Mighty, and may Allah's benediction be upon Muḥammad and his pure Household."

Chapter 6: Theory on Worship

﴿ وَمَا خَلَقْتُ الْجِنَّ وَالْإِنسَ إِلَّا لِيَعْبُدُونِ ﴾

I did not create the *jinn* and humans except that they may worship Me. (51:56)

One of the theories regarding the human being's moral actions is the theory on worship. It is said that the set of human actions [which is different][1] from the natural actions, which all individuals sanctify and praise, and which they regard as honourable and humane actions beyond natural actions, is of the category of worship. In the previous theories we have mentioned, it became clear that some of these actions are considered a sort of affection and love; some are akin to the intellect, knowledge and understanding; others are related to the willpower; others pertain to the voice of human conscience; others are relevant to the domain of beauty. Now, I say that there is another theory about the nature of such human being's sacred actions and that is, such

1. [Missing part in the audio cassette recording.]

actions are of the category of worship; of the category of the worship of God though an unconscious form of worship. For example, the one who has regarded moral actions as a form of beauty say that since beauty is not limited to the tangible beauty and that rational beauty is also [a form of] beauty, anyone who performs a good deed can sense the rational beauty and elegance of moral action, and this beauty or elegance draw it toward himself in the same manner that the ugliness of immoral and wicked actions makes him abhor them. There is attraction toward moral actions which is a kind of attraction of beauty and there is repulsion to immoral actions which is a kind of repulsion to ugliness.

This theory, however, is an amazing theory and the reason is as follows: The one who performs a good deed – even the one who does not consciously recognize God and does not acknowledge His existence or assumingly acknowledges it but consciously does it not for the sake of pleasing God, and this is not an act of worship of God – his moral action is a form of worship and it is an unconscious act of worship.

Outward Sense and the Unconscious Sense

It may possibly be asked, "Is it possible to worship God unconsciously?" The reply is, "Yes, in fact we have also unconscious knowledge about God. In fact, in their innermost beings, and in today's jargon, in the 'unconscous realm', all people recognize their God. The difference among individual people in the knowledge about God is in the 'conscious realm'. This point, if it were made yesterday, i.e. in the past centuries, it would have been more difficult to believe; today, to believe it is quite easy. In other words, today this point [has been proved] that the human being has two types of consciousness: outward sense and unconscious sense; that is, the former is the sense which the human being is aware of or informed about while the latter is the sense which is a kind of consciousness itself but the human being's outward sense is not aware of. Today, even psychoanalysis authorities believe that the major part of human sense is the unconscious one and the minor part of the human sense is the one which the person is aware of. For example, if we inwardly look at ourselves and inspect our own inner beings, we will find a bit of feelings, pieces of knowledge, bits of information, inclinations, hatreds, affections, and such things, and we suppose that there is other than this. Now that the pieces of knowledge, bits of information and documents as well as extreme feelings and inclinations have settled in the depth of our souls, and we are not aware of it. In other words, the main part of my 'self' which is presently talking to you is hidden and the main part of your 'self' which is currently listening to me is hidden. As a parable, it is said, "If you throw a watermelon into a pond of water, how much part of it will above water?" It is very small part of it. Perhaps, ninth part of it is submerged in water while only one part of it is above water. Or, if you throw a big ice cube into a pond of water, how much part of it is under and above water? Obviously, the human conscience whose part is also apparent is such in relation to the part which is hidden.

The world is also such. The relation of this world of nature – which in the words of the Qur'an is the world of testimony – in opposition to the world of the Unseen and hidden truths, is the same relation, if not much more than that. Since the human being does not know the world of nature with all the galaxies, stars and this atmosphere, the question is, where will it end up? It is said that it is an infinite atmosphere and perhaps it is indeed infinite – in relation to the world which encompasses this world; that is, in relation to that part of the world which is hidden, it is so small and in the words a *ḥadīth*, it is like throwing a ring in the desert. What is a ring in relation to a desert? It is nothing.

Now, regarding this thing that we call 'unconscious worship', one should not be surprised asking, "Is unconscious worship possible?" The living person who does not want a proxy or delegate, the 'I' that knows myself that I do not worship God, I do not recognize God at all. Yet, now, are you trying to say that my moral action is a form of unconscious worship?! The reply is, "Yes, you do not know so many things; you do them yourself yet you are not aware of. You do not [even] know your own self.

Presently, we are saying that the gist of the hypothesis is that according to this theory, all moral actions of a person are forms of unconscious worship. In order to explain this subject, I have to mention a set of preliminary points.

What is Worship?

Just as we have said in the section about beauty, the first question is: What is 'worship'? Define 'worship'. Mention its genus and differentia. Give your analysis. Tell its constitutive parts and elements. If what is meant by 'worship' are the human being's actions; that is, those actions which are done by him as [forms of] worship. For example, he prays; he fasts; he performs Ḥajj pilgrimage; he supplicates; he establishes good relations with relatives for the sake of God. If it refers to the devotional acts of a person, the explanation is quite clear. One form of worship, for example, is the ritual prayer (*ṣalāh*); the ritual prayer, in turn, is a set of utterances, actions and intentions. There is bowing down; there is prostration; there is standing straight (*qiyām*); there is *dhikr* (recitation) and the like. If worship, however, is in reality a way of giving form and structure to these acts which are determined for us by God, the Exalted, and an intrinsic manifestation of that which exists in us, and in other words, if it is a form, framework and organ which is determined for us and made for a truth which exists in us – a truth which exists in the depth of our natural disposition whether we understand it or not, whether we can explain it or not – yes, if worship is such as indeed it is such, then its definition is not that simple.

As we have said earlier, philosophers express inability to define justice; they express inability to define beauty – which according to them is one of the human instincts; they even express inability to define knowledge. If you happen to go over the books of philosophers, you will see that they have defined knowledge in a hundred ways. One says that knowledge pertains to quality; another says that it pertains to relation (*iḍāfah*). A third one would say that it is not confined to any category, etc. To define [something] is not an easy job; neither is it necessary. Whenever we want to understand the existence of a reality, we define whenever we can and we do not if we cannot. However, just as we cannot [duly] define beauty and yet we can identify certain things within it, in worship we can also identify certain things. There is attention in worship; there is sanctification.[1] In worship

---

1. Sanctification (*taqdīs*) means to consider a Truth to be immune from any form of defect and suspicion of defect. Whenever we want to give form or structure to that Truth with expressions, we do so with such expressions as *Ṣubhānallāh* (Glory be to Allah), *Ṣubḥāna rabbiya'l-aẓīmi wa biḥamdih* (Glory to the All-mighty Lord and to Him is the praise), *Ṣubḥāna rabbiya'l-a'lā wa biḥamdih* (Glory to the Exalted Lord and to Him is the praise), and even *Allāhu akbar* (Allah is the greatest), which all imply that He is above and immune from any form of defect, suspicion of defect and every deficiency.

(*'ibādah*), there is praise and appreciation of perfections. Just as a nightingale tends to be appreciative in front of a flower, the human being praises in worship the Essence of the Worshipped Being. In worship, to be outside the small confine of the 'self', or to be outside the small confine of hope and wishes is limited and temporary. In other words, in worship the human being makes an exit from a small confine of wishes and hope. In worship, there is recourse; there is curtailment. In worship, there is asking for assistance, getting strength and seeking for help. In worship, the human being really goes out of the confines of selfishness, self-worship, desires, wishes, and trivial matters and soars high. This is the very meaning of seeking proximity [to God] (*taqarrub*). When we say, "We perform prayer *seeking nearness to Allah* (*qurbatan ilallāh*)," this wording is not a word of compliment. In fact, when a person is in a state of ritual prayer (*ṣalāt*) he is actually outside this small confine and soars high to the Real (*al-ḥaqq*).

There is no need, therefore, to tire ourselves out and attempt to define worship – that manifestation of the human being's spiritual want – but all these things exist in worship. The greatest, noblest, glorious, and magnificent human state is the state of worship which overwhelms him.

Is Worship Limited to Man's Conscious Worship?

There is another issue. Concerning beauty, we ask, "Is beauty – as the less informed suppose – something connected to the sexual instinct of animals and can only be felt in relation to the opposite sex?" Or, it is something broader, encompassing the whole nature; it is beyond nature, encompassing mental concepts which we cite in eloquence, rhetoric, poetry, and the like. It is even beyond that; it encompasses rational beauty – forms of beauty which are beyond the limits of the sensory perceptions, imagination and the like. We have said, "Of course, it goes beyond." You can see that we read in the supplication, thus:

اللّهُمَّ اِنّي اَسْأَلُک مِنْ جَمالِک بِاَجْمَلِهِ وَكُلُّ جَمالِک جَميلٌ.

> "O Allah, I ask You to give me from Your refined beauty that makes more beauty, and all Your beauties are gracefully beautiful."[1]

Regarding the Attributes of God, Muslim theologians (*mutakallimūn*) have coined the terms 'Positive Attributes' (*ṣifāt al-thubūtiyyah*) and 'Negative Attributes' (*ṣifāt al-salbiyyah*). Others, however, especially the Muslim mystics (*'urafā'*), their [coined] terms are 'Attributes of Beauty' (*ṣifāt al-jamāliyyah*) and 'Attributes of Glory' (*ṣifāt al-jalāliyyah*). Instead of 'Positive Attributes,' they say, 'Attributes of Beauty' and instead of 'Negative Attributes,' they say, 'Attributes of Glory'. The reason for this is that the essence of Beauty and Glory exists in the former terms. That which exists in the latter terms is a manifestation of that which exists in the former.

1. Shaykh 'Abbās Qummī, *Mafātīḥ al-Jinān*, "*Du'ā' al-Saḥar*."

Exactly the same point is true in the case of worship. Is worship limited to the human beings, and that it is only the human beings who worship God – and to be more precisely, some of them? We have said that it is not so. First of all, it is the conscious worship which some people do while others do not. In the unconscious realm, all do perform worship. As a matter of fact, worship is a reality which exists in all creatures in the universe and there is no creature in the universe which does not worship God. It is stated in the Qur'an that there is not an iota in the universe which does not worship God, just as there is no human being – though unconscious – who does not worship God. It is not only you who glorifies, extols and sings His praises. All things glorify, extol and sing His praises. In this regard, we have the following verses:

﴿ سَبَّحَ لِلَّهِ مَا فِي السَّمَاوَاتِ وَالأَرْضِ وَهُوَ الْعَزِيزُ الْحَكِيمُ ﴾

> Whatever there is in the heavens glorifies Allah and [whatever there is on] the earth and He is the All-mighty, the All-wise. (57:1)

﴿ سَبَّحَ لِلَّهِ مَا فِي السَّمَاوَاتِ وَمَا فِي الأَرْضِ وَهُوَ الْعَزِيزُ الْحَكِيمُ ﴾

> Whatever there is in the heavens glorifies Allah and whatever there is on the earth and He is the All-mighty, the All-wise. (59:1)

﴿ يُسَبِّحُ لَهُ مَا فِي السَّمَاوَاتِ وَالأَرْضِ وَهُوَ الْعَزِيزُ الْحَكِيمُ ﴾

> Whatever there is in the heavens glorifies Him and [whatever there is in] the earth, and He is the All-mighty, the All-wise. (59:24)

﴿ يُسَبِّحُ لِلَّهِ مَا فِي السَّمَاوَاتِ وَمَا فِي الأَرْضِ لَهُ الْمُلْكُ وَلَهُ الْحَمْدُ﴾

> Whatever there is in the heavens glorifies Allah and whatever there is in the earth. To Him belongs all sovereignty and to Him belongs all praise. (64:1)

There is another verse:

﴿ وَإِن مِّن شَيْءٍ إِلاَّ يُسَبِّحُ بِحَمْدَهِ وَلَكِن لاَّ تَفْقَهُونَ تَسْبِيحَهُمْ ﴾

> There is not a thing but celebrates His praise, but you do not understand their glorification. (17:44)

Of course, I do acknowledge that the level of the subject is very high but I want to point out that this is the logic of the Qur'an. Worship, therefore, in the logic of the Qur'an, is not limited to the conscious worship of the human beings and perhaps in many human beings, it is the most defective acts of worship that, for example, we face the *qiblah* and perform two circles (*rak'ahs*) of prayer while our spirit is totally absent in prayer and is preoccupied somewhere else. We outwardly do bend [and perform prayer]. In this regard, Fārābī – the well-known Muslim philosopher who lived one thousand and one hundred years ago and whose millennium birth anniversary Iranians and non-Iranians have recently commemorated – has this statement:

صَلَّتِ السَّماءُ بِدَوَرانِها وَ الْارْضُ بِرَجَحانِها وَ الْمَطَرُ بِهَطَلانِهِ وَ الْماءُ بِسَيلانِهِ.

> "The sky's prayer is its [cloud's] movement, and the earth's [prayer] is its shaking, and the

> rain's [prayer] is its pouring, and the water's [prayer] is its flowing."

We shall set aside this subject for I do acknowledge that it is a high level one. What I have stated is just enough so that whenever we say that every moral action is an act of worship itself, our mind will not immediately think about the conscious acts of worship which we do as a duty. At any rate, this a fact and the People of the Hidden (*ahl al-bāṭin*), the People of the Heart, claim that if a person advances in the levels of spiritual perfections, and accordingly, if the ear of his heart is opened, he will be able to perceive and hear the creatures' praises and glorification [of God].

جمله ذرات عالم در نهان با تو مي گويند روزان و شبان
ما سميعيم و بصيريم و خوشيم   با شما نامحرمان ما خامشيم
چون شما سوي جمادي مي‌رويد   محرم جان جمادان چون شويد

> "We have hearing and sight and are happy,
> With you, the uninitiated, we are mute."
> For as much as you are going towards inanimateness,
> How shall you become familiar with the spiritual life of inanimate beings?[1]

The fact is that 'consciousness' is not peculiar to the human being and animal alone. It also exists in the plants and it is not even exclusive to the plants. There are also

1. Mawlānā Jalāl al-Dīn Rūmī,*Mathnawī-ye Ma'nawī*, Book 3, lines 1019-1020.

certain degrees of consciousness in the inanimate objects. It is one of the issues acknowledge in today's world. Its proponents believe that every speck of atom in the universe has a sort of consciousness.

Moral Consciousness as not Separate from Consciousness of God

As we have said, it is claimed that morality pertains to worship, but the unconscious one. This means that intrinsically and instinctively the human heart recognizes his Creator. In order to cite a parable for consciousness and unconsciousness, [I say that] its likeness is that of a child who is instinctively as follows:

همچو میل کودکان با مادران   سرّ میل خود نداند در لبان

> Like the inclination of babes towards their mothers,
> It does not know the secret of its desire for being suckled.[1]

One or two days after an infant is born, when he cannot open his eyes yet, definitely he is not conscious of the presence of his mother. In other words, he has no image of his mother yet in his mind and he is not aware of having a mother. Whenever he is hungry, he would continuously swirl his head and he would curl his lips this way and that way. These lips are unconsciously looking for the mother's mammary gland. In other words, if

1. Mawlānā Jalāl al-Dīn Rūmī,*Mathnawī-ye Ma'nawī*, Book 4, line 3641.

someone would demand an explanation from this child as to what he is looking for, he could not be able to explain. His mind is not yet developed at all; his mind is not yet receptive to images and figures. Even if he could talk, still he could not say anything about it, yet he is unconsciously looking for something that exists; he is unconsciously looking for his mother's mammary gland. Moreover, these [instincts] are very weak in the human being; they are stronger in the animals. In animals, especially in insects, these instincts are very strong. In many aspects of the human being, there is such extent of instinct.

Now, what is the meaning of saying that moral actions pertain to worship?

We have said that since the human being intrinsically regards moral actions as noble and lofty even if it involves self-sacrifice, is incompatible with the logic of nature and even with the logic of practical reason in that sense (that is, the reasoning which dictates a person to protect himself and his interests). Yet, a person still does these actions and in these actions he can discern a kind of nobility and greatness; he can discern loftiness and prominence. He feels that by doing these acts, he is making himself great; examples [of such actions] are self-sacrifice, altruism and justness.

To be just and fair is an amazing issue. A person faces his rival; for example, a physician faces another physician. A well-known and experienced physician gives an opinion regarding the diagnosis of an ailment. Another physician who is young and inexperienced also gives his own opinion. When the people who are present are presented with these two opinions, they will never give preference to the opinion of the young physician over that of famous and veteran physician. This [veteran] physician himself, however, knows that the young physician's opinion is correct. As the neophyte begins to explain his opinion, the first person to understand the subject is no other than the veteran physician. It is here that a person will be in a state of dilemma: "Shall I undermine and trample upon my personality and fame by saying that 'This gentleman understands better and the prescription I gave is incorrect and the [correct] prescription is the one he gave'?" This is what they call 'justice.' He may trample upon his sense of justice and say, "What are you (young physician) saying?! Mind your own business." He may change his prescription so that his patient's life will not be endangered, but he will not confess but rather he will try to justify his act [of changing his prescription].

The human being has these two states. Sometimes he acts justly and this happens many times in the world. It is mentioned in the corpus of *ḥadīth* that one of the human being's excellent moral traits (*makārim al-akhlāq*) is to just in dealing with rivals. This state is something unconscious in a person in view of the fact that he knows God and there is a set of issues which intrinsically and unconsciously are [part of] God's *Islam*, i.e. God's Law. *Islam* means submission to God's Law. God has two types of Law. One refers to the laws which are ingrained in man's natural disposition (*fiṭrah*) and another type refers to the laws which are not ingrained in his natural disposition, but rather derived from those intrinsic laws and they are declared by the prophets only. Apart from confirming intrinsic laws, the prophets also bring another set of laws for mankind. Through a special sensory perception, the depth of human soul, the human being's natural disposition, or the bottom of his heart unconsciously knows these laws just as it knows God. He knows God's pleasure and he intrinsically does something for the sake of pleasing God, he himself does not know he is taking a step along the path of pleasing God. As such, this question is raised: Are such actions which are unconsciously done for the sake of pleasing God but not so consciously deserve spiritual reward or not? For example, an idolater may possible do so, as Ḥātam al-Ṭā'ī and his likes did. In this regard, we have many traditions (*aḥādīth*) about unbelievers who have done so. The Prophet (S) or an Imām (A.S.) would be asked, "Are such deeds devoid of any reward from God?" He would reply, "No. They are not devoid of reward." It is true that the main rewards belong to the human being's conscious actions, but the fact is that the person responds to his moral sense; moral sense is something which is not separated from the sense of knowing God. This is contrary to what some have imagined that the sense of knowing God is something different from the sense of morality. The sense of morality is the same sense of knowing God but it is a sense of duty of knowing God; it is the sense of knowing God and a sense of duty of knowing God. In other words, it is a sense through which a person recognizes the intrinsic *Islam*; he intrinsically comes to know that forgiveness is pleasing to the Worshipped Being (*ma'būd*); he intrinsically comes to know that rendering service to God's creatures and offering sacrifice for the sake of God's creatures are pleasing to the Worshipped Being; he intrinsically comes to know that just and fair dealing is pleasing to the Worshipped Being; he intrinsically comes to know that non-submission to humiliation and ignominy is pleasing to the Worshipped Being.

Correct Justification of Morality

The claim of the one who says, therefore, that the root of morality lies in the human conscience is both correct and incorrect. It is correct in the sense that the human heart really inspires them to him. At the same time, it is incorrect in the sense that a person imagines that conscience is a sense separate from the sense of knowing God and whose function is to determine the duty (*taklīf*) for us without identifying the duty-bound (*mukallif*) to us; the duty-bound is itself; it independently determines the duty for us and we must identify its duty.

The only flaw of Kant's statement is that he wanted to present [the voice of] conscience as a duty – a determinant duty – which springs from man's innermost being and not beyond his innermost being. It is not so. Man's innermost being discerns the duty just as it discerns the Giver of duty. Conscience and its inspirations all stem from man's nature of knowing God. This is the logic of the Qur'an, which thus states:

﴿ وَنَفْسٍ وَمَا سَوَّاهَا * فَأَلْهَمَهَا فُجُورَهَا وَتَقْوَاهَا ﴾

> By the soul and Him who fashioned it, and inspired it with [discernment between] its virtues and vices. (91:7-8)

Taqwā [here] means wariness of Allah (*taqwallāh*) and nothing else. *Fujūr* [here] means to go outside the bounds of Allah's decree and nothing else.

The theory of conscience, therefore, is a very correct theory, but its flaw is that it has not taken a step further and said that it is impossible that man is created at once and a power which is independent from everything is embedded in him and whose only function is to say, "Such and such is your duty." It is not so; the human conscience is linked to the Source and the entire universe. It has derived his duty from somewhere else and gives it to you; it is the heart's sense of perception. The heart has a sense of perception through which one recognizes God and intrinsically knows his duty to Him. We call these inspirations as 'intrinsic Islam':

﴿ وَأَوْحَيْنَا إِلَيْهِمْ فِعْلَ الْخَيْرَاتِ ﴾

> And We revealed to them the performance of good deeds. (21:73)

As inferred in the Qur'anic exegesis *Al-Mīzan*, it does not state,

وَأَوْحَيْنَا إِلَيْهِمْ افْعَلُوا الْخَيْرَاتِ

"And We revealed to them: 'Perform good deeds,'" which shall technically be called 'legislative duty' (*taklīf al-tashrī'ī*). The Qur'an rather states, "*And We revealed to them the performance of good deeds.*" That is to say, "We have revealed and inspired the performance of good deeds into the hearts of people." It states, "We have given 'revelation' (*waḥy*) to every person." Incidentally, one of the other things which are universal is *waḥy* (revelation or inspiration). Just as beauty and worship are universal, *waḥy* is also universal in the logic of the Qur'an. Is *waḥy* limited to that form of revelation which is given to the great prophets? That constitutes the most perfect degree of *waḥy*. The Qur'an states, "We have sent revelation to every person but only to that limit."

﴿ وَنَفْسٍ وَمَا سَوَّاهَا * فَأَلْهَمَهَا فُجُورَهَا وَتَقْوَاهَا ﴾

> And inspired it with [discernment between] its virtues and vices. (91:8)

﴿ وَأَوْحَيْنَا إِلَيْهِمْ فِعْلَ الْخَيْرَاتِ ﴾

> And We revealed to them the performance of good deeds. (21:73)

It is not only to every person but the Qur'an states, "We have given 'revelation' to the bees:

﴿ وَأَوْحَىٰ رَبُّكَ إِلَى النَّحْلِ ﴾

And your Lord inspired the bee. (16:68)

"Not only to the bees and animals did We send 'revelation' but also to the plants and inanimate objects."

﴿ وَأَوْحَىٰ فِي كُلِّ سَمَاءٍ أَمْرَهَا ﴾

And He revealed in each heaven its ordinance. (41:12)

This 'revelation' which is given to common people, however, is not conveyed by [Archangel] Jibra'īl (Gabriel) (A.S.); it has another form. It is like light; the light of five candles is also light; the light of the sun is also light; yet, light is light after all. The 'revelation' (*waḥy*) given to the Holy Prophet (S) is like the sun's light while the 'inspirations' (*ilhāmāt*) given to all individuals are like the light of a number of candles; it is something like that.

Meanwhile, is the theory which claims that morality pertains to beauty correct or not correct? It is both correct and incorrect at the same time because it supposes that spiritual beauty is only limited to that point. In other words, it assumes that the human soul is created so as to be able to discern the spiritual beauty of only a set of deeds such as honesty, trust, altruism, chastity, bravery, perseverance, justice, and fortitude. The mistake lies here. It unconsciously discerns the Total Beauty, or the Source and Origin of beauty which is the Sacred Essence of God. As a result, it sees as 'beautiful' His wills and means of pleasure which are the means of our felicity because it wants them and sees through Him. In essence, rational beauty (*jamāl al-'aqlī*) and rational goodness and evil (*ḥusn wa qubḥ al-ʻaqlī*) is actually rooted in 'heart-based goodness and evil' (*ḥusn wa qubḥ al-qalbī*). The intellect (*ʻaql*) pertains to the perceptions (*adrāk*) and not to the feelings (*iḥsās*). In reality, all forms of goodness and evil which are called 'rational goodness and evil' are goodness and wickedness of the heart because goodness is beautiful while evil is ugly, and these pertain to the feelings and not the perceptions which are the intellect's function. The feelings are the heart's function. In his unconscious disposition, a person can perceive the beauty of what God wants from him, because he sees this duty in his innermost being as emanating from God and whatever he sees as God's is beautiful for him. In the same manner, whenever we perceive God through our outward senses, we perceive as beautiful whatever perceive to be God's. It is thus said,

به جهان خرم از آنم که جهان خرم ازوست
عاشقم بر همه عالم که همه عالم ازوست

> I belong to the pleasant world as the pleasant world is from Him.
> I am in love with the entire world as the entire world is from Him.[1]

The one who regards morality as pertaining to love must move a bit forward. By the way, how comes that a person happens to love a thing or another person that is totally different from himself and has nothing to do at all with

1. Shaykh Muṣliḥ al-Dīn Saʻdī, *Kulliyāt Saʻdī, ghazal* 13.

him? This love cannot be logically justified in any way. Yet, a person loves his fellow human beings; he loves animals; he loves many other things, [but] not in the way he loves himself. It is beyond that consideration. He loves something as if it is part of his being. In other words, just as he wants to serve himself, he also wants to render services to them. He loves them not because he could utilize them for his own interests; rather, he loves them to the extent of his willingness to serve them. Why? Is it an illogical matter that happens to a person, or not? Of course, it has its own logic. Its logic (justification) is also God; it is the same intrinsic Islam; it is Divine duty. Through the sense of perception of his heart, a person feels that his Real Beloved is the One that loves him. It is for this reason that he loves his Beloved. As such, the correct explanation for morality is the same [theory of worship].

Morality as Pertinent to Worship and Devotion

Each of these theories – as you have seen – has part of the truth but not the whole truth. The whole truth is that morality pertains to worship and devotion (*'ibādah*). Just as a person unconsciously worships God, he also unconsciously follows a set of Divine orders to the same magnitude. Once his unconscious senses turn into conscious senses – for which the prophets have been sent[1]

1. The prophets have come in order to draw us toward our own natural disposition and transform those unconscious senses and matters into conscious senses and matters.

– all his actions, and not only a limited number of actions, shall become ethical; his sleep shall also become ethical; his eating food shall also become ethical. In other words, once we arrange our life program according to the Divine pleasure and duty to God, then our eating, our sleeping, our walking, our talking, and in sum, our life and death will all be ethical; that is, they will all be sacred works:

﴿ قُلْ إِنَّ صَلَاتِي وَنُسُكِي وَمَحْيَايَ وَمَمَاتِي لِلَّهِ رَبِّ الْعَالَمِينَ ﴾

> Indeed my prayer and my worship, my life and my death are all for the sake of Allah, the Lord of all the worlds. (6:162)

Everything shall be for the sake of Allah and everything shall be 'ethical'.

Regarding ethics, there is another set of theories and initially my intention was to mention them as well and then I would deal with the theory of worship, but I sensed that these will turn us away from our main topic because those theories want to rob the human being of the highest nobilities and these [theories] want the people to believe that there is really no set of moral and noble deeds in the world at all and without desiring for their own interests, they perform theses deeds for the sake of their sense of nobility and sanctity. In reality, these are rejecters of morality in this sense. We shall examine those theories later. For example, God willing, we will examine the theory of Bertrand Russell who regards morality as pertaining to consciousness, Marxist morality, or existentialist morality, but these have brought down ethics from its apogee while they [still] subscribe to human nobility and humanity.

Morality as Only Explainable in the Theistic School of Thought

Of course, let me point this out as well: All those who deny [morality in this sense] are forced to acknowledge it at a particular instance. For instance, Bertrand Russell reaches a point where he would talk about humanity and human nobility. Yet, their philosophies could in no way be able to confirm and explain human nobility. The issue of ethics, human and moral nobilities could not be confirmed and explained except in the theistic school of thought. It is only this school of thought which can explain it, and basically, ethics or moral nobility itself is one of the windows of spirituality in the human being's existence. In other words, it is one of the windows which familiarize the human being with the world of archetypes (*'ālam al-ma'nā*) and make him believe the world of religion (*'ālam al-madhhab*).

Degrees of Worship

In this regard, since we touched on worship, there is another point which I must mention and that is, some have written in their books that religion can never be compatible with ethics in the sense of moral nobility because religion implies that the human being has to worship God and worship of God is only because of fear of the hellfire or desire for paradise. It thus refers back to man's material cravings and now 'moral action' is a noble action in the sense that it is done only for the sake of its nobility and sanctity. We have to explain this subject.

According to the sacred religion of Islam, worship has degrees. The highest degree of worship is the one which is devoid of all these things. In other words, there is no desire for paradise or fear of the hellfire in it. Yet, there are also degrees of worship which have [elements of] desire for paradise or fear of the hellfire. Let me briefly explain. We have this subject in *Nahj al-Balāghah* and many [other] traditions (*aḥādīth*). The Commander of the Faithful 'Alī (A.S.) says the worship the people perform is of three types. Some [people] worship God due to the desire for reward and that is the worship of the merchant.[1] This is a business-like worship. In other words, they want to make a [business] transaction with God; to give something and to get something more [in return]. In his dealings, a trader always gives something in order to get something more than his original capital (that is, the original capital plus profit). The Imām (A.S.) said that this is a business-like worship, and that others worship God out of fear. Accordingly, this is a servant-like worship; it is the worship of the servants. It is like the actions of the servants who are under the mercy of their masters which determine works for them. They are afraid

1. Imām 'Alī, *Nahj al-Balāghah*, Saying 229.

of their masters' whip whenever they fail to perform their assigned works. Yet, accordingly, there are those who worship God in gratitude (*shukran*) (or in some traditions, 'in love' (*ḥubban*) instead of 'in gratitude'). In other words, they worship God solely because they love Him. In reality, their natural dispositions are reflected in their conscious senses; they worship God as their God-cognizant dispositions demand. Since they love God, they worship Him. Even if God did not create paradise and hell, they will still worship Him.

إلهي ما عَبَدْتُک خَوْفاً مِنْ نارِک وَلا طَمَعاً في جَنَّتِک بَلْ وَجَدْتُک اهْلًا لِلْعِبادَةِ فَعَبَدْتُک.

> "O Allah, neither do I worship You because of fear of Your hell nor do I worship You because of desire for Your paradise; rather, I consider You the One worthy of worship; so I worship You."[1]

This phrase 'worthy of worship' (*ahlan li'l-'ibād*) is so meaningful. "Only because You are who You are and I am who I am, [I do worship You.] The most natural of things in this world is that You are the Worshipped Being and I am the worshipper and devotee." I do not know if you pay attention to the contents of *Du'ā' Kumayl*,[2] this

1. Muḥammad Bāqir Majlisī, *Biḥār al-Anwār*, vol. 41, section (*bāb*) 101, p. 14. [It is Imām 'Alī's (A.S.) statement. Instead of 'Your hell' (*nārik*) and 'Your paradise' (*jannatik*), what are in the text are 'Your punishment' (*'iqābik*) and 'Your reward' (*thawābik*), respectively.]
2. *Du'ā' Kumayl* (Supplication of Kumayl): The supplication of Prophet Khiḍr (A.S.) taught by Imām 'Alī (A.S.) to one of his loyal

supplication full of lofty contents. Study the contents of this supplication from the beginning until the end:

أَللّٰهُمَّ اِنّي اسْأَلُكَ بِرَحْمَتِكَ الَّتي وَسِعَتْ كلَّ شيءٍ.... وَ سَلَّمَ تَسْليماً كثيراً.

> "O Allah, I ask You by Your mercy which embraces all things... and give them abundant peace!"

Know what 'Alī (A.S.) says and know the meaning of worship of love and gratitude and the concept of being separated [from Him]. In view of the fact that there is not even an iota of hyperbole and exaggeration in the logic of 'Alī (A.S.) especially when he talks with his Lord, we will encounter certain statements which are totally unimaginable for us. Regarding the fire of hell, the Imām (A.S.) says,

وَهَذَا مَا لا تَقُومُ لَهُ السَّمَاوَاتُ وَالأَرْضُ

> "And these cannot be withstood by the heavens and the earth."

The fire of hell is not a kind of fire in this world. It is a kind of fire which the heavens and the earth cannot withstand. At the same time, the Imām (A.S.) also says elsewhere:

←

companions and staunch supporters of Islam, Kumayl ibn Ziyād. Usually offered on every night preceding Friday [*Laylat'ul-Jum'ah*] individually or in congregation after *Ishā'* prayers, this supplication envisages divine teachings and solid foundations of religion in order to enable everyone to follow the right path for becoming a worthy Muslim. [Trans.]

فَهَبْنِي... صَبَرْتُ عَلَى عَذَابِكَ، فَكَيْفَ أَصْبِرُ عَلَى فِرَاقِكَ وَهَبْنِي صَبَرْتُ عَلَى حَرِّ نَارِكَ، فَكَيْفَ أَصْبِرُ عَنِ النَّظَرِ إِلَى كَرَامَتِكَ.

> "Then suppose, I am able to endure Your chastisement, how can I endure separation from You? And suppose that I am able to endure the heat of Your fire, how can I endure not gazing upon Your generosity?"

This is the worship of love. 'Alī (A.S.) cannot endure such a state of affairs. This is the worship of devotion. The human being's station is far higher than this. It is not limited to 'Alī (A.S.). There are many people in the world who reach the point which Ḥāfiẓ thus describes:

در ضمیر ما نمیگنجد بغیر از دوست کس
هردوعالم رابه دشمن ده،که ما را دوست بس

> In our heart, none can be contained but the Friend.
> Give both worlds to the enemy as the Friend is enough for us.

ولا حول ولا قوة الّا باللّه العلي العظيم وصلّي اللّه علي محمّد وآله الطاهرين. بإسمک العظيم الاعظم الاجلّ الاكرم يا اللّه...

> "And there is neither power nor might except that of Allah, the Exalted and Mighty, and may Allah's benedictions be upon Muḥammad and his pure progeny. By Your Exalted, Great, Majestic, and Honourable Name, O Allah..."

وعجّل في فرج مولانا صاحب الزمان.

> "And expedite the advent of our chief, the Master of the Time."

Chapter 7: Islamic Ethics and Morality

﴿ وَلِلَّهِ الْعِزَّةُ وَلِرَسُولِهِ وَلِلْمُؤْمِنِينَ ﴾

> Yet all might belongs to Allah and His Apostle, and the faithful. (63:8)

A discussion surrounding this subject is about moral sanctities - in other words, human inclinations to sacred dispositions - as pertaining to worship, and we have explanations [in this regard]. Now, we would like to discuss Islamic ethics and morality while taking into consideration the Book (Qur'an), the *Sunnah* and sayings of the leaders of religion. I have mentioned earlier that the question as to which category morality belongs to is not merely a theoretical issue. Every theoretician has no option but to identify his stance in moral training and education. For example, the one who regards morality as pertaining to the emotion is forced to rely on emotion and nothing else, and the one who considers it pertaining to willpower has to rely on something else, and the one who treats it as pertaining to the conscience has to point to another thing, and so on and so forth. Now, we would like to understand on which thing we rely mostly in Islamic ethics and morality. If we refer to the Holy Qur'an, the sayings of the leaders of religion, *Nahj al-Balāghah* and other Islamic sources and references, we will find out that in Islamic ethics and morality, most attention is given on the human soul.

The World of Human Soul

The human soul is an amazing world. The most amazing realm of the universe is the realm of the human soul or spirit. Sometimes, I liken by myself the human soul to an audio recording devise, but not an audio recording device in which only one [cassette] tape could be put and record any sound. Consider an audio recorder - and perhaps there are such audio recorders - which can contain tens, nay hundreds of tapes, and in every tape a particular sound is recorded. You may push any of the buttons and one of the tapes will spin and you will hear one particular sound or voice. For example, you push a particular button and you will hear Qur'an recitation by 'Abd al-Bāsiṭ.[1] You push another button and another tape will play, and for example, a speech, a religious speech; you push yet another button and yet another tape will play, and for instance, a song is sung. It depends on which button you push.

---

1. It refers to the world renowned Egyptian Qur'an reciter (*qārī*) 'Abd al-Bāṣiṭ 'Abd al-Ṣamad. [Trans.]

In reality, the human soul is such. In other words, God, the Exalted, has the human being with various talents. Each group of the teachers of humanity pushes one of the buttons of those skills. As a result, one time you will see a nation comes to the fore and whose voice as a whole, for instance, is political struggle and national fanaticisms, and they have nothing other than these. And it is as if only one audio tape could be able to play in their cassette of existence. You can also see another nation and because another button of their spirit is being pushed, all of them talk about asceticism and self-mortification. Yet another nation talks about something else. In the same manner, every person talks about something. All these talents exist in every individual, but one or two buttons of these talents are being pushed and the corresponding audio tapes begin to play while other tapes do not. Every school of ethics pushes the button of one of the distinctive features of the human soul.

Now, of all these buttons, is there one which, if you push, will play all the tapes and harmoniously do its function, or none? This is another question. Any school of thought which could determine its stance and by doing so, it could be able to harmonize all human talents without going to extremes is a comprehensive school of thought. You have to initially consider this subject as a preliminary point before proceeding to another subject. Then, let us see what conclusion we can have.

Contempt and Praise for the 'Self'

In the Qur'an and [other] Islamic sources, we come across a line of argument which, if we will not tackle, we may think that there is some kind of contradiction. In the Qur'an, for example, whenever the human being's *nafs*, i.e. the 'self,' is talked about, sometimes it is done in this manner: One must combat the desires of the *nafs*; one must struggle against the *nafs*. The *nafs* prompts human beings to evil (*ammāratun bi's-sū'*).

﴿ وَأَمَّا مَنْ خَافَ مَقَامَ رَبِّهِ وَنَهَى النَّفْسَ عَنِ الْهَوَى * فَإِنَّ الْجَنَّةَ هِيَ الْمَأْوَى ﴾

> But as for him who is awed to stand before his Lord and forbids the soul from [following] desire, his refuge will indeed be paradise. (79:40-41)

﴿ فَأَمَّا مَنْ طَغَى * وَآثَرَ الْحَيَاةَ الدُّنْيَا * فَإِنَّ الْجَحِيمَ هِيَ الْمَأْوَى ﴾

> As for him who was rebellious and preferred the life of this world, his refuge will indeed be hell. (79:37-39)

﴿ أَفَرَأَيْتَ مَنِ اتَّخَذَ إِلَهَهُ هَوَاهُ ﴾

> Have you seen him who has taken his desire to be his god? (45:23)

Have you seen someone who has taken his carnal desire as his object of worship? In the same manner, Prophet Yūsuf (Joseph) (A.S.), the truthful, is also thus quoted to seemingly have a negative opinion about his 'self' (*nafs*):

﴿ وَمَا أُبَرِّئُ نَفْسِي إِنَّ النَّفْسَ لَأَمَّارَةٌ بِالسُّوءِ ﴾

> Yet I do not absolve my [own carnal] soul, or the [carnal] soul indeed prompts [men] to evil, except inasmuch as my Lord has mercy. (12:53)

In relation to the incident which is a source of scandal, in which he had no hand at all and for which he never committed any sin, yet he still seemed to say, "I do not want to absolve myself and say that I am innately not such a person. I do not want to absolve myself because I know that the [carnal] self prompts a person to evil."

[Based on these verses,] therefore, that which is called *nafs* or 'self' in the Qur'an is something which must be treated negatively and be fought against; it should not be allowed to dominate and to which one should not yield or surrender.

On the contrary, we also come across other verses which praise *nafs* which also means the 'self':

﴿ وَلَا تَكُونُوا كَالَّذِينَ نَسُوا اللَّهَ فَأَنْسَاهُمْ أَنْفُسَهُمْ ﴾

> And do not be like those who forget Allah, so He makes them forget their own souls. (59:19)

Well, if this 'self' is the same 'self' (mentioned earlier), then it would be better to be always forgotten.

﴿ قُلْ إِنَّ الْخَاسِرِينَ الَّذِينَ خَسِرُوا أَنْفُسَهُمْ ﴾

> Say, 'Indeed the losers are those who ruin themselves'. (39:15)

That is, "The losers or the bankrupt are not those who have lost their properties and wealth (as it is a minor loss). The major loss is when a person loses his own 'self'.

In the jargon of today's existentialists, [the major loss is] when he loses his own primordial self. Wealth is not that important asset; the greatest asset in the world for a person is his own self. If a person loses his self, it is as if he owns nothing – an expression which we also have in the Qur'an. Expressions such as ''forgetting one's self,' 'losing one's self' and 'selling one's self' are exceptionally strongly condemned – that one should not forget his self; that one should not lose his self; that one should not sell his self. On the other hand, one must struggle against his 'self' which prompts him to evil. One passage is when the Qur'an says, 'Have you seen him who has taken his desire to be his god?'

'Self' (*Nafs*) in the Sunnah and *Ḥadīth*

Now, let us examine the *Sunnah* and *ḥadīth*; for example, let us take a look at *Nahj al-Balāghah*. In one place, we can see that the 'self' and carnal desires are strongly denounced, and there are many instances of it:

> [إِنَّ] الْمُؤْمِنُ لايمْسي وَلا يصْبحُ الّا وَنَفْسُهُ ظَنونٌ عِنْدَهُ.
>
> "[Indeed] the believer does not allow [daytime] to reach night time and [night time] to reach daytime without being suspicious of his 'self'."[1]

That is, he always looks at it with suspicion. He is like a person who has a treacherous neighbour. He does not

---

1. Imām 'Alī, *Nahj al-Balāghah*, Sermon 175, 566.

trust him and he is always thinking of ways to prevent his neighbour from committing treachery. Imām 'Alī (A.S.) says that the believer must always treat his 'self' as a traitor and someone who cannot be trusted and someone who must be treated with suspicion. In this regard, there are so many [such examples] in Islamic literature – whether in Arabic or Fārsī. Sa'dī thus says:

مرا شيخ داناي مرشد شهاب
دو اندرز فرمود بر روي آب
يكي اينكه در نفس خوشبين مباش
دگر اينكه در غير بدبين مباش

> The learned guide (murshid) Sheikh Shahāb gave us,
> Two pieces of advice on water,
> One is that, 'Do not be optimistic of your self'.
> The other is that, 'Do not be pessimistic of others.'

That is to say, "Do not treat people with suspicion; instead, be suspicious of your own self."

On the other hand, in *Nahj al-Balāghah* we come across with statements in which the 'self' (*nafs*) has been profusely praised and honoured.

In his last will and testament to his honourable son, Imām Ḥasan al-Mujtabā (A.S.), Imām 'Alī (A.S.) thus writes:

وَأَكْرِمْ نَفْسَكَ عَنْ كُلِّ دَنِيَّة وَإِنْ سَاقَتْكَ إِلَى الرَّغَائِبِ، فَإِنَّكَ لَنْ تَعْتَاضَ بِمَا تَبْذُلُ مِنْ نَفْسِكَ عِوَضاً.

> "Keep yourself away from every low thing even though they may take you to your

> desired aims, because you will not get any return for your own respect which you spend."[1]

That is to say, "O my son! Honour and respect yourself by not entangling it with any mean thing because if you lose something from yourself, nothing can be able to replace it. If you lose your body (physical wellbeing), it is still remediable, let alone losing wealth and properties. Whatever you lose can be replaced by something else [and that is yourself]. Anything you lose can be substituted by something else, but there is something which, if you lose, is irreplaceable (or irreparable) [and that is your own self]. If you give away anything from your own self, you will not get anything in return. Similar in content is a poem from Imām al-Ṣādiq (A.S.). In *Biḥār al-Anwār*, in the section on the biography of Imām al-Ṣādiq (A.S.), this poem is quoted:

أُثامِنُ بِالنَّفْسِ النَّفيسَةِ رَبَّها وَلَيسَ لَها فِي الخَلْقِ كلِّهِمْ ثَمَنٌ

That is to say, "I shall not equate myself with anything. If you want to do bargain with myself, I shall not give it in exchange for anything except my Lord; in exchange, I shall only take Him. Other than this, I am not willing to give this asset of mine and my primordial self. I shall not exchange this priceless gem with the entire world and what it contains, all that Allah originates."[2] And we have many similar quotations [in our sources]. Imām al-Sajjād

1. *Ibid.*, Letter 31.
2. Muḥammad Bāqir Majlisī, *Biḥār al-Anwār*, vol. 75, section (*bāb*) 21, 135.

(A.S.) was once asked:

مَنْ اعْظَمُ النّاسِ خَطَراً؟

"Who is the greatest of people?"

The Imām (A.S.) said:

مَنْ لَمْ يرَ الدُّنْيا خَطَراً لِنَفْسِهِ.

"It is he who does not treat the world as greater than himself."[1]

Also, the Commander of the Faithful (A.S.) said as recorded in *Nahj al-Balāghah*:

مَنْ كَرُمَتْ عَلَيهِ نَفْسُهُ هانَتْ عَلَيهِ شَهَواتُهُ.

"He for whom his self is honourable his desire is insignificant for him."[2]

That is, "For him whose self or soul is honourable for himself, or for him who really knows himself and his own worth and honour, carnal desire (*shahwah*) is so insignificant and to go against it is not that difficult for him." There are so many traditions (*aḥādīth*) with similar content and which contain such expressions as self-esteem, self-respect, self-honour, preciousness of the self, respect for oneself. One must read some of these traditions.

Self-esteem and Self-honour as the Pivot of Islamic Ethics and Morality

Approximately thirteen years ago, on the occasion of the 3rd of Sha'bān, I was invited by the Higher College to deliver a speech about Imām al-Ḥusayn (A.S.). I can

1. Muḥsin Amīn, *Fī Riḥāb A'immat Ahl al-Bayt*, vol. 4, 76.

2. Imām 'Alī, *Nahj al-Balāghah*, Saying 441, 1293.

remember that I talked about "The Issue of the Self in Ethics" there.[1] Since that time, I had this thought and the more I study the more I came to believe that in Islamic ethics and morality, the pivot around which moral precepts revolve, or – in tonight's expression of ours – the point in the human soul to which Islam pays special attention for the revival of human morality and drawing a person toward ethics and morality, is self-respect or self-honour. There is no option but to mention to you some of the Qur'anic verses and traditions in this regard, and unless we quote them, we cannot be properly acquainted with them.

Regarding self-honour, [the Qur'an thus states:]

﴿ وَلِلَّهِ الْعِزَّةُ وَلِرَسُولِهِ وَلِلْمُؤْمِنِينَ ﴾

> Yet all honour belongs to Allah and His Apostle, and the faithful.(63:8)

That is, the faithful must be always honourable as they are honourable.

The Holy Prophet (S) said:

أُطْلُبُوا الْحَوائِجَ بِعِزَّةِ الأنْفُسِ.

> *"Seek for the needs by [preserving] the honour of the selves."*[2]

A person will be in need of his fellows. Is to be in need of other people good or bad? Some schools of thought maintain that it is good, especially due to the fact that the

---

1. [A transcription of the speech is included at the latter part of this book.]
2. Abu'l-Qāsim Pāyandih, *Nahj al-Faṣāḥah, ḥadīth* 325, 218.

more a person expresses his need, abjectness and inadequacy, the more his self is debased and degraded. It is good for self-purification (*tahdhīb al-nafs*).

The Cynics and *Malāmiyyah*

There was a group in ancient Greece whose members were called the cynics (*kalbiyyūn*). In the realm of ethics and morality, they used to promote baseness and ignominy, and the more a person debases himself the more he becomes ethical according to them. There were also such individuals in the world other than the cynics. In ethics, our Sufis have also such statements but not a lot because they are influenced by Islamic ethics and they have also many statements about self-esteem and self-honour. At any rate, they are also human beings; there are mistakes in their words. Sometimes, in our Sufi code of ethics, contrary to this Islamic expression can be seen. Basically, a group of Sufis who were called followers of the Path of Blame (*malāmiyah*) emerged. Their approach was that in order to abase the commanding or base self (*nafs al-ammārah*),[1] accordingly, we have to humiliate ourselves as much as we can,[2] so that no one would give importance to us and we would lose our self-honour in the process.

---

1. See Qur'an (12:53). [Trans.]
2. Perhaps the 'abject dervishes' as they are even called now – at least in name – are remnants of the said group.

The Mistake of Sa'dī and Some Sufis

I have said time and again that this poem of Sa'dī (below) has an inaccurate expression. Although Sa'dī has extremely beneficial pieces of advice derived from Islamic sources, the following points also exist in his statements:

من آن مورم که در پایم بمالند   نه زنبورم که از نیشم بنالند

> I am an ant whom they trample under feet.
> I am not a bee whose sting makes them cry.[1]

That is to say, "I am proud to be like an ant to be crushed by hands or trampled under feet. Nor am I a bee whose sting makes people cry." This [way of thinking] is incorrect. A Muslim's standing is as follows:

نه آن مورم که در پایم بمالند   نه زنبورم که از نیشم بنالند

> I am not an ant, whom they trample under feet,
> Nor am I a bee whose sting makes them cry.

Is it an issue of either-or that a person must be either an ant or a bee?! One could neither be an ant nor a bee. Sa'dī then says:

چگونه شکر این نعمت گزارم   که زور مردم آزاري ندارم

> How could I give thanks to this blessing
> That I have no power to annoy the people?[2]

That is to say, "I thank God for having no power to annoy anyone." Well, to have no power to annoy [others] is not a virtue in itself. That which is meritorious is to

---

1. Shaykh Muṣliḥ al-Dīn Sa'dī, *Mawā'iẓ*, couplet 32. [Trans.]
2. *Ibid.*

have power yet you do not annoy anyone. A Muslim's standing is as follows:

چگونه شکر این نعمت گزارم   که زور دارمو وآزاري ندارم

How could I give thanks to this blessing,
That I have power yet I do not annoy?

These are the same extreme moral tendencies of some of the Sufis and followers of the Path of Blame, which are unacceptable in Islam.

It is also mentioned in some books that a certain famous dervish[1] said:

> "I had never been as happy as I was on three occasions. One occasion was I was sick and I slept in a mosque. It was then the time to expel beggars. The *mu'adhdhin* (caller to prayer) who was also the spreader of carpets told me, 'Rise up and go outside.' I was sick and I could not rise up. He sensed that I could not rise up and he took me by my feet and dragged me outside the mosque. I was so glad that in his view, I was so ignominious. On another occasion, it was winter. I was looking for my fur cloak. I found so many lice in it

---

1. It refers to Ibrāhīm Adham (Abū Isḥāq) who was an emir but later abandoned his status and became a Sufi, as reportedly mentioned by Ibn Abi 'l-Ḥadīd in *Sharḥ Nahj al-Balāghah.* See Murtaḍā Muṭahharī, *Training and Education in Islam*, trans. Mansoor Limba (Tehran: ABU and IHCS, 2011), pp. 181-182. [Trans.]

> such that I did not know which was more – its lice or wool. It was another occasion when I was so happy in that I was able to abase myself. The third occasion was when I mounted a ship in which there was a man who made people laugh and the passengers joyfully gathered around him. And I was there. Part of the stories this man was narrating was that [it was as if] we were soldiers fighting in a certain battlefield, capturing enemy soldiers. Then in order for him to show how we captured and gathered them, he looked around and no one was more appropriate than me to be brought in front. He dragged me by pulling my hair, saying, 'We dragged them this way!' I was so happy because I found out that in his view, there was no one more ignominious than me."

These are not correct. On the contrary, some may also go to the extremes of not telling anyone if they are in dire need. The Prophet (S) said, "Seek for your needs..." but "...by [keeping] your self-honour." Go forward in telling your needs to your close friend or confidant so long as your self-esteem, self-respect or self-honour is not trampled upon. Stop whenever doing so would undermine your self-esteem or honour. [In such a case,] to be in need and indigent is better. Similar to this is also mentioned in *Nahj al-Balāghah*:

الْمَنِيةُ وَ لَاالدَّنِيةُ.

"Let it be death but not humiliation."[1]

وَالتَّقَلُّلُ وَلاَ التَّوَسُّلُ.

"Let there be little but not through others."[2]

In one of the speeches which he delivered during the Battle of Ṣiffīn and which is included in *Nahj al-Balāghah*, Imām 'Alī (A.S.) talked about victory and triumph, saying that death is better than life of subservience and inferiority, and death with such victory is a thousand times preferable. The latter part of his epic speech is as follows:

فَالمَوْتُ فِي حَيَاتِكُمْ مَقْهُورِينَ، وَالْحَيَاةُ فِي مَوْتِكُمْ قَاهِرِينَ.

"Real death is in the life of subjugation while real life is in dying as subjugators."[3]

The Qur'an itself thus states:

﴿ وَأَنتُمُ الأَعْلَوْنَ إِن كُنتُم مُّؤْمِنِينَ ﴾

You shall have the upper hand, should you be truthful. (3:139)

Self-esteem and Self-honour in the Sayings of Imām al-Ḥusayn (A.S.)

Although very few sayings are reported from Imām al-Ḥusayn (A.S.), compared to the other Imāms (A.S.) he talked a lot about self-esteem and self-honour. Among his pithy aphorisms recorded in *Biḥār al-Anwār* is as follows:

1. Imām 'Alī, *Nahj al-Balāghah*, Saying 390, 1273.
2. *Ibid.*
3. Imām 'Alī, *Nahj al-Balāghah*, Sermon 51, 138.

مَوْتٌ فِي عِزٍّ خَيرٌ مِنْ حَيوةٍ فِي ذُلٍ.

"Death with honour is better [and more preferable] than life in humiliation."[1]

هَيْهَاتَ مِنْ ٱلذِّلَّةُ.

"May humiliation be far from us!"[2]

It is amazing, and it is one of the sayings whose light and flame will persist until the Day of Judgment. It continuously nurtures heroism, self-honour, self-esteem, self-respect:

أَلا وَأَنَّ الدَّعِي بْنَ الدَّعِي قَدْ رَكَزَ بَينَ اثْنَتَينِ بَينَ السَّلَّةِ وَالذِّلَّةِ وَهَيهات مِنَّا الذِّلَّةُ! يأْبَي اللَّهُ ذلِک لَنا وَرَسولُهُ وَالْمُؤْمِنون وَحُجورٌ طابَتْ وَ طَهُرَتْ وَانوفٌ حَمِيةٌ وَنُفوسٌ ابِيةٌ مِنْ انْ نُؤْثِرَ طاعَةَ اللِّئامِ عَلي مَصارِعِ الْكِرامِ...[3]

"[On the day of *'Āshūrā'*, Imām al-Ḥusayn (A.S.)] would sometimes ride on a horse or talk with people. There was a time when he wanted that his voice be heard by everybody; so he mounted a camel which was taller (like a person on top of the pulpit and was above the rest because they were riding on horses) and he could be able to see everybody at the middle of the field. Then he uttered this statement:

هَيْهَاتَ مِنْ ٱلذِّلَّةُ.

"May humiliation be far from us!"

---

1. *Balāghat al-Ḥusayn*, 141.
2. Khwārizmī, *Al-Maqtal*, vol. 2, 7.
3. Khwārizmī, *Al-Maqtal*, vol. 2, 7-8; *Tuḥaf al-'Uqūl*, 171 with a slight variation; Ibn Ṭāwūs , *Al-Luhūf* (with translation), 97-98.

That is to say, "Where are we in relation to humiliation? It is heaven and earth apart. Our Lord does not desire humiliation for us; the Prophet does not desire so; the laps on which we were brought up – the laps of 'Alī and Fāṭimah – does not allow so. If you ask the believers until the Day of Judgment which they accept for Imām al-Ḥusayn (A.S.), humiliation or sword, all believers in the world will say, 'We prefer the sword over humiliation.' They could not accept that we would prefer obedience to the mean and ungenerous over the deathbeds of the honourable (that is, over being slain and killed).

The following is also part of the Imām's speech on the day of '*Āshūrā'*:

لا وَ اللّهِ لا اعْطيهِمْ بِيدي اعْطاءَ الذَّليلِ وَ لا افِرُّ فِرارَ الْعَبيدِ

> "Nay, by Allah, I shall not pay allegiance to them like an abject person, nor shall I flee like a slave."[1]

The Imām (A.S.) also said, thus:

الصِّدْقُ عِزٌّ وَ الْكِذْبُ عَجْزٌ

> "Truthfulness is honour and lying is weakness."

(We have many similar sayings from the other Imāms (A.S.).) We shall gradually elucidate all the points in this regard. Such an expression is so meaningful. For this reason, one must seek truthfulness for truthfulness is honour and everyone seeks honour and nobility. In the same manner, one must keep aloft from lying for lying is

1. *Al-Insāb al-Ashrāf*, vol. 3, 188.

inability and weakness. A liar tells a lie because of the weakness, inability and impotence that he feels within himself. In other words, it is impossible for a person to have a sense of honour, strength and nobility, and at the same time, has the audacity to tell a lie.

Imām 'Alī (A.S.) is reported to have said:

الْغيبَةُ جُهْدُ الْعاجِزِ

> "Backbiting is the effort of the weak."[1]

That is, a noble person, a strong person, a person who has a sense of honour, power, strength, and nobility, the same honour and nobility of his will not allow him to do such a mean practice of backbiting people. It is the contemptible, weak, abject, debase, impotent, and powerless people who spend their time backbiting others. Backbiting is a product of weakness.

Self-esteem in the Words of Imām al-Ṣādiq and Imām 'Alī (A.S.)

Imām al-Ṣādiq (A.S.) thus said (in *Tuḥaf al-'Uqūl*):

وَلا تَكُنْ فَظّاً غَليظاً يَكرَهُ النّاسُ قُرْبَک وَلاتَکُنْ واهِناً يُحَقِّرُک مَنْ عَرَفَک.

> "Never be so crude that people desist from approaching you, and never be so humble that you will be disgraced by whoever knows you."

That is to say, "Be moderate in dealing with. Do not be harsh and rude in that they will dislike getting close to

1. Imām 'Alī, *Nahj al-Balāghah*, Saying 453, 1297.

you, and do not be lenient or weak in that they will despise you. A believer is not supposed to behave in such a way that he would seem despicable in the eyes of others."[1] In *Wasā'il al-Shī'ah*, Imām 'Alī (A.S.) is reported to have said:

لِيجْتَمِعْ فِي قَلْبِک الْافْتِقارُ الَيٰ النّاسِ وَالْاسْتِغْناءُ عَنْهُمْ.

> "Combine in your heart pride toward the people and independence from them."

That is to say, "There must be two contradictory feelings in your heart at the same time: 'I am in need of the people; I am not in need of them.' At what time should I consider myself in need of them and what time not? The answer is: When you deal with them; when you talk to them, do not treat them lightly; do not speak to them harshly and do not abuse them. Speak to them softly and meekly. At that time, assume that you are in need of them."

يكونُ افْتِقارُک الَيهِمْ فِي لينِ کلامِک وَ حُسْنِ بِشْرِک، وَ يکونُ اسْتِغْناؤُک عَنْهُمْ فِي نَزاهَةِ عِرْضِک وَ بَقاءِ عِزِّک

> That is to say, "But at a time when your integrity, honour and dignity are at stake, say, 'I am not in need of even the universe.' When your honour is to be undermined, we must take the chance to say that you are not in need of even the whole universe."[2]

It is thus recorded in *Nahj al-Balāghah*:

---

1. *Tuḥaf al-'Uqūl*, 316.
2. *Tuḥaf al-'Uqūl* (with translation), 201, *ḥadīth* 21.

ما احْسَنَ تَواضُعَ الْاغْنِياءِ لِلْفُقَراءِ طَلَباً لِما عِنْدَ اللّهِ، وَ احْسَنُ مِنْهُ تيهُ الْفُقَراءِ عَلَي الْاغْنِياءِ اتِّكالًا عَلَي اللّهِ.

"How good it is for the rich to show humility before the poor to seek reward from Allah, but better than that is the haughtiness of the poor towards the rich with trust in Allah."[1]

We thus read in *Du'ā' Abū Ḥamzah al-Thumālī*:

الْحَمْدُ لِلّهِ الَّذي وَكَلَني الَيهِ فَاكرَمَني وَ لَمْ يكلْني الَي النّاسِ فَيهينوني.

"All Praise is for Allah who dignified me by becoming the Disposer of my affairs instead of making me rely on others who then would humiliate me."[2]

Again, [there are very amazing and meaningful sayings] in *Nahj al-Balāghah*:

قَدْرُ الرَّجُلِ عَلَى قَدْرِ هِمَّتِهِ، وَصِدْقُهُ عَلَى قَدْرِ مُرُوءَتِهِ، وَشَجَاعَتُهُ عَلَى قَدْرِ أَنَفَتِهِ.

"The worth of a man is according to his courage, his truthfulness is according to his balance of temper; his valour is according to his self-respect."[3]

Bravery is different from physical prowess. Bravery signifies strength of the heart and not strength of the muscle. It is the opposite of cowardice and temerity. It means not to be afraid of and not to be careful at the same

1. Imām 'Alī, *Nahj al-Balāghah*, Saying 398, 1277.
2. Shaykh 'Abbās Qummī, *Mafātīḥ al-Jinān*, "*Du'ā' Abū Ḥamzah al-Thumālī.*"
3. Imām 'Alī, *Nahj al-Balāghah*, Saying 44, 1110.

time. One's bravery is measured by the extent of his manliness.

عِفَّتُهُ عَلَى قَدْرِ غَيْرَتِهِ.

> "His chasteness is according to his sense of shame."[1]

(This is a very amazing statement.) That is, the unchaste are those who have no shame. It is impossible for an unchaste person who does not care about the honour of others to be such if he cares about his own honour. Whenever you see an unchaste and immodest person, know that he is devoid of shame even with respect to his own honour. As such, the Imām (A.S.) also said elsewhere:

مَا زَنَى غَيُورٌ قَطُّ.

> "A self- respecting man never commits adultery."[2]

Whoever commits adultery has respect, and in reality, he does not even give importance to himself in that he would tarnish the honour of others.

Again, [take a look at] the Imām's statement to [his son,] Imām al-Ḥasan (A.S.):

وَلاَ تَكُنْ عَبْدَ غَيْرِكَ وَقَدْ جَعَلَكَ اللهُ حُرّاً.

> "[My son!] Do not be the slave of others for Allah had made you free."[3]

In the declaration of human rights issued by France, its golden passage begins with this sentence: "God has

1. *Ibid.*
2. *Ibid.*, Saying 297, 1232.
3. *Ibid.*, Letter 31 (Part 46), 929.

created all human beings free." One thousand and two hundred years before, the Commander of the Faithful (A.S.) said, "Do not be the slave of others for Allah had made you free."

Now, we will gradually embark on explaining and elucidating them.

Does the Human Being Have Two Types of the 'Self'?

We have said that it is encouraged in Islam, on one hand, to struggle against and combat the self (*jihād al-nafs*), nay to let it die:

"Die before you die."

That is, "let your commanding self die." On the other hand, there are many admonitions on self-honour, self-respect, self-esteem, freedom of the self, and the like. Does the human being have two types of the 'self'? Does he have two types of primordial self? Does he have two types of the self and must he let the first type of the self die while honouring and endearing the other type? If it is so, then we have to accept what psychology claims about 'multiple personality' in its real sense; that is, we must accept every person, in reality, has two types of the 'self,' two kinds of 'I' and two personalities. Definitely, that is not the point. In fact, in a single body, there are no two distinct I's; there are no two personalities.

One assumption is that there are two personalities in a human being; there are two I's; there are two primordial selves facing each other. One of them must be weakness and killed; the other must be honoured. It is not so. Another assumption is that the human being has two types of 'self' but not in the sense that he has to distinct 'selves'; two I's alongside each other. He has rather two real self and an imaginary self which is non-self but the person thinks that the non-self is the self. Is such a thing possible? It is said that it is possible. When it is said, "Struggle against the self," the 'self' referred to is the imaginary and unreal self. That which you imagine to be 'you' is not the real you. There is the real and original self which is the Real Self. The imaginary self must die so that the original and real self must manifest in a person. Is it so? No.

We can also express the same in another way: One self is the real self while the other self is a subordinate and parasitic self.

Theory Attributed to Heidegger

There is another theory in this regard and it is a theory which some people want [to infer] from the views of Heidegger, a German materialist philosopher, who is still alive.[1] He has laid much emphasis on the point that the

1. It is really amazing. We can see that on spiritual issues, humanity has all these scientific and philosophical efforts and it has recently discovered some of the truths which have been disclosed fourteen hundred years ago. For example, up to this extent, at least, they discern that there seem to have two types of the 'self'. Now, as to how these two types of the 'self' should be described, they have made some descriptions. Yet, as a whole, it can be said that our time is a time which is in search of the 'self'. Of course, this notion has

human being has two types of the 'self': the individual, personal and particular self, and the collective self. For instance, I have one 'self' by which I am this individual and this person, and you have one 'self' by which you are that individual and that person that you are, with such distinct features and characteristics, namely, the identity of your parents and individual characters, traits and information. And there is another 'self' which is within every person, which is the 'collective self' and not a personal or individual self; it is the 'human self'. For example, there are two types of 'self' in this 'I' that I am. One 'self' is the 'I' who is A son of B, and the other 'self' is the person which exists in this 'I'. You have also two types of the 'self'. There is one 'individual self' which is you while the other is a person which exists in this 'you'. The others are also like that. This is another assumption.

←

precedence but today it has somehow reached its peak. The issue of alienation from the self or separation from the self is an issue which is highly discussed nowadays and apparently, the first person to have brought it forth was Hegel. From Hegel onward, this issue has been discussed and not it is hotly debated.

Fourteen hundred years ago, the Qur'an talked about "forgetting about the self." By the way, can a person forget his own self? A person believes that he may forget everything, but not his own self. To forget one's own self is tantamount to death. Is it possible for a person to forget his own self?! But the Qur'an says that it is possible; a person may forget his own self. As to how this is possible, we will discuss later.

At any rate, it is discussed today that human being loses himself; he forgets his own self; he sells his own self; he confuses non-self with his own self.

The Qur'an says that one must struggle against a certain 'self' while honouring, loving and respecting another 'self'. And it is by means of honouring this 'self' that all noble traits in a person are nurtured and evil traits are kept away from him. If this 'self' is being honoured, it will find its esteem and this will be nurtured in a person. Thereafter, it will not allow the person to turn away from honesty and take on dishonesty instead; abandon trustworthiness and adopt treachery; abandon honour and adopt abjectness; abandon kind words and adopt backbiting; so on and so forth. Now, is this 'self' the same [collective and human] 'self', or is it something else? This is the question we posed tonight – what are these two types of the 'self' and how can they be explained. And we shall present to you the answer to it tomorrow night, God willing.

* * *

Other Statements of Imām al-Ḥusayn (A.S.) about Self-honour

I have said that in the transmitted sayings of Imām al-Ḥusayn (A.S.), the issue of human honour, nobility and respect occupies a special place, and the secret behind such sayings from the Imām compared to the transmitted sayings from the other Imāms is that the event in Karbalā' was a fertile ground for the spirit of Imām al-Ḥusayn (A.S.) to manifest into words in this aspect. It is written that when the Doyen of the Martyrs was heading toward Karbalā', he would meet individuals and each of them would say, "Don't go; it's dangerous for you." The Imām (A.S.) would reply to each of them, and of course, his reply to all of them was somehow this: "No, I have to go." When meeting the Imām, one of them said, "It's not expedient; don't go." The Imām said, "I shall give you the same reply of one of the companions of the Messenger of Allah to someone who wanted to dissuade him from participating in *jihād*." Then the Doyen of the Martyrs recited these poems to him:

سَأَمْضي وَما بِالْمَوْتِ عارٌ عَلَي الْفَتيٰ
إذا ما نَويٰ حَقّاً وَجاهَدَ مُسْلِما
وَواسَي الرِّجالَ الصّالِحينَ بِنَفْسِهِ
وَفارَقَ مَثْبوراً وَخالَفَ مُجْرِما

That is to say, "I will go. Death for a chivalrous man is not a shame if he performs *jihād*, exerts efforts while being a Muslim (that is, his intention is good and performs *jihād* while being a Muslim) and console, coordinate and sympathize with the righteous men, and on the contrary, separates his path from the ill-fated wretched, culpable and sinful people."

فَانْ عِشْتُ لَمْ انْدَمْ وَ انْ مِتُّ لَمْ ا لَمْ
كفي بِک ذُلّاً انْ تَعيشَ وَ تُرْغَما

That is to say, "Either I shall remain alive or die; there is no third option. Both results of this path I am going to tread are good and felicity for me. If I remain alive, I cannot be blamed because I did not escape from death and I emerged successful in this trial. I was not afraid and I remained alive. Such a life for me is ignominious and condemnable. If ever I die, neither can I be reproached. For you, this ignominy and wretchedness is enough that you remain alive and your nose is dragged on the ground. There is no ignominy and wretchedness worse than this [kind of] life."[1]

There are other poems which are either composed by the Imām or by his blessed father, Imām 'Alī (A.S.), and which are recorded in *Dīwān Mansūb beh Amīr al-Mu'minīn* (*Collection of Poetry Attributed to the Commander of the Faithful*), but at any rate, he was whispering the following to himself:

فَانْ تَكنِ الدُّنْيا تُعَدُّ نَفيسَةً فَدارُ ثَوابِ اللَّهِ اعْلي وَ انْبَلُ

That is to say, "Although the world is considered so beautiful and attractive in that a person does not want to turn away from it, the abode in the Hereafter is thousand times higher and more magnificent. The one who shall be imprisoned by the world is he who is not familiar with the other worlds."

وَ انْ تَكنِ الاَمْوالُ لِلتَّرْک جَمْعُها فَما بالُ مَتْروک بِهِ الْمَرْءُ يَبْخَلُ

That is to say, "If the endpoint of the wealth and riches of the world is dying and extinction, why should a person be stingy and parsimonious so long as he is alive?! Why does he not perform compassion and kindness; why does he not help and assist?!"

وَ انْ تَكنِ الاَبْدانُ لِلْمَوْتِ انْشِئَتْ

فَقَتْلُ امْرِيٍ بِالسَّيفِ فِي اللَّهِ افْضَلُ

That is to say, "If these bodies of ours will be

---

1. Aḥmad ibn Yaḥyā Bilādhurī, *Al-Ansāb al-Ashrāf*, vol. 3, 171.

extinguished in the end, and no matter how we keep distance from the swords, the endpoint is that suffering from fever or infection with microbes make us die. Yes, if this body is meant for dying, then is there anything more beautiful than this that this body be cut into pieces in the way of God, the Exalted."[1]

Now, you embody the spiritual state of this person who whispers these poems to himself and only then that his body would be practically cut into pieces in Karbalā'. It is exactly like the situation of a person who entrusts himself to a barber and the barber is beautifying him. When he sees that this blood whose end is to be spilled on the ground is currently spilled in the way of God, this forehead shall be struck in the way of God, this breast shall be targeted by poisonous arrows in the way of God, [he will have a beautiful feeling.] In the first portion of his body, hundreds of wounds by swords, spears and arrows could be counted. In other words, hundreds of [budges of] pride, hundreds of decors, and hundreds of medals were placed on Ḥusayn's chest. For him, it is embellishment, pride and medal. According to the opposite view, it is crime. He commits a crime; his crime for this person who extends brotherhood is [budge of] pride and model.

Abū 'Abd Allāh (Imām al-Ḥusayn) was in his last moments [of his life]. It was then that the Imām fell down.

---

1. 'Alī ibn 'Asākir, *Tārīkh Damishq*, 164; *Maqtal Khwārazmī*, vol. 1, 223; Abū 'Abd Allāh Muḥammad ibn 'Alī ibn Shahr Āshūb Sārawī Māzandaranī, *Manāqib*, vol. 4, 72.

Since the ground was somewhat deep, it is called 'the cliff of death.' It was a moment when the Imām was somewhat far. [The *Ahl al-Bayt* (A.S.)] could not see him and were not aware of his condition. It was the last moments. The wounds, spilling of blood and thirst so much overpowered the Imām that he could no longer be able to stand. The sky already seemed dark and gloomy to him. The enemies wanted to rush to him while lying and they could not dare least the Imām was only pretending to be weak. It is because they knew that if the Imām were strong enough, no one of them could be able to confront him. Someone wanted to behead him [but] he could dare approaching him. There was such a scheme that Ḥusayn was believed to be a brave (*ghayūr*) man – the honour of Allah (*ghayrat Allāh*). It is impossible that the soul is in his body and yet he could tolerate people rushing to his family's tent while he was still alive. In order to test whether Ḥusayn was still alive or not, a troop suddenly rushed to his family's tent. The Imām sensed it. He tried to stand up by his knees, apparently by holding his sword. He was reported to have shouted (in which he also talked about nobility and freedom):

وَيلَكمْ يا شيعَةَ آلِ أبي سُفْيانَ! أنَا اقاتِلُكمْ وَانْتُمْ تُقاتِلونَي وَالنِّساءُ لَيسَ عَلَيهِنَّ جُناحٌ

That is to say, "O mercenaries of the Family of Abū Sufyān! You are fighting with me and I am fighting with you. What are the faults of the children and women?! If you do not know God; if you do not believe in the Day of

Resurrection, what happened to the sense of nobility that a person is supposed to have?! What happened to your sense of freedom and independence?!"[1]

ولا حول ولا قوة الّا باللّه العلي العظيم وصلّي اللّه علي محمّد وآله الطاهرين. بإسمک العظيم الاعظم الأعزّ الاجلّ الاكرم يا اللّه...

"And there is neither power nor might except that of Allah, the Exalted and Mighty, and may Allah's benedictions be upon Muḥammad and his pure progeny. By Your Exalted, Great, Noble, Majestic, and Honourable Name, O Allah..."

"O God! Illuminate our hearts with the light of faith. Embellish our souls with the embellishment of honour and nobility. Keep us away from every type of abjectness and humiliation. Illuminate our hearts with Your love and gnosis. Let us know the value of Islam and the Qur'an. Let us be grateful of the Holy Prophet and his progeny. Shower Your grace and mercy to our deceased ones."

وَعَجِّلْ فِي فَرَجِ مَوْلاَنَا صَاحِبُ الزَّمَان.

"And expedite the advent of our chief, the Master of the Time."

---

1. Ibn al-Mu'ayyad al- Muwaffaq Akhṭab Khārazmī, *Maqtal al-Ḥusayn*, vol. 2, 33; Ibn Ṭāwūs , *Al-Luhūf* (with translation) with a slight variation, 120.

Chapter 8: Self and non-Self

﴿ وَفِي الأَرْضِ آيَاتٌ لِلْمُوقِنِينَ * وَفِي أَنْفُسِكُمْ أَفَلا تُبْصِرُونَ ﴾

> In the earth are signs for those who have conviction, and in your own souls [as well]. Will you not then perceive? (51:20-21)

There was a discussion surrounding this subject. In Islamic ethics, it is a subject which can be taken as the basis and axis of all precepts of Islamic ethics, and as far as I know, in Islamic sources no subject has been given emphasis as the basis and axis more than this subject, and that is the principle of human nobility. Last night I have recited to you enough number of Qur'anic verses and traditions (*aḥādīth*). It is said that in Islam the honour and nobility of the self (*nafs*) and honouring the self has been given much importance while highlighting the word *nafs*. Take, for example, the following sayings of the Commander of the Faithful (A.S.):

اكرِمْ نَفْسَک عَنْ كلّ دَنِيةٍ.

"Respect yourself concerning all wickedness."[1]

---

1. Āmadī,*Ghurar al-Ḥikam wa Durar al-Kalim*, chap. 2, 124, *ḥadīth* 202.

مَنْ كَرُمَتْ عَلَيهِ نَفْسُهُ هانَتْ عَلَيهِ شَهَواتُهُ

> "Whoever honours himself has a sense of abjectness toward his carnal desires."[1]

The one who has sense of nobility and greatness has an inward sense of honour and greatness. He feels a sense of greatness in himself. It is easy for him to combat animalistic desire. Its opposite is a tradition from Imām al-Hādī (A.S.) when he says:

مَنْ هانَتْ عَلَيهِ نَفْسُهُ فَلاتَأْمَنْ شَرَّهُ

That is to say, "If someone has abjectness in himself; if someone loses his sense of self-respect in the sense that if he does not feel a sense of honour as a being – and in today's jargon which is close to this expression – the one who does not have a sense of moral-spiritual personality, beware of his wickedness. For him self-indulgence and pursuit of carnal desires is something detestable and not to indulge in it is easy [and in the words of Imām al-Hādī (A.S.)] it is the opposite. The one who does not have this feeling and does not feel that he is someone, has a sense of personality, has a sense of nobility, and a sense of greatness, is he who has lost this feeling and lost everything."

فلا تَأْمَنْ شَرَّهُ.

Should the 'Self' be Despised or be Held in High Esteem?

Then, this question is raised: How comes that in Islam,

---

1. Imām 'Alī, *Nahj al-Balāghah*, saying 441, 1293.

morally speaking, on one hand, struggle and combat against the self and carnal desire is highly advised and emphasized, and on the other hand, all weight is given to the greatness of the self – try hard not to lose the sense of greatness in yourself; do not lose respect of the self? How can they be reconciled? And we have said that in the origin of the meaning, *nafs* means 'self'. *Nafs* refers to the human 'self'. Should the 'self' be smashed, trampled upon and crushed, or should it be honoured and respected and its nobility be preserved? Do these two refer to the same 'self'? It cannot be so. Are there two types of the 'self' in the human being such that morally one must struggle against one of them, put it under lock and key, restrict its freedom, trample upon it, let it die, and in the expression of our poets – although this expression does not exist in the traditions (*aḥādīth*) – it must be killed and extinguished, and the other 'self' be revived and let live? It cannot also be such in this form. It is obvious that everyone does not possess two 'I's' and two 'selves.' Are there two types of 'self' in the body of each of us?! It is definitely not so. We have then said that it is an issue is not only applicable to Islam and Islamic morality. For others, it is discussed that the human being has and shows two types of the 'self,' to one of which he must struggle against and to which his humanity does not depend. He has also another 'self' which is noble, and from which human essence emanates. However, in explaining and justifying this subject – how comes that the human being has two types of the 'self' – we have said that such is not possible. There is no option, therefore, but to express it in another way. Firstly, we shall mention the Islamic viewpoint. Then we shall also explain other views.

The Islamic View

From the Islamic point of view, this question is already resolved. According to Islam, while the human being is an animal just like other animals, at the same time, in the expression of the Qur'an, the Divine Spirit is breathed unto him; a spark of the Divine realm (*malakūt*) and celestial light exist in the human being. The real 'I' of a person is the 'I'. The human being has also an animal 'I' but the animal 'I' in the human being is the parasitic 'I'; it is not the original 'I'. The original 'I' in the human being is the same celestial 'I' of the human being.[1] That is, that which is in an animal constitutes the real 'I' and reality of the animal in the human being is his parasitic 'I'. I do eat; I do drink; I do sleep; I even do run. All of these depend on one 'I,' but these are degrees lower than this 'I'. The same 'I' – I do eat; I do drink; I do get thirsty; I do get hungry, etc. – and at the same time, I do think; I do remember God; I do love to give preference to others than myself. All

1. The philosophers have a discussion about *māddah* and *ṣūrat* in which they say that the truth of every being is the same last activity of that being, and other than this is not part of his truth and has nothing to do with his activity. It is a philosophical discussion and for the meantime, I will not discuss it.

of these are the same 'I'. But this 'I' has degrees. Whenever the 'I' is highly regarded, it is the human being's high degree of 'I' which we talk about. Whenever we talk about animalistic issues, we refer to the lower degrees of the 'I'.

Inner Debate

Let me cite a parable. One of the distinctive features of the human being is that there is an inner debate between and among the 'I's'. Sometimes, this debate is described as debate of the reason, self or, for example, debate of the moral will and carnal desire. At any rate, such a debate exists in the human being and an inner debate has no meaning for the animals. This scenario more or less exists in every person. It is truer in some while less true in others. A person decides whether he follows his carnal desires or not. That is, his desire is something else. He decides to act contrary to his [carnal] desires. Let me give you a very simple example. The doctor prescribes a food diet to [his] patient, proscribing him some foods or fruits, or setting a limited amount of food. He (doctor), for example, says, "You have diabetes or high blood pressure. Do not eat such and such food." One makes a decision to follow this prescription, but the desire has its own place. The table spread starts to incite the carnal desires, urging the person to eat the same food proscribed to him. Sometimes, one practically goes against his carnal desires; that is, his moral will, and in another expression, his intellect, prevails over his [carnal] self, without listening to the dictates of his desires. Sometimes, the contrary also happens. His desires prevail over moral will, and in another expression, his 'self' prevails over his intellect. These two conditions happen to a person.

Either a person decides to be an early riser and decides seriously. One night, however, he will wake up, leaving his warm bed. [His] moral will say, "Get up!" while his nature or desire says, "Don't get up!" One time, a person moves and does something against his [base] nature. At another time, he would follow his [base] nature. These debates do not exist in the animals. One is an animal and its nature and desires are also animalistic. The animal acts according to the dictate of desires. In the animal, there is no other basis other than the basis of desires which gives a command contrary to the [dictates of] desires. Now, the conclusion I want to arrive at is something else. This is a state which the psychologists refer to and when a person conducts a study, he will see that it is a noteworthy point. Who or what are involved in this inner debate? It is clear that it is between [a person's] ego and alter ego; it is not beyond one's self. A person does not engage in a debate with a stranger. There are two forces within a person which are engaged in debate. One [of these forces] says, "Do not eat this food." The other says, "Eat it." At the time of *saḥar*, one [of these forces] says, "Get up." The other says, "Don't get up." One says, "Do not say so." The other says, "Say so" [as his desires dictate]. This debate is within a person. Obviously, no stranger is involved here. It is a debate of a person with himself. The point, however, is this: when man's natural desires prevail over his moral will, and does something which he decides not to do, what state does it give to a person? It is a state of shame and setback. Within himself, he feels being defeated. It is exactly like a champion who is sent to a battlefront in which he encountered another champion and was defeated. A person really feels a sense of defeat. On the contrary, when the moral will prevails over the natural will, one would leave the dining table and faithfully observe the dietary restrictions. When one wakes up before dawn and sees that in spite of the dictate of nature to resume sleeping, he would, for example, leave his warm bed and engage in his acts of worship that is the time he would feel a sense of victory and triumph. This [feeling] exists in every person. I do not think there is any person who has not tested it in himself and hypothetically it is testable for such a person.

The Original 'Self' and Parasitic 'Self' (Self and non-Self)

What is this feeling in a person? In both states, a person is defeated by himself, and in both states, he prevails over himself. He, therefore, should not feel being defeated or victorious, or at least, he must feel being defeated, on one hand, and being victorious, on the other hand, and now it is no so. When his desires prevail over his moral will, a person really feels being defeated, reproaching himself thus, "Woe unto me. I have realized now that I am nothing." When his moral will, however, prevails over his natural desire, he will feel victorious and triumphant, imbuing a sense of hope to himself. It is the very moment when a person understands that the original 'self,' the real 'self,' [and] the real 'I' is the moral will which is under the dictate of reason and that this desire in 'I' is but a mere tool; it is not the real 'I'. The real 'I' is not this desire and this nature. This is a stranger which is trying to defeat the [real] 'I'. This is a feeling which exists in a person and it is the same feeling with which he discerns that the real 'I' is not the 'I' of these desires and nature. I am not this nature with all these desires; nature with all these desires, tools and means which are given to this 'I' to use. 'I' is the very station that decides; the same intellect and perception; it is the station that understands these [things]. But the station which commands nature to me is a stranger and non-self; I am not this one.

Now, taking into consideration this point, with which 'self' that one must struggle against and combat? One must struggle against the 'self'; which 'self' one must combat? Which 'self' that one must not let loose and be left to itself? It is the same 'self,' the animalistic 'self' which in reality is non-self. In other words, all battles within a person, the conflicts which a person has within his soul from the moral and immoral points of view are in reality a struggle of the 'self' against a non-self; it is not a struggle of the 'self' against the 'self'. When the animalistic desires prevail, absolutely dominating over the human intellect, will and disposition, and one becomes a plaything of desires and anger – that is, the instincts that animals have – the real 'self' of a person is overwhelmed, forgotten, and lost; one must find it. The person in whose existence there is nothing but animalism and things he is in common with animals and nothing rules, in reality has lost his real 'self' [or] his real 'I':

﴿ قُلْ إِنَّ الْخَاسِرِينَ الَّذِينَ خَسِرُوا أَنْفُسَهُمْ ﴾

> Say, 'Indeed the losers are those who ruin themselves'. (39:15)

He has lost himself in this game of chance – the greatest of loss. He has forgotten himself. What is it that is always in his mind? What is it that dominates in his mind? [It is] money, carnal desires, foods, drinks, clothes; nothing other than these dominate in his being. So, what happened to that 'self'? It is relegated to oblivion. Instead of the 'self,' he thinks of the non-self as the 'self'. He himself is not aware that he has forgotten his own self. A person could never believe that he would forget his own self. [He would say,] "Have I forgotten my own self?! I always talk about myself. It is I myself who has such money. It is I myself who ate such-and-such food today." The Qur'an says, "You have lost your own self. This 'self' is not your own self; it is something else. It is your parasitic 'self'. It is your surrogate 'self' and not your original 'self.'

﴿ وَلَا تَكُونُوا كَالَّذِينَ نَسُوا اللَّهَ فَأَنْسَاهُمْ أَنْفُسَهُمْ ﴾

> And do not be like those who forget Allah, so He makes them forget their own souls. (59:19)

That is, do not be like those who forgot God and as a reaction to this forgetfulness – which is the true law, the law of action and reaction – God has made them forget their own selves; they have forgotten their own selves.

Self-reminding (Self-discovery)

This is the issue in the Qur'an called 'forgetfulness of the self' which is something condemnable. Its opposite is self-reminding or remembrance of the self. O human being! Remember yourself. Remembrance of the self is impossible except through remembrance of God. In other words, according to the logic of the Qur'an, these two are inseparable. To be always mindful of God means to be always mindful of the self. It is a fact that the essence of worship is recovery or finding the 'self' though not the animalistic 'self' but rather the real 'self,' the celestial 'self.' It is in the remembrance and worship of God that a person finds his own self and really discovers himself. The Commander of the Faithful Imām 'Alī (A.S.) has a very elegant expression in *Ghurar al-Ḥikam wa Durar al-Kalim* when he thus says:

عَجِبْتُ لِمَنْ يَنْشِدُ ضالَّتَهُ وَ قَدْ اضَلَّ نَفْسَهُ فَلايطْلُبُها.

> "I am surprised by the one who seeks whatever he lost and when he lost himself, he does not look for it."[1]

That is to say, "I am surprised by those who, when they

1. Āmadī,*Ghurar al-Ḥikam wa Durar al-Kalim*, chap. 54, *ḥadīth* 18.

lose something, anxiously look for it. (When one loses his ring, he looks for it; when he loses his coat, he looks for it; when he loses his donkey, he looks for it.) How comes they have lost themselves yet they are not anxious in looking for their selves?! O wretched one! When you lose your coat, you look for it in every corner just to find it. By the way, have you found yourself? When you lose yourself, where will you look for it? Why are you not looking for yourself?! It is indeed surprising."

Rūmī's Words

We have said that although there are pertinent incommensurate expressions in extreme Sufi teachings, excesses which under the rubric of struggle against the self also trample upon self-respect to some extent, many of the discerning ones among them have understood these meanings. Mawlawī [Rūmī] says, "O he who has lost his own self in battle! It refers to the same inner battle, debate and conflict. O he who has lost his real self in the inner conflict due to the victory of the desires and [base] nature! You have failed to distinguish yourself from others. You confuse yourself with a stranger. You think of an 'other' as 'I' and you do not know that the 'I' is not him. He is not you. The fact that you think that the 'I' is you, it follows that you have mistaken yourself as somebody else."

تو به هر صورت که آيي بيستي　　که منم اين، والله آن تو نيستي

You, in whatever form you come and stand,
Saying I am this, by Allah it is not you.

Sometimes, a person comes and stands in front of a mirror, thinking that he sees himself...[1]

یک زمان تنها بمانی تو ز خلق   درغم واندیشه مانی تا به حلق

One time, you will remain alone from the creation,
In grief and thinking you will remain until the throat.

It says that if you want to test yourself whether you have found yourself or you have lost yourself, you can discern it in private moments. If after some days you do not see other persons, you will be frightened by yourself. You always want to see other people [or] other things because you are lost in them and you look for yourself in them. Once you have found your real self, even if you were alone with your real self for a hundred years, you will never feel bored for even a moment.

این تو كي باشي كه تو آن اوحدي
كه خوش و زيبا و سرمست خودي

Who is this 'you' for the sole you ,
Is happy, eyeful and inebriated with yourself?[2]

The question of self and non-self is an important issue. This subject has been mentioned many times in the words of our leaders in religion in various ways.

The Miser Lost Himself

The Commander of the Faithful Imām 'Alī (A.S.) has a

1. [Missing part of the audio cassette recording.]
2. Mawlānā Jalāl al-Dīn Rūmī, *Mathnawī-ye Ma'nawī*,345, line 18.

saying regarding a miser. The miser is one of those people who have lost their real selves. In other words, money and wealth become his 'self.' The real self of a person whose priority and goal is money and wealth, and in today's jargon in psychology, who finds stability and firmness in money in the sense that he is drowned in or succumbed to money, becomes money, and he has no other 'self' other than money because he has misplaced and lost his real 'self'. The result is that he wants his 'self' for the money and not the money for his 'self.' That is, he spends his life, health and time for money, but he is not willing to spend money for his own health, comfort and even life.

The Imām (A.S.) says,

> عَجِبْتُ لِلْبَخِيلِ يَسْتَعْجِلُ الْفَقْرَ الَّذِى مِنْهُ هَرَبَ وَ يَفُوتُهُ الْغِنَى الَّذِى إِيَّاهُ طَلَبَ.
>
> "I wonder at the miser who is speeding towards the very destitution from which he wants to run away and misses the very ease of life which he covets."

That is to say, "I am surprised with the miser who seeks wealth, riches and self-sufficiency and flees from poverty, yet he practically succumbs to the same poverty and keeps away from the same wealth." The explanation for this can be found in *Nahj al-Balāghah* when the Imām (A.S.) says,

> فَيَعِيشُ فِى الدُّنْيَا عَيْشَ الْفُقَرَاءِ وَ يُحَاسَبُ فِى الْآخِرَةِ حِسَابَ الْأَغْنِيَاءِ.
>
> "Consequently, he passes his life in this world

> like the destitute, but will have to render an account in the next world like the rich."[1]

That is, he lives in this world like a poor, wretched and broke person because he is not willing to spend money for himself. He worn and torn clothes; he eats simple food such as plain bread and cheese. Such a person should be asked, "Why do you do this?" Neither does he perform an act of altruism. If he were a person who does not spend for himself but spends for others, he is an altruistic person but here we are talking about a miser who only wants to accumulate [money]. The Commander of the Faithful (A.S.) describes what poverty is: not to have anything. Once a person does not have anything, he cannot afford wholesome food, residence, riding animal, and garment. You are wretched for succumbing to the same state of affairs. For your whole life, you just eat bread and cheese so as not to become poor and be forced to eat just bread and cheese. Now, you also fall prey to the same bread and cheese. For your whole life, you just eat bread and cheese lest you should become poor and be contented with just bread and cheese! This is the very person who has misplaced himself; that is, he has lost himself.

Rūmī's Parable

Mawlawī [Rūmī] has a very elegant parable. Assume that there is someone who has a lot of land in which to

---

1. Imām 'Alī, *Nahj al-Balāghah*, Saying 121,1145.

construct a building. For whatever reason, during the daytime he would not go there to start the construction. At night-time he would send labourers, a bricklayer, an engineer, and construction materials there to construct a building he will reside. He spends money. He constructs a well-equipped and completely furnished house and he is also aware that he has built a very elegant house for himself. On the day that he moves to the new house, he realizes that the house is built in other people's lot. He has built the house but not on his own lot; it is on the lot of other people. How is his lot? It remains bare and uninhabited. What condition does this give to a person? It is said that it is the same condition of a person who shall enter the Day of Resurrection. He will see himself like a barren land. That which did not work for himself was his own self. That which worked for him was somebody else.

در زمین دیگران خانه مکن
کارخود کن کار بیگانه مکن
کیست بیگانه، تن خاکي تو
کز براي اوست غمناکي تو
تا تو تن را چرب و شیرین مي‌دهي
گوهر جان را نیابي فربهي
گر میان مشك تن را جا شود
وقت مردن گند آن پیدا شود

Do not make your home in others' land,
Do your own work, don't do the work of a stranger.

Who is the stranger except your own earthen body?
For the sake of which is your sorrow.
So long as you are giving your body greasy and sweet,
You will not see fatness in your essence.
If the body be set in the midst of musk,
On the day of death its stench will become manifest.[1]

If you always set this body in the midst of musk, once it is dead for two days, it will begin to decay and the people around will be forced to bury it two meters below the ground in order to escape from its stench.

مشک را برتن مزن بردل بمال مشک چه بود نام پاک ذوالجلال

Do not put musk on your body, rub it on your heart.
What is musk? The holy name of the Glorious (God).[2]

﴿ وَلا تَكُونُوا كَالَّذِينَ نَسُوا اللَّهَ فَأَنْسَاهُمْ أَنْفُسَهُمْ ﴾

And do not be like those who forget Allah, so He makes them forget their own souls. (59:19)

Human Soul as the Source of Moral Feelings and Window to Spirituality

From the Islamic point of view, the human being's real 'I'

---

1. Mawlānā Jalāl al-Dīn Rūmī, *Mathnawī-ye Ma'nawī*, Book 2, lines 263-266, with slight variation. [Trans.]
2. *Ibid.*, line 267. [Trans.]

is the same Divine breathe which exists in every person, and one's moral feeling emanates from this 'I'. If such an 'I' – which is not mud but rather a Divine Spirit which comes from a realm higher than the world of natural and materiality – does not exist in the human being and if the real 'I' or the real 'self' of a person does not exist, none of these moral feelings which are incompatible with physical gains would not have existed. It is strange that Europe for reasons which must be dealt with separately (and in which sensual inclinations and carnal desires are actively involved) does not want to acknowledge the existence of a Divine spirit in the human being.[1] On the other hand, they observe that there are inclinations in the human being which are incompatible with his physical nature – inclinations which go against his physical nature.

It is very clear and obvious that the human soul is a window to his spirituality, through which he realizes that he is a spiritual being; he will endure; the real 'I' is immortal and with death the work of 'I' does not end. Yet it (Europe) does not acknowledge it. On the other hand, it cannot deny that there are two inclinations in the human being: natural-physical inclinations and spiritual inclinations. That is, the latter are not compatible with material considerations.

1. Of course, we do not generalize. Many of the Europeans are also 'spiritual'.

William James[1] is a theistic figure and his books translated [into Fārsī] are to a great extent good, especially his book *Religion and Soul.* He is an outstanding psychologists and philosopher, and regarded as one of the great thinkers in the world. Perhaps sixty years have not yet passed since his death. In the said book, this unprejudiced man has some good observations. He says that there is set of instinct in the human being which is incompatible with materialistic considerations (and he categorically acknowledges it). Physical instincts connect and supposed to connect us to the physical world. These are channels between us and the physical world. If there is the feeling of hunger in us, for example, this is a channel of communication between us and nature, because had it not been for this feeling, we would have been looking for food. He then says that in view of the existence of instincts in us, we are connected to nature. For this reason, there are instincts in us that are not compatible with our physical nature, and it is these instincts which connect us to the other world. Out of our existence, we have reason and way to another world which is different from the world of nature. With his natural instincts, the human being has a set of needs which is incompatible with his nature, and with metaphysical instincts (as termed by William James) he

1. William James (1842-1910): a pioneering American psychologist and philosopher trained as a medical doctor. Among his best-known works is *The Varieties of Religious Experience*. [Trans.]

fulfils a set of other needs which is beyond his physical nature and is compatible with his non-material nature. In other words, these instincts connect the human being to his metaphysical nature so as to fulfil a set of spiritual needs which exists in him.

This is a reasonable argument. But let us see how those who do not want to acknowledge this fact explain the non-material instincts of the human being.

Explanation of non-materialist Inclinations in Europe

They say that the human being is in pursuit of two things. He is either in pursuit of gain or in pursuit of value. The material inclinations are called 'gain' while spiritual inclinations are called 'value'. They think that by changing the name, they could change the truth. They say that sometimes the human being is in pursuit of gain while at other times he is in pursuit of value. Let us ask, "What is value?" They reply that value is anything which is not beneficial to a person; it is of no use to him; it does not address any of his needs; it is also incompatible with logic; in fact, it goes against the dictate of logic; the least is that it is non-logical. Yet, it does exist; for instance, altruism. That a person performs an act of altruism is not logical. That which is logical is for a person to look for gain. Human reason also dictates that one must look for his gain. Yet, on the other hand, they cannot deny the fact that such inclinations also exists in the human being: inclination to selflessness, inclination to self-sacrifice, inclination to justice, inclination to freedom, inclination to fairness, inclination to meekness, and inclination to tolerance, most of which are basically incompatible with the human being's material interests. They acknowledge that these are incompatible but these do not constitute gain; they constitute value. The human being is in pursuit of a set of values.

Let us ask, "What is value?" It means cost or price; cost by itself is nothing. A person believes in a value or cost for a thing. What is that? Unless something is connected to the essence of the human being, one cannot value to it. Such a thing is impossible.

Islam says that there is something valuable in you and it is the most valuable, and that is the Divine spirit of yours. We have earlier read in traditions (*aḥādīth*) that it is even described as exquisite (*nafīs*). Imām al-Ṣādiq (A.S.) says,

اثامِنُ بِالنَّفْسِ النَّفيسَةِ رَبَّها

> "I set its Lord as the price of the exquisite soul."[1]

Or, when Imām al-Sajjād (A.S.) is asked, "Who is the greatest of people?" he says, "It is he who does not give any importance to anything with respect to his own self." The human being feels the most valuable of realities within himself and that is his real self. It is the hallmark of his possession. He considers it valuable as it is he himself. He also regards his body as valuable, just as he regards his soul valuable. According to them, lofty moral feelings are

1. Muḥsin Amīn, *Fī Riḥāb A'immah Ahl al-Bayt*, vol. 4, 76.

valuable for a person. They do not want to confess that these are spiritual goodness (*khayr*) while materialities are material goodness. Our philosophers call the materialities man's material goodness while spiritualities are called spiritual goodness. In this way, the issue shall be resolved and this is the contention. They do not want to say that material goodness and spiritual goodness, like inner realities and truth, are at work, and they do not want to acknowledge it. They say that 'goodness' is that which is material; its name is 'gain'. What is 'spiritualities'? This is not goodness; this is not 'gain'; it is only value and cost; it is not truth. Islam says that it is also goodness; as you do a moral act, you also pursue goodness, but this goodness is something which your animalistic nature does not pursue. It is your celestial nature which is in pursuit of it.

It is here that ethics or moral feeling is a window so as for the human being to know his immaterial soul, and by knowing the immaterial soul, he will be aware of the celestial and unseen world, for he is a ray of the celestian and unseen world. From here the root of moral feelings can be found. As the human being is a celestial spirit, his genus is that of majesty [for] the celestial genus is majestic. When a person senses the celestial self, he will not yield to abjectness:

> كَرُمَت عَلَيهِ نَفْسُهُ هانَتْ عَلَيهِ شَهَواتُهُ
>
> "Whoever honours himself has a sense of abjectness toward his carnal desires."[1]

1. Imām 'Alī, *Nahj al-Balāghah*, saying 441, 1293.

It is for this reason that we always emphasize that whoever has a sense of self-respect will not yield to abjectness - and we have cited pertinent traditions (*aḥādīth*) earlier. When a person senses his 'self' which originates from the world of majesty and majestic itself, he will not yield to abjectness. It is like the case of a person who sees a very exquisite tableau, say the Portrait of Rafael.[1] He knows its value and it is impossible for him to allow it to be tarnished or tainted because he senses its great value. As the human being senses his own self through intuitive knowledge which emanates from the realm of power, he detests weakness and impotence. Once self-honour feels itself, it will not yield to weakness, humiliation and inability. He (who has self-respect) does not backbite because - according to a tradition (*ḥadīth*) we have read earlier - he feels that backbiting is [a sign of] inability and impotence. He does not get jealous because he feels that jealousy is rooted in inability and impotence. He is not arrogant because he understands that arrogance stems from abjectness of the self. He will not become arrogant unless he has abjectness of the self:

ما مِنْ رَجُلٍ تَكَبَّرَ اوْ تَجَبَّرَ الّا لِذُلَّةٍ وَجَدَها في نَفْسِهِ

"No man will ever be arrogant or unjust

1. It refers to Raffaello Sanzio da Urbino (1483 - 1520), an Italian painter and architect of the High Renaissance, whose work is admired for its clarity of form, ease of composition, and visual achievement of the Neoplatonic ideal of human grandeur. [Trans.]

except that he has a sense of abjectness in himself."[1]

An arrogant person has not found his real self. If a person finds his real self, he will no longer feel a sense of abjectness; he will feel a sense of power and greatness; he will no longer act arrogantly or unjustly because it is incompatible with his spirit. Why a person is pleased with knowledge and dislikes ignorance? It is because his essence, his real self, emanates from the realm of knowledge and knowledge itself, and it detests ignorance. Why munificence for a person is a value as they call it and a spiritual goodness as we call it, although it involves spending for others? It is because munificence signifies mercy and giving, and the person himself feels that he is from the realm of mercy and to be from the realm of mercy necessitates giving and sharing of blessings.

It is a fact that in the Islamic school of thought, all moral feelings emanate from finding the 'self' and its real feeling. If a person finds his real self, he can see all moral values – as they call them – and immoralities also find meaning. After a person realizes that all Islamic narrations [on the issue of ethics] have a specific philosophy, and ethics in Islam revolves around the axis of self-knowledge and sense of respect in the real self, and the Islamic ethics is founded on this basis. It became clear, therefore, that according to Islam, there are really

1. Abū Ja'far Muḥammad ibn Ya'qūb al-Kulaynī , *Uṣūl al-Kāfī*, vol. 3, 426, *ḥadīth* 17.

two types of 'self' in the human being but this does not mean that there are two distinct I's in him. [The two types of 'self' are] the real 'self' and the parasitic and imaginary 'self'; that is, it is actually non-self and one assumes it to be his own self. The 'self' which one must struggle against and from which self-conceit (*'ujb*), jealousy (*ḥasad*), arrogance (*takabbur*), sensuality, and injustice emanate is the human being's real self. The real self is inspired by the intrinsic Islam:

﴿ وَنَفْسٍ وَمَا سَوَّاهَا * فَأَلْهَمَهَا فُجُورَهَا وَتَقْوَاهَا * قَدْ أَفْلَحَ مَن زَكَّاهَا * وَقَدْ خَابَ مَن دَسَّاهَا ﴾

> By the soul and Him who fashioned it, and inspired it with [discernment between] its virtues and vices: one who purifies it is felicitous, and one who betrays it fails. (91:5-8)

This is the explanation of the subject from the Islamic point of view.

A Survey of Materialist Views

We have said that others – even the materialists – have also reached the point that one cannot limit the human 'self' to this so-called 'formal self'. In essence, human personality is such that even the ultra-materialists believe in para-personal identity to a person. They have no option but to also look for explanation that the human being has a higher and greater self. However, in reply to this question – what is this greater self? – they look for other explanations.

One of these schools of thought says something which on account of its relevance to very important philosophical questions, we have no option but to concisely mention and refute. It is said that there are two I's in the human being: an individual 'I' and a collective 'I'. The individual 'I' feels yourself as an individual, while the collective 'I' is the same so-called natural collective 'I' which exists in all individuals; that is, the human being. It is for this reason that a person is humanitarian; that is, the reason why a person is humanitarian in nature is that two types of 'self' exists in him: the individual self which is particular and limited, while the other self is general.

This contention is so incorrect. They have not understood the meaning of 'general'. The preeminent philosophers, the Muslim philosophers in particular, have very valuable research works on general issues and general-natural essence – from Abū 'Alī Sīnā to Ṣadr al-Muta'allihīn (Mullānā Ṣadrā)[1] – and we shall refrain from dealing with it. They think in such a way that the 'I' which is noble in the human being and feels a sense of nobility is the 'I' of other human beings which is also not outside nature; it is the same physical humans. It is said that whenever I feel myself, it is the same filthy 'self' which must be relinquished, and whenever I feel human, again I

1. Ṣadr al-Dīn Shīrāzī (1572-1641), better known as Mullā Ṣadrā or Ṣadr al-Muta'allihīn: the foremost representative of the Illuminationist (*ishrāqī*) School of Islamic philosophy whose magnum opus is *Al-Asfār al-Arba'ah* (*The Four Journeys*). [Trans.]

do feel the self but I do feel the self within a general human, and it is the sacred self. We say that the general human is the same other humans; it is nothing other than these. Moreover, the general human in an individual is the same individual and not some part of the individual. It is a long story.

Sartre's Statement

Some like Jean-Paul Sartre[1] have made a different remark. They say that the human being himself is not to have the self. The human being has a real self and a virtual self which is non-self. His real self is not to have the self. Whatever self you assume for a person, you have regarded it as nature, essence and disposition for him. In essence, the human being is a being who is devoid of any mould and nature; an existent who lacks absolute identity and freedom. The human essence is absolute freedom from everything including having an identity. Your real self is not to have the self. As you found a self, you have lost your real self.

This is also an irrelevant remark but it is explainable and justifiable. Later on, we shall explain and elucidate it, if God wills.

---

1. Jean-Paul Sartre (1905-80): French philosopher, dramatist, novelist, political journalist, and leading exponent of existentialism whose writings reflect his vision of the human being as master of his or her own fate, with each life defined by a person's actions: "Existence precedes essence." [Trans.]

The Marxists' Theory

There is another theory in this regard, which is that of the Marxists. In the end, they have also no option [except that] they have to identify two types of 'self' in a person, because these two inclinations in the human being cannot be denied. They claim that the filthy self in the human being which one must combat is the private self, while the noble self in him is the collective self. They express that there had been periods in humanity in which there was no ownership and for this reason, there had been no I's and we's. There had been no dividing walls. All selves were but a single self and that was the human self. It is like the individuals in a family which all constitute a single 'self' and we call it the 'family self'. This limited self – the 'I' with which we say, "My property," "My clothes," "My house," "The document of my ownership," etc. – means putting division between and among individuals. With such ownerships, individual human beings become separate from one another. These individuals who were before like the water of the sea and who were unitied with one another, in the words of Mawlawī [Rūmī] [became like drops of water as a consequence of ownerships.] Of course, Mawlawī has a loftier point:

منبسط بودیم و یک گوهر همه　　بي سر و بي‌پا بُدیم آن سر همه
یک گهر بودیم همچون آفتاب　　بي گره بودیم و صافي همچو آب

Simple were we and all one substance;
We were all without head and without foot yonder.

> We were one substance, like the Sun;
> We were knotless and pure, like water.[1]

He speaks about a mystical truth, while they talk about a social matter. They say that in the beginning, mankind used to live communally. All individuals were like the sea water. This ruthless ownership came and made this water into pieces or drops. From here the individual self came into being. The self that one must struggle against is the individual and private self. As you fight against ownership, you uproot moral corruption. All moral corruptions are rooted in ownership. Establish collective ownership; put up a collective identity and thereafter all moral goodness which is related to the collective identity will be observed.

Criticism of this Theory

This is also another remark which is more akin to poetry. For the meantime, I shall only discuss to you one aspect of it. If there is any opportunity, I shall elaborate on it later.

We have one question to them: Is the thing which divides individuals and separates the I's from one another limited to ownership? Are all endowments in life limited to those which are rooted in wealth? Or, are there also other endowments in human life? Let us assume that the members of a family who have collective ownership live together. Will the I's and we's among the siblings be

1. Mawlānā Jalāl al-Dīn Rūmī, *Mathnawī-ye Ma'nawī*, Book 1, lines 686-687.

totally extinguished? Or, will there be some other things which will create the I's and we's among them? In a society, even in a collective society, as the wealth and riches are collectively and equally divided - which they do not as there are issues about it and they do not in practice - are things such positions, ranks, posts, fame, popularity, and power also equally divided? Does a certain worker in a certain steel company that only receives a pastil bread and cheese [for his work] have the same power of, say, Mr. Brezhnev?[1] Is power not the basis of humanity? A person sacrifices wealth before the altar of power. How about the women? Were they able to establish equality among women? No. They wanted to, but they realized that such a thing is impossible. Is this not an endowment? And there are thousands of other endowments. In addition, moral values are a set of values which is incompatible with collectivity. How is it related to a person, for example, who sacrifices himself for others in a battlefield or who is just to others when it comes to the truth? Regarding this subject, I shall also make some explanations later, if God wills.

From the Islamic point of view, therefore, the crown of all moral feelings of the human being is the sense of respect, nobility, honour, power, and greatness within himself and in his real self - real respect, power and

1. Leonid Ilyich Brezhnev (1906-1982): Chairman of the Presidium of the Supreme Soviet of the Union of Soviet Socialist Republics (USSR), from 1960 to 1964 and 1977 to 1982. [Trans.]

greatness and his real self is the same 'breathed into him of My spirit' (15:29) as expressed by God, the Exalted, in the Qur'an. Islam's perfect human beings in terms of morality are individuals who have more knowledge of themselves than others; they have sensed more nobility and honour in themselves than others.

***

We have said earlier that all the epic campaigns of Imām al-Ḥusayn (A.S.) revolve around the axis of respect, honour, nobility, and exquisiteness of the self. His bidding of good and forbidding of evil is also of this type of feeling. He said:

الا تَرَوْنَ انَّ الْحَقَّ لايعْمَلُ بِهِ وَ انَّ الْباطِلَ لايتَناهي عَنْهُ لِيرْغَبِ الْمُؤْمِنُ فِي لِقاءِ اللَّهِ مُحِقّاً.

That is to say, "O people! Can your eyes not see? Can't you see how good things are being overlooked and abandoned and not acted upon? Can't you see how wickedness has become prevalent? Any believer in Islam, any man of nobility, would prefer death over life in which he will always face filthy scenes and will never see lofty panoramas of humanity. In such conditions, a believer must crave for meeting Allah; that is, he must basically detest this world." The Imām (A.S.) had also this expression:

انّي لا ارَي الْمَوْتَ الّا سَعادَةً وَ الْحَياةَ مَعَ الظّالِمينَ الّا بَرَماً.

> "Indeed I do not see anything in death but success and in life with the oppressors but boredom."

What kind of feeling is this in a person? Life with the oppressors, life in which I only meet the oppressors, mingle and cooperate with them, for me this life is no life at all; it is death; it is boredom. For me success is not to be in such a state of affairs. Death in such a state of affairs is success for me.

On the day of '*Āshūrā*' the Imām (A.S.) would come and stand at the door of the tent, addressing his honourable sister, thus:

يا اختاه! ايتيني بِوَلَدِي الرَّضيع حَتّي اوَدِّعَهُ.

> "O sister! Bring my sucking child so that you bid farewell to him."[1]

Although the mother of this child was present there, Abū 'Abd Allāh (Imām al-Ḥusayn) (A.S.) wanted to prove that the leader of the caravan after him shall be Zaynab; hence, he addressed his sister. Zaynab run and brought to him his sucking child. Ḥusayn looked at the face of the child. For some days, his mother [was not able to drink] and as usual, once the breastfeeding lady is not in good mode, she does not produce plenty of milk, let along being unable to drink for how many days and night. Sponteneously, Abū 'Abd Allāh sensed signs of hunger and thirst in the child. Ḥusayn who was an embodiment of love would carry the child to kiss him. The enemy would command one of his soldiers, thus: "Let us see what good target have you found? If you can show your feat, show it

1. Ibn Ṭāwūs ,*Al-Luhūf* (with translation), 117.

now." He (the soldier) asked, "What should I show?" "The child," the commander replied. As the child was in the hands of Abū 'Abd Allāh, at once you could see that he became like a slaughtered chicken. But what Ḥusayn – that formidable mountain – did was that he collected all the blood in his fist and threw it toward the sky:

> هَوْنٌ عَلَي ا نَّهُ بِعَينِ اللّهِ
>
> That is to say, "It is in the way of pleasing Allah who sees it. It is no longer unpleasant for Ḥusayn."
>
> ولا حول ولا قوة الّا باللّه العلي العظيم وصلّي اللّه علي محمّد وآله الطاهرين. بإسمک العظيم الاعظم الأعزّ الاجلّ الاكرم يا اللّه...
>
> "And there is neither power nor might except that of Allah, the Exalted and Mighty, and may Allah's benedictions be upon Muḥammad and his pure progeny. By Your Exalted, Great, Noble, Majestic, and Honourable Name, O Allah..."
>
> "O God! Illuminate our hearts with the light of faith. Honour us with the Islamic noble traits. Keep us away from moral impurities. Grant all the Muslims individual, moral and collective honour. Make them triumph over their enemies. Grant the legitimate requests of this assembly. Shower Your grace and mercy to our deceased ones."
>
> وَعَجِّلْ فِي فَرَجَ مَوْلاَنَا صَاحِبُ الزَّمَان.
>
> "And expedite the advent of our chief, the Master of the Time."

Chapter 9: Knowledge of the Self

﴿ وَفِي الأَرْضِ آيَاتٌ لِلْمُوقِنِينَ * وَفِي أَنْفُسِكُمْ أَفَلا تُبْصِرُونَ ﴾

> In the earth are signs for those who have conviction, and in your own souls [as well]. Will you not then perceive? (51:20-21)

One of the oldest words of wisdom in the world which have been conveyed by the great prophets to humanity and also mentioned by great men of wisdom in the world and whose credibility it has always preserved, nay its value has been gradually discovered, is this famous statement: "O man! Know thy self." In our narrations and traditions, this expression has been repeated time and again. It is thus reported from the Noble Messenger (S) as well as from the Commander of the Faithful 'Alī (A.S.) in different wordings:

مَنْ عَرَفَ نَفْسَهُ فَقَدْ عَرَفَ رَبَّهُ.

> "Whoever knows himself has known (or knows) his Lord."[1]

---

1. Āmadī,*Ghurar al-Ḥikam wa Durar al-Kalim*, chap. 77, *ḥadīth* 301.

And there are also other expressions similar to this; take, for example, this one: "O man! Be your own physician." Of course, this does not to be one's own physical doctor or healer, but this is a command [after all]. For instance, Imām al-Ṣādiq (A.S.) thus says in a tradition recorded in *Tuḥaf al-'Uqūl* and so elaborate, and in which there are many sayings full of wisdom and apparently it is narrated by 'Abd Allāh ibn Jundab:

انَّکَ قَدْ جُعِلْتَ طَبیبَ نَفْسِکَ [وَ عُرِّفْتَ آیةَ الصِّحَّةِ] وَ بیَّنَ لَکَ الدّاءُ وَ دُلِلْتَ عَلَي الدَّواءِ.

> "[O man!] You have been made the physician of your own self [and the sign of wellness has been shown to you] and the pains have been mentioned to you and you have also been guided to [their] cures."

The point is that this expression and similar expressions can be found a lot in the words of great men in the world. Socrates who lived approximately two thousand and five hundred years ago has left this important saying: "Know thy self." What is the importance and value of knowing the self and for what purpose that it is encouraged? It has been encouraged for two purposes. One purpose is for you to know yourself so as to know your Lord. Before, I have quoted a statement from Gandhi, our contemporary, when he said, "Out of reading the *Upanishads*, which are the oldest religious-mystical books in Hinduism, I have learned three things which became my guide in life. One is that there is only one knowledge in the universe that

that the knowledge of the 'self'. The second is whoever knows himself has known his God and the universe..."[1]

As such, in the *Upanishads* which pertain to thousands of years ago, we see that one of the oldest issues and admonitions which have been left to humanity is knowledge of the self, and even nowadays – especially in the past century and at the present – the question of man, knowledge about him and sciences pertaining to him are considered the most important and valuable human sciences.

Knowledge of the Self as Preliminary to Knowledge of God and Morality

Now, for what purpose that they have said, "Know thy self"? Where will knowledge of the self end up to? In other words, knowledge of the self is a preliminary to what? We have said that they have encouraged it for two purposes. One purpose is that if you know yourself, you will find out the most important issue ever raised in humanity and the ultimate secret of the universe (that is, God). Secondly, know yourself so that you will know what you should do and how you should behave in your life in this world; attitude and action. If you do not know yourself, you will not know how to behave and conduct oneself in this world; that is, how you are supposed to be.

1. [And the third one is throughout the universe, there is only one power (the power to dominate one's self) and one goodness (to love others).]

As morality is a set of traits, it is traceable to how one is supposed to be and how to behave. As such, in order to find out the greatest secrets in the universe and the most important question in the human mind (that is, God), you should know yourself. And for the most important question in terms of practical human development – how I should be and how I should behave (that is, God) – you should also know yourself. In the first part I want to explain a bit how a person will know God once he knows himself.

The Qur'an has also opened a separate account for knowing the self, in the sense that in the Qur'an – and in the Qur'an only – the entire world of creation is a sign and lesson for knowing one's self. In other words, it is not limited to the human being that he should only know himself so as to know God. From the point of view of the Qur'an, all happenings in the universe, all units of the creation – be they heavenly or earthly – all the things in the universe are signs (*āyāt*). That is, they are signs and manifestations of the sacred existence of God:

﴿ إِنَّ فِي خَلْقِ السَّمَاوَاتِ وَالأَرْضِ وَاخْتِلاَفِ اللَّيْلِ وَالنَّهَارِ لآيَاتٍ لِّأُوْلِي الألْبَابِ ﴾

> Indeed in the creation of the heavens and the earth and the alternation of night and day, there are signs for those who possess intellects. (3:190)

There are many such verses in the Qur'an. While the Qur'an, however, regards the whole universe as the Book of God, the Exalted, such that each line of this book points to the knowledge, wisdom and cognizance of the Author, it has opened a separate account for the human soul. That is, from the Qur'anic perspective, this chapter of the Book of Creation whose name is 'human being' has lessons for a person that are higher and more, for example, than the trees have. It is true that

برگ درختان سبز در نظر هوشیار
هر ورقش دفتري است معرفت کردگار

The green leaf of tree for the intelligent,
Is a book of God's gnosis.[1]

However, the human soul or 'self'– which is closest to the human being compared to anything else – has lessons which cannot be found in other than him. What are these teachings which are peculiar to the human soul and meant for the human being? Of course, the human being has some component parts which every natural being also possesses, and functionally, physiologically and anatomically, just as the leaves of a tree [point to] God's gnosis, the finger or nail of a person also point to the same. In fact, in every hair in the human body or in every blood of the human body, it points to the same. From this perspective, the human being is similar to the other things. There are teachings, however, which are peculiar to the human soul in that we have said that the Qur'an has also opened a separate account [for the human soul in terms of knowing God].

1. Shaykh Muṣlīḥ al-Dīn Sa'dī, *Dīwān-e Ash'ār*, "ghazaliyāt," with slight variation. [Trans.]

One example why we say 'separate account' is this: 'In the earth are signs for those who have conviction' (51:20) – those who want to reach the station of certainty. It is obvious that the human being is on earth and he is not outside of it, yet concerning him, it is thus said: '...and in your own souls [as well]' (51:21). It specifies. It is also stated in another verse, thus:

﴿ سَنُرِيهِمْ آيَاتِنَا فِي الآفَاقِ وَفِي أَنْفُسِهِمْ حَتَّى يَتَبَيَّنَ لَهُمْ أَنَّهُ الحَقُّ ﴾

> Soon We shall show them Our signs in the horizons and in their own souls until it becomes clear to them that He is the Real. (41:53)

It mentions separately the account of horizons (external world). It could mention the human being as an integral part of the horizons, but it mentions a separate account for the human 'self' (soul) – *"and in their own souls."*

Lessons of the Human Soul in Knowing God

What are those particular lessons and teachings? These lessons are so many. I have nothing to do with the mystical teachings with which a mystic person may reach after a lot of contemplations – in which the eyes and ears of his heart are open and inwardly witness the metaphysical world – at least the station of Maryam bint 'Imrān (Mary the daughter of Amran) who would converse with angels while in worship, or of Zakariyyā (Zechariah) or others from among the prophets and non-prophets. It is because these are related to the individuals who have at least engaged in a certain amount of mystical wayfaring (*sayr wa sulūk*), self-contemplation (*murāqibah*) and lifting up of mystical veils. If we talk about them, you will say that we are not like them; they are a selected few. It is not so. We talk about issues which are related to all individuals.

The World of Nature as a Continuous Flux and a Single Motion

Among them is the fact that day by day science has proven more that the world of nature is a continuous flux; that is, nothing in the world is in a single state in two moments. You may possibly say that this is sophistry; last night we came and saw this mosque in the same state that it has tonight; what change does it have? The answer is very clear. If all changes were tangible changes, then the issue has been solved already, but our senses can perceive the changes in the universe up to a certain extent. Our eyes, ears or faculty of touch can only perceive between two extents; it cannot perceive if it (extent) is lower; the same if it is higher. For example, if someone tells us that now there are sounds in the air, can we accept? We will say, "What are you saying?! You say contrary to the obvious; we have also ears yet we do not hear any sound." That is not so. Our ears, we, human beings, can [only] perceive certain waves in the atmosphere. Apparently, it is said that if the number of vibration of a wave is lesser than sixteen thousand per second, our ears cannot perceive it (just like a radio receiver which cannot receive the [sound] wave. That wave exists but we cannot perceive it. A certain animal may hear it.) And if it is more than thirty two thousand, it may be a deafening sound but we cannot hear it at all, and we may engage in our study, for example, in utmost peace of mind. Yet an animal may hear it. In the same manner, our eyes can [only] perceive certain extent of movements in the world. Let us consider these very simple instances of locomotion. The human eyes can [only] perceive certain speed, say one-tenth millimetre per second, of the movement of objects, but if the movement is slower than this, it is [still] a movement but the human eyes cannot perceive [it]. For example, the human eyes can perceive the movement of the watch's second hand. The movement of the minute hand which turns around in every watch can perhaps be perceived by some people if they were meticulous enough, whereas it is also in constant movement. But even if you look at the hour hand of a watch for an hour, you will not perceive at all that it moves although you know for a fact that an hour ago, it was on the number 7, for example, and not it is on number 8; it has moved very slowly. As far as your eyes are concerned, it is static in the sense that your eyes cannot perceive its movement, but your intellect tells you that this moves for the reason that an hour ago, it was on the number 7 and now it is on the number 8, and you know that it is not that the eyes failed to observe that it jumped from number 7 to number 8 at once.

The universe is in constant flux. Those who have proved

transubstantial motion (*ḥarikat-e jawhariyyeh*) and those who have proved other motions have established that there are things which you and I suppose to be static such the water of the river are actually in fast motion, but if we look at a distance I think that it is stationary. That a thing is in motion means that every amount of that thing at a given moment is no longer the same at another moment. The movement's components are hidden from one another. At the same time, the same motions in the universe follow a specific system.

Can the 'Self' be Changeable?

Let us deal with our own body. Our body is also in constant flux, from cells to atoms to those particles that constitute an atom. Some cells of our body are constantly dying and they are replaced by new cells. And those that do not die are in constant flux; that is, to be accurate, even the body an hour ago is different from that of the present. The old folks used to say that the body would change every seven years. Accurately speaking, however, even the body an hour ago is not the same body of the present, let alone the body after a year. In a person aged eighty, for instance, the body of the past eighty years has already been changed, and if ever we would compromise a lot, we have to say that it has been changed many times. But how about the 'I'? Has the 'I' been changed? If I am fifty years old, is the 'I' of today really and actually the same 'I' fifty years ago? Is it such that I am the same 'I' but that 'I' has already gone and another 'I' has replaced it? This is the answer: The body which is part of nature is in constant change but the 'I' evolves and progresses without changing, and it does not mean that another 'I' comes [as replacement].

The Story of Bahmanyār and Ibn Sīnā

This is a popular story and has been written in our own books. Abū 'Alī Sīnā has an outstanding student named Bahmanyār Azerbāijānī who is from Azerbaijan. He was a Zoroastrian (for belonging to a family of Zoroastrians) but he became Muslim later on. It is said that Abū 'Alī Sīnā discovered this student. One day Abū 'Alī was in a bakeshop. Bahmanyār who was then a small kid came and told the baker, thus: "I need some fire for fire-shovel. I want to bring home some fire; please give me." The baker said, "Fire cannot be brought just like that. Go and bring back a container here." This child immediately filled his hands with ashes and said, "Put the fire here." Abū 'Alī discovered that this was a clever child. He went to the child's parents and said, "It is unfortunately for this child to just die like that; entrust him to me and in the future he will become a learned man."

Bahmanyār is a student who has presented many of the ideas of Abū 'Alī. He himself has written a book entitled *Al-Taḥṣīl*. Perhaps this book was printed by me for the first time (we printed it for the first time in Iran) and it is a thick book. He has discussions with his teacher Abū 'Alī.

Bahmanyār believed that all things do change; not only the human body, but also the human soul does change. Just as the body in a moment is different from the body of the subsequent moment, the 'I' of this moment is also different from the 'I' of the subsequent moment. One day, he was debating with his teacher Abū 'Alī regarding this issue. Abū 'Alī said that it is not so; the body does change but the 'I' does not change; the 'self' is fixed. He insisted on his view. When he asked a question, Abū 'Alī remained silent without hinting any reply. "Why didn't you answer?" he asked. Abū 'Alī said, "The Abū 'Alī to whom you asked question is no longer the same in the subsequent moment. Also, the questioner of the earlier moment is no longer the same questioner of the subsequent moment. In every moment that you ask question, you are a particular person and you talk to a particular person. In the subsequent moment, you are another person and the earlier 'you' no longer exists. As such, in the subsequent moment it is no longer you the questioner and it is no longer the 'I' who is supposed to give answer." At this point, Bahmanyār remained silent.

Knowing the 'Self' Being an Inalterable Truth as Precursor to Knowing God

If a person knows his real 'I' as a person and a real unity,[1] if a

1. It is contrary to this nonsense talk: "The 'I' is a set of imaginations which come one after the other. I imagine that I am a particular thing; I am a million things. In essence, the 'I' of this hour is

person knows his self, he will see it as a fixed reality in this fluid nature, and then he will see that the universe which is also in constant flux is a reality whose unity has been preserved. The sun, moon, stars, and earth, if we look at their nature, they are always in a state of change, but there is the Real that keeps the universe intact. Just as this 'I' is the keeper of the body, keeping its unity, and the identity of the body emanates from the real identity of the human soul. The identity of the universe also depends on the identity of that inalterable metaphysical Real. Mawlānā Rūmī thus sings:

خلق را چون آب دان صاف و زلال
واندر آن تابان صفات ذوالجلال
گشت مُبدَل آب این جو چند بار
عکس ماه و عکس اختر برقرار

> Know that (the world of) created beings is like pure and limpid water,
> In which the attributes of the Almighty are shining.[1]
> The water in this channel has been changed many times,
> The reflection of the moon and of the stars remains unaltered.[2]

different from the 'I' of that hour. The 'I' is a set of imaginations which come one after the other; it is like a thread ball once it is opened; it is nothing but a thread ball. The human being is but a set of imaginations." Anyone who says so has not recognized himself.

1. Mawlānā Jalāl al-Dīn Rūmī, *Mathnawī-ye Maʻnawī*, Book 6, line 3173. [Trans.]

2. *Ibid.*, line 3178, with a slight variation. [Trans.]

The Existence of Spiritual Inclinations in the Human Being as a Sign of Knowing God

Another reason why the human soul is a sign for knowing God is the issue of human being's spiritual inclinations:

مَنْ عَرَفَ نَفْسَهُ فَقَدْ عَرَفَ رَبَّهُ.

> "Whoever knows himself has known (or knows) his Lord."

I have quoted to you before a very excellent statement by William James. Of course, it is something also mentioned by others but he has uttered through a very elegant expression. He is an experimental psychologist and he is a person who introduced psychology, especially religious psychology, into the level of experimentation and test. For approximately forty years, this man has experimented on the psychic-religious manifestations of the mind; that is, he has examined and studied the minds from the religious perspective, and he has done so not through analogy and reasoning but through experimentation and test. The outcome which this great psychologist of the world has arrived at from forty years of test on the human mind in terms of the spiritual inclinations is this: "In the human existence, just as there is a set of inclinations to nature and materiality which links him to nature and serves as the criterion for his link with nature, there is another set of inclinations which cannot be compatible with material considerations; rather, they are contrary to the considerations related to the human being's link with nature because his link with nature is meant to make him benefit from it, but these inclinations cannot be compatible with these ideas. The human being has a set of desires in this world which are incompatible with the natural and physical dimension of his existence." He also adds, "These are the reason for the existence of the other world and these feelings connect us to the other world. Spiritual and heavenly inspirations, quest for God, pursuit of piety, inclination toward goodness, and looking for spirituality have always existed in humanity, and they are inextinguishable and irreplaceable. Tomorrow night which will be the last session, I intend to discuss to you "Spiritual and Moral Vacuums in the Present Age," if God wills. Today, what problem has been brought to humanity by this extent of spiritual and moral emptiness resulted from the waves of materialism in the world and this campaign against man's natural disposition?

As such, another path for "Whoever knows himself has known (or knows) his Lord" is these spiritual inclinations, tendencies and attachments of the human being.

Fanaticism toward Materialism

This wave of materialism which surfaced in the world and subsequently brought miseries to humanity is more a violent reaction in the West against ignorance, violence and misbehaviours of the Church, and now we are paying the price of the Church's penalties. In the book *'Ilal-e Girāyesh beh Māddigarī (Causes of Tendency Toward*

Materialism),[1] this subject has been elucidated to some extent. The Church's ignorance and unawareness – its wrong interpretations about God, Resurrection and soul; its violence and policies of suppression, detection of the Church doctrines, its anti-freedom and democracy stances – dragged the world toward this state in which we have to accept either science or God (because the Church created contradiction between science and God); we have to accept either God or a life of comfort and wellbeing; we have to accept God or democracy. It is obvious that once God is placed on one hand and hundreds of other innate needs of man on the other hand, naturally most of the people would choose the latter; of course, some may possible side with God. At any rate, for various reasons this violent wave of materialism swept the Western world, and gradually it has also more or less spilled over the Eastern world, and the people of the East do not think that the conditions the Westerners had are different from the conditions that we have. Little by little bias in favour of materialism came into being just like the Church's fanaticism toward religion. In other words, just as the Church wanted to justify religion at all cost without the use of logic and reasoning, they also want to justify materialism at all cost. They are afraid lest materialism

1. The book's partial English translation, "The Causes Responsible for Materialist Tendencies in the West," is published in four parts in *Al-Tawḥīd Journal* (Tehran: Islamic Thought Foundation), vol. 12, no. 2, pp. 159-174; vol. 12, no. 3, pp. 139-166; vol. 12, no. 4, pp. 129-152; vol. 13, no. 1, pp. 127-146. [Trans.]

should be taken away from them and – as they say – they would return back to the Middle Ages. They say, "If materialism is taken away from us, then we have to return to the Middle Ages." As such, notwithstanding the openness of the path for humanity through nature and human soul toward God, they strive at all cost – by force or persuasion – to say that these paths are not trustworthy. One of these [paths] is this path of spiritual tendencies.

Maurice Maeterlinck's Statement

Now, I am going to cite two examples for you:

Maurice Maeterlinck[1] has many books. He has written a book on the bees[2] and another book on the termites,[3] and perhaps all his books have been translated [into Fārsī] in Iran because he has been a good writer. Here in Iran, he has been labelled, in a sense, and introduced as a great philosopher. At any rate, he has been a learned man and a very prolific writer. In Europe literature and philosophy are fused together. As this mixing of literature and philosophy enriches the former – which is more based upon intellectual tastes and imaginations; that is, it has more to do with human taste rather than thinking – and

1. Maurice Polydore Marie Bernard Maeterlinck (1862 – 1949): a Belgian playwright, poet, and essayist who was a Fleming, but wrote in French, and awarded the Nobel Prize in Literature in 1911. [Trans.]
2. *La Vie des abeilles* (*The Life of the Bee*) (1901). [Trans.]
3. *La Vie des termites* (*The Life of Termites*) (1926). [Trans.]

impoverishes philosophy, this mixture has enriched European literature and impoverished European philosophy. The fact is that this man is a good writer. I have been always saying that our very own Iranian, Muḥammad Mas'ūd, if he were only in Europe, he would have become known as a philosopher, because he was a writer like Maeterlinck and they could be at par with each other. Here in Iran, however, such [figures] shall never be recognized as philosophers and they cannot be recognized as such.

The life of bees is an amazing one and cannot be explained from a materialistic perspective – how these animals have such amazing awareness. No one has so far explained this subject. Meanwhile, the Qur'an explicitness states, thus:

﴿ وَأَوْحَى رَبُّكَ إِلَى النَّحْلِ ﴾

And your Lord inspired the bee. (16:68)

That is, there is this inward inspiration in this animal. The Qur'an has also astonishing words about the bees and ants, and today, these two insects have been recognized in an exceptional manner. More astonishing are its words about the ants. When Prophet Sulaymān (Solomon) (A.S.) reached an ant colony, [an ant said something] from which it can be deduced that basically the ants have a faculty of perception and understanding which is higher than that of the bees, and there is even an exchange of ideas, conversations, announcements, and reporting taking place among the ants. Nowadays, it was only fifty years ago that the knowledge about this subject was discovered.

﴿ حَتَّى إِذَا أَتَوْا عَلَى وَادِ النَّمْلِ قَالَتْ نَمْلَةٌ يَا أَيُّهَا النَّمْلُ ادْخُلُوا مَسَاكِنَكُمْ لا يَحْطِمَنَّكُمْ سُلَيْمَانُ وَجُنُودُهُ وَهُمْ لا يَشْعُرُونَ ﴾

When they came to the Valley of Ants, an ant said, 'O ants! Enter your dwellings, lest Solomon and his hosts should trample on you while they are unaware'. (27:18)

But Prophet Sulaymān (A.S.) who endowed by God, the Exalted, with the language of birds and others was aware of them and talked to that ant. Nowadays, science has proved that through their antennas the ants send and receive waves (of messages) in communicating with each other. The Qur'an [mentions] this subject while taking into consideration that these animals do not go to any school and receive no training. Thousands of research works have been made. There is no training and education among them, and for example, the engineers from among the bees have not put up a technical school in which to train their students; rather, their baby engineers were born engineers. The Qur'an categorically says, thus:

﴿ وَأَوْحَى رَبُّكَ إِلَى النَّحْلِ ﴾

And your Lord inspired the bee. (16:68)

Mankind has failed to give another answer to this question as it cannot be anything other than a Divine inspiration (*ilhām*).

Mr. Maurice Maeterlinck mentions all these things, but when it reaches the issue of origin of these astonishing pieces of knowledge, he says, "The beehive's spirit inspires it." You think of God and how silly this statement is! The beehive is nothing other than these bees. If we take away the bees, the beehive is nothing but some inanimate objects. What does the beehive's spirit mean?! He says, "The beehive's spirit inspires it." Well, from where did the beehive's spirit learn? Moreover, the beehive's spirit is not higher than the bee's spirit. Why does he say so? It is because he does not want to make mention of God, thereby to be condemned for bringing God to the sphere of science. In this way, it is the case of A, to be followed by B which, in turn, is to be followed by C, to be followed by D, thereby entailing thousands of responsibilities. And [he will be told,] "Mr. Maurice Maeterlinck, you can no longer live freely the way you want to."

The Story of Clever Pupil and School

It is said that a clever pupil was sent to the school. The teacher told him, "You say, 'A'." He remained silent. The teacher said, "This is simple; you say, 'A'." He would not utter anything no matter how his teacher insisted. Others came. His parents [also] came and said, "Son! You are an intelligent child. You can easily utter 'A'. You say 'A'." In the end, they asked, "Why do you not utter?" He said, "Well, if I utter 'A' you will ask me to utter 'B'. Once I utter 'B' you will ask me to utter 'C'. As I finished uttering 'C' you will ask me to utter 'D'. From the beginning I will not utter 'A' so that I will be free until the end, for you will send me back home and I will be totally free. Once I utter 'A,' this will continue until such time that I will be spending my youth studying in the school."

Now, in order to avoid bringing the issue of God to the front, this gentleman says, "It is the beehive's spirit that inspires the bees."

Repentance (*Tawbah*)

The human being's spiritual inclinations cannot be reconciled with any materialist consideration. From the perspective of the individual, these moral inclinations, which we have elaborated earlier, is based upon [personal] harm and loss: offering one's life for the society, to be just in dealing with others, to be fair in the sense of non-transgression, to rise up against one's self, and to combat the self, which in religious parlance, is called 'repentance' (*tawbah*). There was a time when I collected verses of the Qur'an in this regard; I found out that the logic of the Qur'an is exactly this: to revolt against one's self. Strange! A person revolts or goes against himself; he stages a revolution against himself, with all the constitutive elements of a revolution; he puts himself in trial; he exacts punishment against himself. How sweet and elegant Imām 'Alī's (A.S.) statement was! Someone came to him and said in his presence:

اسْتَغْفِرُ اللّهَ رَبِّي وَ اتوبُ الَيهِ.

> "I ask the forgiveness of Allah, my Lord, and to Him do I turn.

He thought that repentance (*tawbah*) means to verbally ask for Allah's forgiveness (*istighfār*). Imām 'Alī (A.S.) turned to him and said:

ثَكِلَتْكَ أُمُّكَ، أَتَدْرِي مَا الاسْتِغْفَارُ؟ إنَّ الاسْتِغْفَارَ دَرَجَةُ الْعِلِّيِّينَ.

> "Your mother may lose you! Do you know what *istighfār* is? *Istighfār* is meant for people of a high position."[1]

Then the Imām (A.S.) elucidates *istighfār*, thus: "The first is to repent over the past; the second is to make a firm determination never to revert to it; the third is to discharge all the rights of people so that you may meet Allah quite clean with nothing to account for; the fourth is to fulfil every obligation which you ignored (in the past) so that you may now do justice with it."

Thereafter, he uttered two sentences which exactly mean revolution and uprising against the self and punishing the same. He says, "The fifth is to aim at the flesh grown as a result of unlawful earning, so that you may melt it by grief (of repentance) till the skin touches the bone and a new flesh grows between them; and the sixth is to make the body taste the pain of obedience as you (previously) made it taste the sweetness of disobedience." This is repentance. Such have been the penitents in the world, and they have always such individuals.

In one of his writings, the late Ḥājj Mīrzā Jawād Āqā Malikī Tabrīzī, one of great people of gnosis (*ahl al-*

1. Imām 'Alī, *Nahj al-Balāghah*, Saying 409, 1285.

ma'rifah) in our time – who passed away fifty two years ago and whose grave is in Qum and whenever I visit there I always wish to pay homage to his grave – talks about his great teacher, the late Ākhūnd Mullānā Ḥusayn-Qulī Hamidānī who was one of the marvels of the people of inner world (*ahl al-ma'nā*). He writes that someone came to the late Ākhūnd and the late Ākhūnd taught him how to repent. Forty eight hours afterward when he came [back], we did not recognize him. He was so changed facially and physically that we could not believe that he was the very same person forty eight hours earlier.

I do study this from the perspective of human character. What is the explanation for this transformation of the said penitent person in the presence of Ākhūnd Mullānā Ḥusayn-Qulī Hamidānī, who was heading to a certain direction and suddenly diverted to the opposite direction, staging an uprising, revolution and upheaval against himself? Who stages an uprising, revolution and upheaval against whom? These are meant to be a lesson for mankind – a great lesson:

مَنْ عَرَفَ نَفْسَهُ فَقَدْ عَرَفَ رَبَّهُ.

> "Whoever knows himself has known (or knows) his Lord."

Where do these strong inclinations come from? Where are their roots and origin? Concerning moral inclinations – one of which is repentance – there are other inclinations which are totally incompatible with the interests of an individual and whose name is 'service to the society and humanity,' such as to sacrifice oneself for the survival of society, depriving oneself for the welfare of society, and self-deprivation for the comfort of society. These cannot be reconciled with any material consideration.

Is it the Collective Spirit that Inspires Moral Inclinations?

Now, whenever they want to explain these inclinations, what do they say? Some have said that it is the collective spirit that inspires; the collective spirit inspires a person to do a certain thing. "The collective spirit inspires" means that it is the collective spirit that deceives and this has no meaning other than deception. It is the same statement of someone about the bees, saying that it is the spirit of beehive that inspires the bees to perform such amazing works. This gentleman whose committee is lame in spiritual inclinations says that it is the spirit of society that gives inspiration. What is society? Society means a group of individuals with a particular composition. The society has no existence separate from individuals unless it is just metaphorical existence, and metaphorical existence is devoid of any spirit. Let us assume that it has spirit, from where did this collective spirit get this inspiration? Who gave this inspiration to the spirit of society? Moreover, the theologians who say that it is God, the Exalted, who gives inspiration (*ilhām*) to mankind, maintain that the just God shall not allow any work to have no recompense:

﴿ لِلَّذِينَ أَحْسَنُوا الْحُسْنَىٰ وَزِيَادَةٌ ﴾

> Those who are virtuous shall receive the best reward and an enhancement. (10:26)

It is impossible for God to say to the human being: "O man! Sacrifice your felicity; sacrifice your existence for the sake of nothing." Rather, there is the subsequent reward. According to the Real Being who gives inspiration, that is, God, such an action is a wise action and it shall not be devoid of a reward. But once we say that there is no transcendent existence and it is the spirit of society which gives inspiration to the misfortunate person to throw himself on fire for the sake of saving others and after throwing yourself on fire, you will be gone for nothing. This means that it is the spirit of society that deceives.

The Reason behind Expressing Materialist Views

As I have said, apprehension for the extinction of materialism and the popularization of God and religion is the reason behind expressing these views. Some of them say, "If God and religion come [to the fore], what will happen to freedom of action that I want?" Others say, "May the Middle Ages not come back! If we do not say, 'materialism,' it means that we have accepted that the Middle Ages have to come back." Well, this statement is not that surprising for the Westerners; for our people it is surprising. What is surprising is that sometimes our people talk about [returning to] the Middle Ages. There is a talk about [returning to] the Middle Ages in Iran! The Middle Ages belong to Europe. For Europe the Middle Ages mean the period of decline and degeneration. The period which is the Middle Ages for him is the period of civilization, culture and honour for you. One thousand years ago mean the period of Abū Rayḥān Bīrūnī,[1] Abū 'Alī ibn Sīnā, Fārābī, Ibn Rushd,[2] Ibn Haytham,[3] and others. It is one of the most brilliant periods of human civilization and culture which belongs to you. Why do you associate his history to you?! He says, "We want the Middle Ages not to come back!" If the Middle Ages come back, it is of utmost honour for you. If Abū 'Alī ibn Sīnā existed in the world today, they will gather to his monument. If Abū Rayḥān Bīrūnī were alive, they will kiss his feet. They say, "Middle Ages." We also say, "Yes, Middle Ages." They say,

---

1. Abū Rayḥān Muḥammad ibn Aḥmad al-Bīrūnī (973-1048): a Persian Muslim scholar and polymath of the 11th century. [Trans.]
2. Abū 'l-Walīd Muḥammad ibn Aḥmad ibn Rushd better known as Ibn Rushd, and in European literature as Averroes (1126-98): an Andalusian Muslim polymath; a master of Aristotelian philosophy, Islamic philosophy, Islamic theology, Malikī law and jurisprudence, logic, psychology, politics, Arabic music theory, and the sciences of medicine, astronomy, geography, mathematics, physics, and celestial mechanics. [Trans.]
3. Abū 'Alī al-Ḥasan ibn al-Ḥasan ibn al-Haytham, known as Ibn al-Haytham, Alhacen or Alhazen (965 – c. 1040): a Muslim scientist and polymath who made significant contributions to the principles of optics, as well as to physics, astronomy, mathematics, ophthalmology, philosophy, visual perception, and to the scientific method. [Trans.]

"The Middle Ages should not come back." We say, "The Middle Ages should come back." They have the Middle Ages, but basically we do not have the Middle Ages. Of course, we have a period of degeneration but ours is not similar to their Middle Ages. Their Middle Ages are our new ages; that is, the past five or six centuries. It is the period which they call 'the Middle Ages'. Their Middle Ages are our period of culture and civilization; the period of our honour.

Among the issues which they avoid [out of fear of the return to the fore of God and religion] is the issue of the 'self'. Since time has already passed, let me summarize in a few words. This issue has also been clarified nowadays. The statement we made about the 'self' is in the Qur'an. It is not that of one of the Muslim scholars such that we could say that perhaps today it has been learned from others. It has been in the Qur'an for the past one thousand and four hundred years; nowadays, they have recently found it out. If we are supposed to say that someone has learned it from somebody else, we must say that these have been taken from the Qur'an. The Qur'an of the past one thousand and four hundred years could not have taken it from them. That issue is that the human beings loses himself; he forgets himself and thinks of non-self as his own self; and that morality is the human being's return to his original and real self. As to what is the human being's real self, I have discussed before to a certain extent.

Sartre's View Regarding the Real Self

Some have claimed that the human being's real self is selflessness and freedom. In this world, the human being is freedom, nay the freedom itself. He is not a free being, but rather a being that is freedom itself. And it is interesting to note that instead of building the thesis of God's existence from the human freedom and independence,[1] Mr. Sartre says, "Since man is free, I therefore say God must not have existed because if God does exist, he can no longer be free." How? He says something which one will basically find surprising how he and his likes are so uninformed and unaware! He says, "If there is God, it means that God has a mind and he has had conceived our nature in His mind, and if ever I were conceived in His mind, I, therefore, cannot be free as I am supposed to be under compulsion. I must be as I have been supposed to be in His mind. Does 'God's mind' make sense at all?! [If He has such, then] He is not God. He must be just a creature like you Sartre which you call 'God'.

The Relationship between Man's Freedom and God's Existence

The question of freewill and predestination is a question

1. If there is only matter and nature, freedom has no meaning for the human being and he cannot be anything in the world other than an account of matter and nature. The human freedom and freewill itself is one of the manifestations of "Whoever knows himself has known his Lord."

which has been solved more than one thousand years ago and has not least contradiction at all with human freedom. In fact, it is only through the affirmation of God, freewill and predestination that one can talk about human freedom. As a Divine breath (*nufikhah*), the human being can be free from the constraint of nature. If the human being were mere body and his will were naturally born out of the movements of atoms and the like, then he is nothing else but a 'compelled' (*majbūr*) one. Sartre says, "The human being is a free will." Let us ask [him], "Where it this will come from? If the human mind and will were automatic peculiarities of nature and matter, then what would freedom mean?! Let anyone says that he believes that the human being has a metaphysical power in the sense that he does not regard the human being as subdued by nature; he considers the human being dominant over nature and he does not regard nature as the root and the soul as the secondary element. In fact, there is no talk about the primary and the secondary elements. He believes in the human being as having two types of power (natural and supernatural), and since the human being is a metaphysical flame and emanation, he can dominate over his nature and his decision could be something other than the very movements of atoms; he can manipulate nature and prevail over nature. "The human being has no self other than freedom!" What?! Of course, to say that the human being has no disposition (*sarshat*) and nature has a shade of truth in it, and tonight

I intended to deal with the subject through Islamic philosophy. The subject which he has discussed under the label 'the primacy of existence' is not recognized by the Muslim scholars as such. They have rather discussed some of his words under a different name – that the human being builds and chooses his own self. In other words, he is not like other things in nature. That which is in nature is the same thing which has been created, with the exception of the human being that is what he wants to be. This does not mean, however, that the human being is devoid of any disposition, temperament and nature; it rather means that the human disposition is such a disposition and it is not that he possesses no disposition and persona [at all]. The human 'self' is such a self that dictates so; it is not that the human being is such since he has no 'self'.

Since I promised last night to deal with this discussion, in order for me not to hold [the discussion] in total silence, I shall only briefly touch on two sections.

The Human Being Is What He Likes to Be

Concerning the fact that the human being is what he himself thinks of or the human being is what he likes to be, our scholars have had a better discussion than Mr. Sartre. In Islamic philosophy, Ṣadr al-Muta'allihīn had the best exposition. The fact is rooted in the Qur'an that every being is its very own self with the exception of the human being who shall be summoned in various forms:

﴿ يَوْمَ يُنْفَخُ فِي الصُّورِ فَتَأْتُونَ أَفْوَاجًا ﴾

> The day the Trumpet will be blown, and you will come in groups. (78:18)

And only a group of the people will be summoned as humans. Other groups of people will be summoned in various forms of animal. The human being is not compelled to be human; rather, he may mould himself as human and he may turn himself into a wolf, dog, pig, or rooster; he may acquire whatever trait for himself. Concerning the notion that the human being is what he thinks of, Mullānā [Rūmī] very beautifully says, thus:

اي برادر تو همه انديشه‌اي   مابقي تو استخوان و ريشه‌اي
گر بود انديشه‌ات گل، گلشني   ور بود خاري تو هيمه گلخني

> O brother, you are the same thought;
> As for the rest, you are flesh and bone.
> If your thought is a rose, you are a rose-garden;
> And if it is a thorn, you are fuel for the bath-stove.[1]

If we ask Mullānā [Rūmī], "What is a human being?" he will say, "He is what he thinks of." If you ask, "Who am I?" He will say, "Tell me what you think of so that I could tell you what you are. If you think about the truth, then you are truth. If you think about God, then you are godly. If you think about 'Alī, then you are 'Alī-like. If you think

1. Mawlānā Jalāl al-Dīn Rūmī, *Mathnawī-ye Ma'nawī*, Book 2, lines 277-278. [Trans.]

about an act of a dog, then you are a dog. Tell me what you think of so that I could tell you what you are."

Concerning the notion that the human being is whatever he wants and whatever he desires, in our traditions (*aḥādīth*) this has been much emphasized:

مَنْ احَبَّ حَجَراً حَشَرَهُ اللّٰهُ مَعَهُ

> "Whoever loves a stone, Allah shall summon him along with it."[1]

It is because he shall also become stone-like. A person shall become whatever he likes.

Enduring many difficulties, someone from the far-flung Khurāsān came to Imām al-Bāqir (A.S.) [in Madīnah] (as the love for *Ahl al-Bayt* (A.S.) drew him there) while on foot; his shoes were destroyed; his feet cracked; his heels having large gaps. He came to the Imām (A.S.) with love and ardent desire. He thanked God for being able to fulfil his goal. He then showed his feet with blood in the cracks and said, "O son of the Messenger of Allah! Do not draw us here except the love of you *Ahl al-Bayt* by which I have come here on foot from Khurāsān." The Imām (A.S.) made this statement: "Whatever one wants, he shall become such and shall be summoned along with it." As the poet says,

1. Shaykh 'Abbās Qummī, *Nafs al-Mahmūm*, 36, as quoted from Shaykh al-Ṣadūq's *Al-Āmālī*, 79, session (*majlis*) 27 with the following phrase:

فَلَوْ انَّ رَجُلًا تَوَلَّي حَجَراً لَحَشَرَهُ اللّٰهُ مَعَهُ يَوْمَ الْقِيامَةِ.

"If a man loves a stone, Allah shall summon him along with it on the Day of Resurrection."

گر در طلب گوهر کاني، کاني ور در پي جستجوي جاني، جاني

That is to say, "If you are looking for a jewel, a land mine and an inanimate object, you are an inanimate object, and if you want an animate object and you are looking for life and meaning, then you are an animate."

من فاش کنم حقيقت مطلب را هرچيز که در جُستن آني، آني

That is to say, "You are whatever you are looking for. If you ask this poet, therefore, 'What am I?' He will say, 'Tell me what you are looking for so that I could tell you what you are.'"

As I have promised, God willing, tomorrow night I will discuss to you "Spiritual and Moral Vacuum in the Contemporary World" whose outcome are these materialistic inclinations.

***

The *Ahl al-Bayt* (A.S.) were brought to the court of Ibn Ziyād. It is written that Zaynab was of tall stature. While entering the court of Ibn Ziyād, the womenfolk were gathering around her and like a signet, they surrounded her. Ibn Ziyād knew who this magnificent woman surrounded by others like maidservants was. He was expecting that Zaynab would greet him as she entered, but Zaynab did not greet him. Zaynab wanted to proved and she proved (and proved even more afterward) thus, "O Ibn Ziyād! Do not think that though you cut our bodies into pieces, or you made us captives and enchained us, you can also make our spirits your captives. Our spirits are the sound human spirit; it is the spirit that knows no defeat; it is God's breathe. Our spirits cannot be captured. Our spirits are inextinguishable. Our spirits cannot be enchained." She did not give salutations. He angrily asked:

مَنْ هذِهِ الْمُتَكَبِّرَةُ؟

"Who is this arrogant woman?"

No one replied. He repeated the question twice or thrice. Finally, someone answered him, thus:

هذِهِ زَيْنَبُ بِنْتُ عَلي بْنِ ابي طالبٍ

"She is Zaynab, the daughter of 'Alī ibn Abī Ṭālib."[1]

Thereafter, she reproached Ibn Ziyād so much that he could not say anything and he had no make such executioner's decision as he had no other option. He said, "They have still tongues! Cut off their heads!"

When Zaynab entered the court of Yazīd, she had also showed the same magnificence. That is, these forty stations of captivity still failed to cut Zaynab into pieces; Zaynab's spirit was impregnable. In fact, its glory further manifested there. Believe me, the sermon delivered by Lady Zaynab in the court of Yazīd is one of the unique sermons in the world. I shall only quote one sentence from it. She said:

كدْ كيدَک وَ اسْعَ سَعْيک انَّک لا تُميتُ وَحْينا.

That is to say, "O Ibn Mu'āwiyah! You can craft any trick and do whatever you want but I can assure you that this light is inextinguishable. That which shall be extinguished

1. Muḥammad Bāqir Majlisī, *Biḥār al-Anwār*, vol. 45, section (*bāb*) 39, 115.

in this world is you and your political apparatus. That which shall remain is my brother. That which shall inspire all the pious in the world is my brother. That which shall enthral the world is my brother. This assurance is an assurance to human disposition. God has created the human being truth-seeking." Although Yazīd was one of the eloquent and fluent Arabs, he could not say anything against the logic of Zaynab, and since the ambassadors of non-Muslims countries, the court guards and the notables were present at that time, he was so embarrassed. He wanted Zaynab to remain silent but she did not remain silent. Finally, he resorted to a criminal scheme, as if telling himself, thus: "I have to incite the emotions of this woman; I have to shut her mouth through her emotions." I shall no more mention what crime he committed, but it is enough to say that one of those who were seated was so touched that he thus shouted, "O Yazīd! Take away these sticks. By God! I saw with my own eyes the Prophet kissing these very lips."

> ولا حول ولا قوة الّا باللّه العلي العظيم وصلّي اللّه علي محمّد وآله الطاهرين. بإسمک العظيم الاعظم الأعزّ الاجلّ الاكرم يا اللّه...
>
> "And there is neither power nor might except that of Allah, the Exalted and Mighty, and may Allah's benedictions be upon Muḥammad and his pure progeny. By Your Exalted, Great, Noble, Majestic, and Honourable Name, O Allah..."

"O God! Illuminate our hearts with the light of faith. Embellish our hearts and souls with the Islamic noble traits. Cleanse our souls of all impurities and filths. Illuminate the lights of love and gnosis of You and Your saints (*awliyā'*) on our hearts. Shower Your grace and mercy to our deceased ones."

وَعَجِّلْ فِي فَرَجِ مَوْلاَناَ صَاحِبُ الزَّمَان.

"And expedite the advent of our chief, the Master of the Time."

Chapter 10: Spiritual and Moral Crises in the Present Age

﴿ فَأَمَّا الزَّبَدُ فَيَذْهَبُ جُفَاء وَأَمَّا مَا يَنفَعُ النَّاسَ فَيَمْكُثُ فِي الأَرْضِ ﴾

As for the scum, it leaves as dross, and that which profits the people remains in the earth. (13:17)

I promised to deal with the spiritual and moral crises in the present age tonight.

The Academic and Practical Values of a Theory

At the outset, let me give a short a short introduction and that is, the value of any belief is twofold: one is theoretical or academic value and the other is practical value. The theoretical value of a belief means the degree of its compatibility with the truth and reality. The academic value of a philosophical, social, global, or so theory is this: Is this theory compatible with the reality or not? The way to know whether a theory is compatible with the reality or not is experiment, observation and test in some cases while rational argumentations in other cases.

Ptolemy, for example, had said that the earth is the centre of the universe and the planetary bodies revolve around the earth. Later on, scientists came and changed this theory. "The theoretical value of the Ptolemaic notion" is this: Is the earth really the centre and all the planetary bodies and stars revolve around it, or not? [Does theoretical value belongs to the Ptolemaic notion] or not? Theoretical value belongs to the Copernican idea that the earth is the centre of the universe; the sun is the centre; not the centre of the universe but the centre of our solar system.

Practical value means that "Well, it does not matter to me which of them is compatible with the truth or reality; in actuality, which of them is more useful for mankind? Is the former notion more useful and beneficial to mankind, or is it the latter? Or, is there no difference between them in this regard? Religious beliefs are included in them. The first fundamental religious belief is that of God's existence and His Oneness. This has two values. One is 'theoretical value'; that is, the subject is really and actually such; in other words, proof, evidence and reasoning also affirm the matter and that is the truth. And the other is 'practical value'; that is, what effect does this belief have on human life? Is such a belief beneficial to humanity or not?

In general, religion must be discussed and is discussed from two perspectives or ways. One is the theoretical value of religion; that is, its being the truth and realistic.

Scholastic theology (*'ilm al-kalām*) deals with this subject. Scholastic theology – especially the classical one – is not concerned with the practical value; it is only concerned with the theoretical value; it pursues ways and justifications, for example, for the Oneness of God (*tawḥīd*), prophethood (*nubuwwah*), Divine justice (*'adl*), Imāmate (*imāmah*), and the Resurrection (*ma'ād*). It presents proof that these [beliefs] are the truth. Practical value, however, means that "Well, whether we have concluded that these are the truth, or not, let us see what does this thinking, belief or faith offer to mankind; that is, what effect it has on human life?

The second point is this: Is the perpetuity of an idea or belief depends on its theoretical value or practical value, or both? If a belief wants to remain among the people, does it mean that it must have both values, or is just one of these values enough? Or, is it that none of these values is necessary for its perpetuity and that none of these values is a prerequisite for it to endure? In other words, it is possible for an idea or a belief to be not the truth and not beneficial to mankind; yet it endures. I shall reply to this question later.

To be True as Equal to be Useful

Another [question] is this: Can these two be separated from each other? In other words, can an idea or belief be the truth and yet harmful to humanity, while another idea or belief is senseless and yet beneficial? No. (I shall say this concisely pending my pertinent discussions.) According to the Qur'an, to be the truth or theoretical value is equal to being beneficial or practical value. Whatever is the truth, any belief or idea which is founded on truth is not harmful to mankind. It is not that an idea or faith is correct and true as well as realistic, yet it is better not to be believed by people. On the contrary, they must believe in the opposite idea which is non-sensical yet beneficial to mankind. On the other hand, a belief or faith is nonsense and futile yet it is beneficial to a person and if he believes in it, it will be beneficial to him. No. It is not so. It is possible for a nonsense talk, a false statement to be beneficial to some individuals – and not all individuals – for a limited period of time, but this is the same thing describes by the Qur'an as 'falsehood' (*bāṭil*), saying that it is not beneficial to mankind; neither will it last. Once we understand that the truth (that is, what is true and real) is identical with being good (that is, to be useful), the reply to the second question becomes clear, and no one can say that a certain thing is the truth yet harmful. How can something be beneficial yet unrealistic? No. We have no more than two alternatives. Either a belief or faith is the truth and good, or it is nonsense and at the same time, harmful to humanity.

The question, therefore, must be posed in this way: Is to be nonsense and harmful equal to be the truth and good in terms of the chance to perpetuate? Or, is it that in the universe, just as if, for some reason, an extraneous limb develops in a body it shall gradually be eliminated by the orderly system of creation, it is possible for thousands of nonsensical and false beliefs to flourish among the people and endure for a limited period of time and the system of creation shall gradually eliminate them and brought them to extinction? This is the same struggle between truth and falsehood mentioned in the Qur'an, saying that falsehood passes by and after sometime it shall cease to exist, while the truth (that is, what is true and real), due to its being beneficial[1] and good at the same time, shall endure forever.

The verse I have recited [in the beginning] refers to this.

﴿ فَأَمَّا الزَّبَدُ فَيَذْهَبُ جُفَاءً وَأَمَّا مَا يَنفَعُ النَّاسَ فَيَمْكُثُ فِي الأَرْضِ ﴾

> As for the scum, it leaves as dross, and that which profits the people remains in the earth. (13:17)

This verse is one of the manifest miracles of the Qur'an; that is, in terms of the substance, it is par excellence and it is impossible for a human, especially an illiterate one, to compose by his own. It gives a parable of the truth and falsehood. It gives the parable of the rain water that pours onto the mountains and valleys and then creates flood. The current of water forms a scum. Later on, the scum covers the water current, and a superficial observer would think that the water which is the real is overwhelmed by the scum which is futile and fleeting.

---

1. That is, beneficial in its general sense, and not only material benefit.

The Qur'an, however, says, that it is not so; the scum shall go and the water shall remain. The water is like the truth while the scum is like falsehood. The truth shall remain because of its being beneficial. That is, here the Qur'an regards the truth as identical with what is beneficial and it does not give distinction between the two. This is the point I would like to highlight as an introduction to the topic "Spiritual Crises in the Present Age" and to discuss it requires more ample time.

Spiritual Crisis as the Greatest Crisis of the Present Age

Now, let me briefly state, however, that today the narrowminded people in the world draw their attention to the fact that the greatest crisis experience now by human society, especially by the so-called advance and industrialized societies, is spiritual crisis, and not political or economic crisis, for example. Of course, there are political crises in today's world, such as the Arab-Israel Issue, the border disputes between China and the Soviet Union, and many others. There are also economic crises such as the issue of global inflation. Now, these crises are not considered unsolvable problems. There was even more threat to world war ten years ago[1] compared to the present. The unsolvable crises whose solution is yet to be found are spiritual crises; that is, it is neither related to

1. Most probably it alludes to the 13-day Cuban Missile Crisis of 1962 between the US and USSR. [Trans.]

the economy nor related to politics nor related to industry, for example. It is related to the spiritual aspects of the human being. Now, I shall mention them to you one by one. Some of existing crises are not spiritual crises per se but they are spiritually rooted.

Increase in Suicide Cases

One of the serious problems in the world today is the daily increase of suicide cases. What research studies show? What is the root cause of suicide incidents? Is it poverty, for instance (although today's poverty itself has also spiritual root and not economic)? What prompts suicide cases? Do they happen in poor and deprived families? If it were so, the problem had another form. Is it traceable from things which have no, or the least, bearing on material aspects? It is [traceable] from spiritual aspects; that is, feeling of futility in life, and in their own words, freedom in senselessness, and "What do I live for? For what purpose have I come to this world? What is the use of this life?" It is a state of irritability and lack of willpower to face problems in life. In other words, a very simple problem, which in the past would not be treated as a problem at all and would not rob a person of even an hour of sleep, will end up today into the point where [it is said that] "There is no other way to live. We have to resign from living." There are statistical data in this regard. From these newspapers of ours which occasionally reflect statistical data, I was seriously touched and I have mentioned some of them in my books such as in *Mas'aleh-ye Ḥijāb*. These statistical data show that there are more cases of suicide in countries which are industrially more advanced and are more in material welfare. Analyses indicate that these are nothing but spiritual emptiness and psychological insatiability.

Idleness During Spare Time

An issue which is frequently discussed today is the issue of idleness during spare time. In very advanced countries, because of the progress in science and technology, the number of the working hours is reduced and naturally the income somehow also increased. Of course, for this reason, it is source of happiness that the salary increases while the hours of work – hard work – are lessened. Yet, this situation has also brought about spare time. How should this spare time be filled? This is a problem in today's world – through which means should space time be filled? The tools which have been brought into being are nothing but tools of self-forgetfulness – cinemas, theatres, tools for self-indulgence, and others. So long as a person is with himself, he feels a sense of futility.

Increase in Nervous Breakdowns and Mental Disorders

What do the statistical data about the problem of daily increase in nervous breakdowns, mental disorders, and even illnesses which are called 'illnesses of civilization' show? Were there more psychological illnesses in the past or now? You may possibly say that we have no statistical data of the past. Yet advanced countries have statistical records for approximately the past two hundred years. Statistical data there specifically show that the more progressive and advanced in material welfare humanity becomes, nervous breakdowns and mental disorders also increase. Mental disorders are broad. Some mental disorders do not end up in nervous breakdown; they only result in physical illnesses such as intestinal ulcers. It is said that ulcers are mostly caused by nervous problems and these are called 'illness of civilization'. Do not make mistake about it; I do not want to conclude here that welfare must be lessened. No. Whether welfare is lessened or increased is inconsequential. The root [of the problem] is the absence of something else. Some day one should not conclude from my lecture that I want to say that since the people are in comfort, they are experiencing mental disorders, and thus it is better for them to be in poverty. It is not so. I want to point out that although the people are in comfort and they are not supposed to suffer from such nervous problems and illnesses, they still have and more than in the past. This is while the people in the past were experiencing more economic deprivations.

Juvenile Delinquency and Hippie Movement

Another issue is that of juvenile delinquency and youth problems. Fortunately, it is of lesser degree among us (and not it is totally non-existent), and that which exists is only blind imitation of others. Our youth are really not rebellious but once they hear that others have done so, they say, "Let us also do it." The hippie movement is to turn back from today's civilization. While all means and facilities are provided for a person, he turns his back from everything about life including hygiene. He abandons all traditions and all manifestations of progress and civilization. He is not willing to wear usual clothes. If you give him a new pair of pants, first he will make some cuts on it and then trample on it. He wears an old pair of slippers. He goes and lives in undergrounds. He indulgences in drug addiction. The issue of hippie movement, its analysis, roots, and solution constitute a discussion which could be tackled, if there were time, in two or three sessions. It is one of the serious problems in the world today and originates from a sort of spiritual emptiness in the sense that this hippie generation has a way of thinking of its own and it has also a fundamental idea and that is, this Western civilization of today is nonsense. Perhaps he also fails to explain the origin of futility of this civilization. Is it the fault of the machine and that it is nonsense? Why the machine is nonsense?! Is science nonsense? Science cannot be nonsense. Yet he understands so much that what exists today as 'civilization' is nonsense. Hippie movement means to turn back from the civilization which this generation considers nonsense. You can see that they have turned their attention to the East, especially in the Far East; they say that in the Far East, there is spirituality and mysticism among the Buddhists. They want to go there and see for themselves if they could satisfy themselves. From this machine, industry and technology which are of no avail, let us go there and see if we can find something there or not.

Emotional Emptiness

Yet another issue is that of emotional emptiness. People have taken the form of machine parts for themselves. This is a terrible kind of poverty in humanity. Mothers do not have such feeling of love to their children; so are the children toward their parents; brothers toward one another; let along neighbours toward one another; let fellow countrymen toward one another; let a human being toward his fellow human being. This problem is a serious problem of today, and there are stories in this regard.

Some years ago, one of our learned friends and scholars was suffering for ulcer and he went to one of the European countries (apparently Austria) as his son was there, so as to see his son and at the same time, undergo medical treatment. He narrated, thus: “One day my son and I were in a restaurant and I just then recently went out of the hospital. We were sitting in front of a table and my son would regularly stand up to serve me foods; he would bring me tea; he would bring me coffee; he would stay around me. A man and a woman apparently aged fifty to sixty. I saw them observing us for a while.

Meanwhile, my son came and passed by them. I saw them talking with him. They asked him some questions and he was answering them. Then my son came [to me] and said, 'They are asking who you are that I am serving. They had no doubt that I am an attendant and I get money for rendering such services. They asked, 'How much money do you get from this person for rendering such services?' I said, 'He is my father.' They said, 'Fortunate is your father. Should a person serve his father without receiving anything in return?!' I said, 'Well, he is my father. I am studying here. He sends money from Iran for my matriculation and living expenses.' They continued, thus: 'He works and sends you money to spend?!' I said, 'Yes.' They could not believe. They gradually became acquainted. They said, 'Yes, we are also a couple. We have a son and a daughter. Our daughter lives in so-and-so (place) while our son lives in so-and-so (place) and now we are living here alone. Later on, upon my son's investigation they confessed that "Thirty years ago, we were acquainted with each other and became in love with each other. We agreed to live together for a while and get married afterward if we see ourselves compatible with each other. Thirty years have passed in such a way and we have no child. This period of our engagement took thirty years and yet to reach a certain point!'"

The issue of emotional emptiness is an amazing problem in the world. They are also human beings and in terms of disposition, they are also like us. God forbid, one day we may also become like them. Just tonight, I happened to read a news report in the newspaper. I was really surprised to realize that once a person loses his humanity, he could become like a machine spare part. It was reported that an aircraft crashed in Egypt and ninety two persons were killed. A person who works in the airport as an air traffic controller, for example, did not give any prior information to the pilot, saying thus: "Yes, when the aircraft was coming and flying at an elevation of around two thousand meters [above sea level] and supposed not to be below three thousand and five hundred meters, I saw it and I knew that it will not take before getting crashed." He was asked, "Why did not you tell this?" He said, "It was not part of my responsibility. I was not in charge of it. I was assigned to a particular job which I did." Well and good, it was not part of your job but you are human. He said, "I knew that if I gave the information – and I could do it – the pilot could save himself along with all the passengers but I did not give the information." You see to what extent emotional emptiness will go and what it will bring to humanity!

Another crisis is the problem of disruption of the family system, alienation of husband and wife to each other, and early marriages followed by divorces. Each of them could be discussed in detail.

Issue of Hunger

As I have said, some of these [problems] are not spiritual

but are rooted in spirituality. In other words, their root is spiritual crisis. One of them is the issue of hunger. You might have read the book *Hungry Man* (*The Geopolitics of Hunger*) by Josué de Castro.[1] In the newspapers, strange statistical data are sometimes written. What is so obvious is that today there are five hundred million hungry people in the world. Moreover, it is said that in some regions this number of hungry people exists; there is no available statistical data for developed regions. It is said, for example, that this number of hungry people exists in Africa, Latin America and parts of Asia, while there are also many hungry people in the developed regions.

Now, there are five hundred million hungry people in the world while it is estimated that if approximately one-fourth, nay [only] one-fifth of the amount spent for armaments is spent for what they call 'Green Revolution,' agricultural development in the world, all these five hundred million will be save [from hunger]. It has been said that in the past three or four years, the amount spent for armaments has reached two hundred four billion dollar, and now fifty million dollar is enough to save the world from the scourge of hunger. Conferences are regularly being held, but according to the report given by the newspapers, in the said conferences, political rivalries are still prevalent. The *Iṭṭilā'āt* newspaper thus wrote, "In

1. Josué de Castro, born Josué Apolônio de Castro (1908 – 1973): a Brazilian physician, expert on nutrition, geographer, writer, public administrator, and activist against world hunger. [Trans.]

seven days that we were there, the important news transmitted by the news agencies - and the most truthful of news in this seven-day conference held in Rome - was that in this whole week the reception to the representatives of various countries who came to think about the hungry in the world was the best of receptions; that is, to the heart's content.

Annually in America, approximately two million dollar is spent for the foods of dogs and cats, and the leftovers are just thrown away, but the hungry people in the world just die one after the other.

Problems on Environmental Pollution

Yet another issue is that of the environmental pollution. Now, we also experience this problem in our big cities, especially Tehran. In other words, the greatest element of human life which is the air is now so polluted and becomes more polluted day by day, and the human being is about to be deprived of the greatest essential in life. And this has become a major problem in the world. What is its root? Is it really what they have said that it is the power of machine and there is no alternative? Are all these machines (in general sense) and all these machine products produced in the world based upon the need of humanity? Not at all. They are not compatible with the needs of humanity. It is only greed and avidity which have brought them in this form. How about consumption? Today, they employ thousands of tricks in the world in order to produce artificial consumptions. All means of mass communications in the world are used at the service of big capitalists in order to create false appetite for consumption; that is, the machines continuously produce products but since humanity is not in need of such amount, they want through various means (music, sexual attractions, films, television shows, and others) to offer the produced products to the people who would be prompted, on one hand, to earn income through whatever means and, on the other hand, to spend it quickly so as for the machine wheels to continue to turn.

Toynbee's Allegory

Perhaps it was one year ago when I read an article in the *Iṭṭilā'āt* newspaper which I liked very much. It was a translation of an article by Toynbee,[1] the great historian and sociologist in the contemporary world. The said article was written in the form of satire. In the Bible, by which he meant the Old Testament, it is written that when our God the Father created Adam He placed him in paradise and all favours were given at his disposal, saying to him thus: "Make use of all these favours. Only one tree was forbidden [for you]. Do not go near this tree and if you do so, all these favours shall be taken away." But our

1. Arnold Joseph Toynbee C.H. (1889 – 1975): a British historian, philosopher of history, research professor of International History, a leading specialist on international affairs, and author of numerous books. [Trans.]

God the Father made Adam commit the wellknown sin as he went near the tree and ate something from that tree. As a result, he was told, "Paradise is no longer your place. You must get out from here." Our God the Father brought Adam here on earth from paradise. Initially, it was so difficult for Adam and his children to live on earth, because here on earth they were obliged to sweat and toil for their daily living. Human beings, however, were able to adapt to the life on earth and they practically made this earth the same paradise for them. They made use of the seas; they utilized the air; they benefited from the jungles and plants; they took advantage of the animals, etc. Gradually, this earth turned into paradise for the children of Adam.

The second mistake was also committed in the second paradise for which the human being is condemned for expulsion from earth. What is the second mistake?[1] The second mistake was the machine. Three or four centuries ago when machine was invented for the first time and they were thinking that they have rendered the greatest service to humanity, did our forebears and predecessors know that they invented a device which will cause human beings to be expelled from earth in the sense that they will no longer be able to live on earth and be condemned to extinction? Day by day the machine improves while the human being gets weaker and weaker; it is like the

1. It is Toynbee who is asking this. Of course, I myself do not accept the way he expresses it. I will mention my reason.

case of silkworm and its cocoon. In his own cocoon, the human being is forced to build and build it until such time that he gets suffocated within. Unfortunately, when our God the Father expelled Adam from paradise, there was the earth in which he lived, but if the human being were to be expelled from this second paradise, he will be condemned to absolute extinction.

Then this historian sociologist had explained the machine's antipathy with nature – what it has done to the atmosphere; what it has done to the jungle; to what extent it has polluted the seas and rivers; how many thousand kinds of fishes it has relegated to extinction; how many birds have been made extinct; how it has made the human being hostile to nature.

Tale of the Magician and the *Jinn*

He mentioned another parable which is included in our old fiction stories. A magician was able to capture a *jinn* and put him in a bottle which he sealed off. Whenever he was bringing this *jinn* of the bottle, he would use him (to perform very amazing acts). Once it was finished, he would bring again the *jinn* back into the bottle. The magician had a student who wished to be like his master and be able also to utilize the *jinn*. He strived hard to learn, without his master knowing it, the secret behind bringing the *jinn* out of the bottle and utilizing him. One day, in the absence of his master, he brought the *jinn* out of the bottle and utilized him. Now he wanted to bring the *jinn* back into the bottle but he forgot the secret behind doing it. He failed to do so no matter how hard he tried. He became a victim of his own making. Since he could no longer utilize the *jinn*, the *jinn* utilized him on the contrary. It was thus written that it is the parable of the machine. The human being has invented the machine but it becomes out of his control.

But we do not accept it as it is and we maintain that the problem is something else.

Scientism as the Primacy of Science

Contrary to the opinion of Toynbee, the human error was not made by the industrialist or the one who invented the steam engine. The human error was made by Francis Bacon and then his innovation was made when he said, "Science is everything for the human being (scientism or the primacy of science); we must look to science for the solution to all problems." By the way, how many enemies do the human being has? It is ignorance; it is physical ailment; it is poverty; it is apprehension and anxiety; it is injustice; it is greed, etc. The mother of all human miseries is ignorance and lack of knowledge. Give knowledge, learning and awareness to humanity and you eliminate the mother of maladies. As ignorance is removed, all of these will also be removed. Such a trend once came into being for the human beings. Knowledge is indeed a sacred truth. But knowledge was separated from its twin which is faith. It is said that all things which were done by faith in the past could be done by knowledge in the future.

What a beautiful expression it is when the Noble Messenger said,

> الْحِكمَةُ ضالَّةُ الْمُؤْمِنِ يطْلُبُها اينَما وَجَدَها فَهُوَ احَقُّ بِها.
>
> "Wisdom (that is, science, knowledge or truth) is a lost property of the believer. He takes it wherever he finds it and regards himself as more deserving of it."[1]

In other words, the position of knowledge is that of a house in which faith also exists. If knowledge is in a house in which its twin (faith) does not exist, then it is not its own house. This expression is an amazing one: "He takes it wherever he finds it and regards himself as more deserving of it." [Imām 'Alī (A.S.) also says:]

> خُذِ الْحِكمَةَ وَ لَوْ مِنْ اهْلِ النِّفاقِ.
>
> "Get wisdom even if it were from a hypocrite."[2]
>
> خُذِ الْحِكمَةَ وَ لَوْ مِنْ مُشْرِک.
>
> "Get wisdom even if it were from a polytheist."

اي برادر بر تو حكمت جاريه است
آن ز ابدال است وبر تو عاريه است

1. Abu'l-Qāsim Pāyandih, *Nahj al-Faṣāḥah*, *ḥadīth* 2195, 618, with this expression:

الحِكمَةُ ضالَّةُ المُؤمِنِ فَحيثُ وَجَدَها فَهُوَ احَقُّ بِها.

"Wisdom is a lost property of the believer. So he takes it wherever he finds it as he is more deserving of it."

2. Imām 'Alī, *Nahj al-Balāghah*, 1122, *ḥadīth* 77.

O brother! Wisdom is current in you;
It is of recompense and borrowed from you.[1]

Knowledge belongs to you. Why does it belong to you? Well, the other person has acquired knowledge. It is thus said: "But knowledge is not situated in its own house; knowledge must be situated in the house of faith and live with its partner (faith) and nothing else.

All miracles are expected to come from knowledge. One enemy of human being is weakness. Knowledge makes him strong. They are also correct in saying that knowledge empowers the human being. Knowledge is power; he who is knowledgeable is powerful. But power against what or whom? It is against nature. Acquire knowledge so that you could uproot sickness. It is a valid remark. Acquire knowledge so that you can fight against poverty. One half of it is correct while the other half is not. In other words, through knowledge the economy can be improved, but poverty is not always caused by economic shortcoming. Acquire knowledge so that you will prevail over apprehensions and anxieties. This is totally wrong. Knowledge fails to fight against human apprehension and anxiety. Acquire knowledge so as to uproot oppression. On the contrary, knowledge became an instrument in the hands of oppression. Acquire knowledge so as to combat greed and avarice; that is, against your [base] self. As nothing is being acquired,

1. Mawlānā Jalāl al-Dīn Rūmī,*Mathnawī-ye Ma'nawī*, 86, line 6.

knowledge became an instrument in the hands of greed and avarice, and its consequences we can observe today.

Ideology

For one or two centuries humanity was engrossed with this [thinking] until the nineteenth century when it was said that knowledge alone is not enough; social philosophy and ideology are also essential. Knowledge alone cannot do anything. An anti-knowledge movement in the sense of insufficiency of knowledge without an ideology came into being. They came to craft an ideology of humanity and different isms. Ideology, however, requires a worldview and anthropology. He must state his view regarding man and the universe so that later on, he could arrive at the ideal sacred conclusions in his social school of thought. He came and negated God in [his] 'worldview'. He denied the soul in the human being. He presented the human being as an economic tool. Thereafter, he wanted to formulate a sacred social idea. It failed. Such a thing is not possible: The person is told that there is no such thing as 'God' in the universe. There is also nothing sacred within him, but you are obliged and required to work for sacred social ideas; you must be commited not to satisfy your greed and avarice. Do not oppress and be concerned with others. It is obvious that these two [stances] are contrary to each other. The basic philosophical teachings of the anthropological worldview are contrary to this social idea. Georges Politzer[1] thus writes in his book,[2] "Although we are Marxists in terms of philosophy, we are idealists in terms of ethics." Is it possible for a person to be Marxist in terms of philosophy and idealist in terms of morality?! Mere claim cannot one such.

For sometime, they entertained themselves with this exercise. But is such a thing possible?! All these efforts are meant to escape from faith. Initially they said, "No to faith; yes to knowledge. But knowledge alone did nothing." Then they said, "No to faith; yes to social philosophy, method and ideology. But on the basis of these worldviews, however, we can see that ideology alone has failed but it has no humane aspect. The victories are the same political victories and the same compromises. Agaim, the disputes are all about the coverlet of Mullā Naṣr al-Dīn. Look at the Eastern Bloc; look at the Western Bloc; look at the latter's imperialism; look at the former's socialism. At the end of day, it returns to the point at the beginning in the past.

Intellectualism

Others came and presented another hypothesis, saying: "Well, it is accepted that nothing can be done with mere

1. Georges Politzer (1903 – 1942): a French philosopher and Marxist theoretician of Hungarian origin, affectionately referred to by some as the 'red-headed philosopher' (*philosophe roux*). [Trans.]
2. Most probably it alludes to his main work *Elementary Principles of Philosophy* (*Principes Élémentaires de Philosophie*). [Trans.]

knowledge and learning, but nothing can also be done with mere social philosophy. They put forth a special kind of intellectualist self-awareness [and in other words,] the issue of intellectualism. They came and made a distinction between the learned and the intellectual. Sartre and others came and put forth the issue of the intellectuals, saying that "Nothing can be done from knowledge and the knowledgeable as well as from culture. You must bring the intellectual to the front." Who is the intellectual? "The intellectual is he who has a particular kind of awareness which draws him toward human goals." Awareness is nothing other than being well-informed. Awareness means awareness. Can awareness and information mould a human being? Our very own Sanā'ī[1] has made the best of remarks, thus:

چو دزدي با چراغ آيد گزيده‌تر برد كالا

> "As the thief came with a lamp, he was able to take away the best of items."

Awareness cannot do anything to a person except making clear the surrounding for him; it does not do anything else. Awareness does not set goal to a person, just as knowledge cannot set goal to him. Knowledge helps a person in achieving him goals but it does not set

---

1. Ḥakīm Abū'l-Majd Majdūd ibn Ādam Sanā'ī Ghaznavī was a Persian poet who lived in Ghazni between the 11th century and the 12th century in what is now Afghanistan, and whose masterpiece *Ḥadīqat al-Ḥaqīqah* (The Walled Garden of the Truth) is the first known Persian mystical epic of Sufism. [Trans.]

the goal itself - to follow this path or that path. Knowledge helps a person in reaching [his] goals. Knowledge thus says, "I shall give the means; for example, I wil give you an automobile. If, in the past it took two whole days to travel to Qum or Qazvīn, now within two hours you can go there. Yet, does knowledge say, "Go to Qum, for example, through this automobile to help the poor, or go there to steal?!" Machine says, "Do whatever you want to do as I am at your disposal. I cannot mould you or set the goal for you. I shall help you wherever you want to go.

Jalāl Āl Aḥmad[1] has a very elegant statement in his book *Gharbzadegī* (*Occidentosis*): "I was translating a piece about a play. I was thinking about its goal for sometime. Finally I reached the point where it says that such-and-such happened. Then everyone could quickly go to wherever he wanted to go. I understood that the role of knowledge is to say, 'The role of knowledge is only to let a person quickly reach the point he wanted to reach,' and it is true."

Nothing can be done by mere awareness. The Qur'an says that the most aware of the wary is Satan, and he was so aware at that. He was even God-wary. The Qur'an does

1. Jalāl Āl Aḥmād (1923-69): a prominent Iranian writer, thinker and social and political critic who popularized the notion of *Gharbzādigī* (xenomania or occidentosis) in his book with that title. See its English translation, R. Campbell (trans.) and Hamid Algar (ed. and anno.), *Occidentosis: A Plague from the West* (Berkeley: Al-Mizan Press, 1984). [Trans.]

not also regard God-wariness as sufficient, and it does not believe in awareness per se except that it clarifies another value. It thus says, "Satan used to know God. He was aware of God. He used to believe in the prophethood of the prophets. He believed in and affirmed the existence of the Resurrection (as it quotes Satan's confessions to all these), and yet he was an unbeliever. Why? [It is because] he was not faithful (*mu'min*). Faith (*īmān*) is something which is based upon awareness but [it is along with] inclination. Faith means submission (*taslīm*); that is, God-wariness signifies inclination and submission in the presence of God.

The only cure to the malady of humanity today is God-wariness that signifies inclination, submission and humility in the presence of God. And it has only one cure. Of course, the Qur'an always maintains knowledge and faith alongside each other. Today's humanity has knowledge; the cure to its malady is faith. One cannot expect anything from intellectualistic and non-intellectualistic awareness. Awareness, after all, is awareness.

They have said all these as a means to escape from faith. They wanted not to mention faith; rather, they wanted to be able to solve the problem through awareness and knowledge. Philosophical awareness did also reach nowhere. Intellectualistic awareness did also reach nowhere. Lately, they have crafted a new devise. Some say that humanistic culture [is essential]. This is while one must be culture-leaning. Is culture humanistic?! For a person, culture is culture. In the end, culture is knowledge for a person. If you [affirm the faith in God] from the strands of culture that they have recommended such as Sa'dī's parable of admonitions, nothing will be left from it.

Mysticism Minus Religion!

Lately, they have paid attention to mysticism (*'irfān*) on account that they regard it as [an example of] 'humanistic' culture. They do not know that the foundation of mysticism is God-wariness and submission to God. They want to separate mysticism from God and still to call it 'mysticism'. Very interesting! In today's writings of Iranians, I can observe that they have inclined toward mysticism – mysticism minus God and religion! This is very interesting! This is not possible. Imām al-Bāqir (A.S.) said:

غَرِّبوا وَ شَرِّقوا...

That is, "Go to the Western world; go to the Eastern world."[1] In the end, you have to come there to kneel down in order to know the truth.

The fact is that the future of mankind has no option but submission to faith; that is, God-wariness coupled with submission and humility. Today's unsolvable crises and problems of humanity are all spiritual and moral crises. What is their root? [It is] lack of faith. In the past,

---

1. Muḥammad Bāqir Majlisī, *Biḥār al-Anwār*, vol. 46, section (*bāb*) 19, 335 with this expression:

شَرِّقا وَ غَرِّبا فَلا تَجِدانِ عِلماً صَحيحاً اِلّا شَيئاً خَرَجَ مِنْ عِنْدِنا.

mankind had experienced many crises whose root was ignorance, unawareness and lack of knowledge, but today, thanks to Allah, this wing of mankind has extensively grown. One of its wings which is the wing of knowledge has grown very well but its other wing which is the wing of faith has remained the same (and any bird cannot fly with only one wing). In the same manner, in some aspects faith grew but in the domain of ignorance and fanaticism, it will not bring anything for humanity except misfortune. The Qur'an counts on both of them: the wings of knowledge and faith, and it is through these two wings that the problems of humanity will be supposedly solved.

Sometimes the Qur'an talks about knowledge and faith separately:

﴿ وَقَالَ الَّذِينَ أُوتُوا الْعِلْمَ ﴾

> Those who were given knowledge said... (28:80)

﴿ وَقَالَ الَّذِينَ أُوتُوا الْعِلْمَ وَالإِيمَانَ ﴾

> Those who were given knowledge and faith said... (30:56)

The extent of clarity that knowledge gives to man is that it makes clear the domain of nature to him; it increases and extends the power of man over nature and sets nature at his disposal. Faith, however, conquers a stronghold which is outside the sphere of knowledge and knowledge is incapable of conquering this stronghold. The said stronghold is what is within a person; it is human 'self' or soul.

In both Sunnī and Shī'ah corpuses of *ḥadīth*, there is a reliable tradition from the Holy Prophet (S), and how appropriate the Prophet says so! He knows the timing when to tell the truth. He wants to bring forth the issue of the struggle against the self (*jihād al-nafs*). He waits for the day when his companions have returned with honour and pride from a battle. He comes in front and congratulates them. He congratulates them in this way:

مَرْحَباً بِقَوْمٍ قَضَوُا الْجِهادَ الْاصْغَرَ وَ بَقِي عَلَيهِمُ الْجِهادُ الْاكبَرُ

> "Blessed are those who have performed the minor *jihād* and have yet to perform the major *jihād*."

They asked, "O Messenger of Allah! What is the major *jihād*?" They were imagining that it is another battle. The Prophet (S) replied: "The *jihād* of the self (struggle against self)."[1] That is, my Islam requires two types of *jihād*: both in the outside front of *jihād* against rebellious and wayward individuals, and *jihād* with the self. Only one of them is not sufficient. Here Mawlawī [Rūmī] has really painted a beautiful panorama in his poems which thus sing:

اي شهان كشتيم ما خصم برون
ماند خصمي زان بتر در اندرون

O kings, we have slain the outward enemy,
There remains within a worse enemy than he.[2]

---

1. Shaykh Muḥammad ibn Ḥasan al-Ḥurr al-'Āmilī ,*Wasā'il al-Shī'ah*, vol. 11, 122.
2. Mawlānā Jalāl al-Dīn Rūmī, *Mathnawī-yeMa'nawī*, Book 1, line 1373. [Trans.]

I am a witness to this poem which says thus:

کشتن این کار عقل و هوش نیست
شیر باطن سخره خرگوش نیست

> To slay this is not the work of reason and intelligence:
> The inward lion is not subdued by the hare.[1]

Do not think that through thinking, reason, philosophy, and knowledge, one can overrun this stronghold of the 'self'; faith can do so; nothing can be done [in this regard] through reason or intelligence.

As such, I have said that the mistake which Mr. Toynbee mentions is not the invention of machine. The mistake is in giving free hand to greed. Giving free hand is rooted in what? Since you have taken away from humanity the only element that keeps it (greed) under lock and key which is faith, this is the reason why we must return to faith, and we have no other option but to return to faith.

***

It is the last night of our session. Let me give two or three remarks about the tragedy. We seek the intermediation (*tawassul*) of the sacred existence of Ṣaddīqat al-Ṭāhirah (Fāṭimah al-Zahrā') (S.A.).

The emotional attachment between 'Alī and Zahrā' is among the historical emotional attachments in the world:

كنّا كزَوْجِ حمامةٍ في ايكةٍمُتنَعّمَين بِصُحْبَةٍ وَ شَبابٍ

That is to say, "We were like a couple of doves that

1. *Ibid.*, line 1374. [Trans.]

cannot be separated from each other. It is fate that made us separated."[1] Sometimes Imām 'Alī (A.S.) would visit her grave at the darkness of the night. He would stand beside it, talking to his beloved Zahrā', extending greetings to her and then he would complain and he would respond to his own complaint through the tongue of Zahrā':

ما لي وَقَفْتُ عَلَي الْقُبورِ مُسَلِّماً قَبْرَ الْحَبيبِ وَ لَمْ يَرُدَّ جَوابي

"I am standing by the grave of my beloved, greeting her, yet she does not respond to me!"

حَبيبُ ما لَک لا تَرُدُّ جَوابَنا

"Beloved! Why do you not respond to me?"

ا نَسيتَ بَعْدي خُلَّةَ الْاَحْبابِ؟

That is to say, "Is it that as you left me you forgot love? Am I no longer in your heart?" Then he himself would respond, thus:

قالَ الْحَبيبُ وَ كيفَ لي بِجَوابِكُمْ وَ ا نَا رَهينُ جَنادِلٍ وَ تُرابٍ

That is, "My beloved answered me thus: 'What kind expectation is that from me? Don't you know that I am locked under the ground?" Zahrā' made his last will thus: "O 'Alī! As you bury me and cover me in my grave, do not immediately leave my grave. Stand for a while. It is that moment that I need you most. 'Alī buried Zahrā' with his own hands. It was with his own hands that he covered his beloved's grave, filling it with soil and levelling the ground. His clothes became full of dust. Soil dusts would fill his

---

1. *Dīwān Mansūb beh Amīr al-Mu'minīn (A.S.)* (*Collection of Poetry Attributed to the Commander of the Faithful*), 15, with this expression: مُتَمَتِّعَين بِصِحَّةٍ

clothes. Now, it was the time for him to stand for a while.

فَلَمّا نَفَضَ يدَهُ مِنْ تُرابِ الْقَبْرِ هاجَ بِهِ الْحُزْنُ.

That is, "As he finished his work, grief and sorrow suddenly engulfed his heart."[1] What should he do? Whom he should speak to? To whom should he tell the pains of his heart? The Prophet's heart is near. There is nothing there better than the Prophet. He turned to the sacred grave of the Prophet and said:

السَّلامُ عَلَيک يا رَسولَ اللَّهِ عَنّي وَعَنِ ابْنَتِک النّازِلَةِ في جِوارِک وَالسَّريعَةِ اللَّحاقِ بِک، قَلَّ يا رَسولَ اللَّهِ عَنْ صَفِيتِک صَبْري.

That is to say, "Peace be upon you, O Messenger of Allah, from me and your daughter! If you ask 'Alī, his patience has become so little. He then continued:

وَ سَتُنَبِّئُک ابْنَتُک بِتَضافُرِ امَّتِک عَلي هَضْمِها

That is to say, "O Messenger of Allah! You daughter will soon tell you how your *ummah* (community) behaved with her after you [left]."[2]

ولا حول ولا قوة الّا باللّه العلي العظيم وصلّي اللّه علي محمّد وآله الطاهرين. بإسمک العظيم الاعظم الأعزّ الاجلّ الاکرم يا اللّه...

"And there is neither power nor might except that of Allah, the Exalted and Mighty, and may Allah's benedictions be upon Muḥammad and his pure progeny. By Your Exalted, Great, Noble, Majestic, and Honourable Name, O Allah..."

"O God! Illuminate our hearts with the light of

---

1. Shaykh 'Abbās Qummī ,*Bayt al-Aḥzān*, 155.
2. Imām 'Alī, *Nahj al-Balāghah*, Sermon 193, 651.

faith. Make us God-wary and real believers. Cleanse our hearts of wicked traits. Embellish your hearts with excellent moral traits. Grant help and victory to the Muslims over their enemies. Acquaint us with the truths of the sacred religion of Islam. Make us be grateful for Islam, the Qur'an, the Prophet, and his progeny. Shower Your grace and mercy to our deceased ones."

وَعَجِّلْ فِي فَرَجِ مَوْلانَا صَاحِبُ الزَّمَانِ.

"And expedite the advent of our chief, the Master of the Time."

Part Two:
Assorted Lectures

Chapter 11: The Criterion for Moral Action

At the outset, I have to state that I had been requested to talk about, for one or two sessions, one of the ethical, social and fundamental discussions of Islam to the seminary gentlemen who are present here. As I came today, I heard that there was a public announcement [regarding the talk]. The truth is that I felt uncomfortable because I am not prepared for something like delivering a [public] speech and I have not prepared [for that]. As I entered here now, however, I observed that all or most of the gentlemen are seminarians like me, and I am glad and fortunate that I can be able to discuss in a seminarian way.

[An issue is raised among the current scholars and] that issue is this: What is the criterion for moral action? In other words, what is the criterion for an action to be called 'moral'? What characteristic an action should possess so as for it to be called a 'moral action'? And naturally, we can understand from here what morality is. In contrast to the moral action, 'natural action' is presented with the argument that a set of human actions are 'natural actions'.

Natural Action and Moral Action

Natural actions are common actions, and a person will not be praised or appreciated for these actions. For example, one eats as he gets hungry; he drinks when he gets thirsty; he sleeps as he feels drowsy; he engages in a sexual activity [as he feels like doing so]. When someone offends him or violates his right, he will defend his right. These are called 'natural actions' or common actions which animals have in common with human beings. There are some other actions, however, which are beyond natural actions. Sometimes, these are called human actions, and they are beyond animal actions; for example, sense of gratitude and thanks-giving. If a person is treated with kindness by someone else at a given time, in an opportune time he will express a sort of gratitude to him. It may be an emotional or practical gratitude; for instance, he will send him a gift without being compelled or required to do so. This is called 'moral action'. In general, services rendered by a person to his fellow human beings without expecting anything in return but only for the sake of doing good to others are called 'moral actions'; an example of which is helping the needy.

The point here is this: What is the criterion for moral action? What is something in the first action because of which it is called 'natural action', and what is it in the second action because of which it is in a higher level and called 'moral action'? There is a question here which is also raised by the Westerners and that is: In the absence of religion, can a moral action be able to exist or not? In other words, if a person has no religion or religious faith, are all his actions natural actions and that none of his actions can be considered 'moral'? Or, is it that it does not matter how a person is being brought up - whether with religion or not - and he can have a 'moral action'? There are actually two views [in this regard]. The first view holds that moral action means an action which is directly sanctioned by religion, while the other view maintains that it is no so; a person can be moulded in such a way that he would acquire traits on account of which he would perform a moral action. Then there is another question here: Is religion essential here for moulding a person in such a way, or not?

Dastayuski's Statement

Some have said that if there is no God (that is, if there is no belief in God and a person thinks that God does not exist) everything is permissible. Dostoyevsky[1] is known to have said, "If there is no God, everything is permission." In other words, the only criterion for a person to have do's and dont's for himself; that this action is good and that action is bad; this action must be done and that action must not be done; and the issue of following his natural faculties of desire and anger is that there must be

1. Fyodor Mikhaylovich Dostoyevsky (1821-81): a Russian writer and essayist, known for his novels *Crime and Punishment* and *The Brothers Karamazov*. [Trans.]

religion. If there is God and religion, all these things become meaningful, and if there is no God and religion, none of them has any meaning at all. This is one theory. For the meantime, we will not deal with this. Now, if religion has any role, we will tackle it. For the meantime, let us enumerate the [pertinent] theories. They have attempted to suggest morality without religion. 'Without religion' does not mean that there must be no religion at all; it rather means that religion must be rationally independent [from religion]. I shall discuss to you the views of those who have wanted to propose rationally independent morality.

What is the Criterion for Moral Action?

Some have said that the criterion for moral action is that others must be the goal. Any action whose goal is the person himself is not 'moral' and any action whose goal is not the person himself, but another person or other persons, is a 'moral' action. Moral action, therefore, refers to any action whose goal is others. Based upon this definition, moral action is defined on the basis of the purpose behind it. You have learned in logic that the definition of a thing is either on the basis of internal factors or external factors. Definition on the basis of external factors means [definition] through genus (*jins*) and differentia (*faṣl*) (matter (*māddah*) and form (*ṣūrat*)) while definition on the basis of internal factors means [definition] through agent-based cause (*'illat-e fā'ilī*) or purpose-based cause (*'illat-e ghā'ī*). On the basis of this definition, morality (*akhlāq*) is defined on the basis of its purpose (*ghāyah*). It is said that moral action is any action whose purpose is for other than the doer himself.

Before criticizing this definition, let me mention another definition which is similar or close to this one.

Some others have defined 'moral action' in a different way. [Accordingly,] moral action is any action which originates from humanitarian feelings. A set of feelings may exist in a person. If the source of an action is a humanitarian feeling, that action is 'moral'. In terms of outcome, this definition is one and the same with the first one, although the former is a purpose-based definition while the latter is an agent-based definition. It is because an action whose purpose is for other [than the doer] is practically impossible without the doer having the feelings of love for others. The main proponent of that theory may possibly hold such a belief, but it is actually impossible. And also, naturally the purpose of an action which originates from feelings of love for others is other than the doer. The difference between these two definitions is that the former is defined on the basis of the purpose while the latter is defined on the basis of the agent (doer), but I observed that they are very close to one another.

Is this definition correct? Can it be said that moral action is an action whose purpose is other [than the doer] or an action which originates from feelings of love for others? It seems that it is not devoid of any problem. [For instance, in view of] the motherly feelings which are not limited to the human beings as they also exist among the animals, can a motherly action be regarded as a moral action? And can it be called 'moral' or it must be deemed 'natural'? Obviously, the purpose of the mother in her motherly selfless acts which also exist among animals is not herself. It is the child, and her action does not also originate from her individual instincts; it originates from feeling of love for others which in this case is her child. Be that as it may, although emotionally speaking a motherly act is so valuable and laudable, it cannot be said that mothers possess excellent morality because inherently, intrinsically and innately any mother has such feelings. In other words, any mother has not acquired (or learned) this state for herself as in the case of individual temper or disposition; she was rather born with such innate characteristic (and for this reason, it cannot also be called 'temper'). It is beyond her control. Just as every person has sexual urge and that attraction to the opposite sex is innate and instinctive in him, desire to protect one's child naturally exists in a mother. This is the reason why they have said – and they are correct – that a motherly action cannot be called a 'moral action'.

As such, what should be said in defining a moral action? Some have attempted to modify the definition with an additional condition. They have said that moral action is any action whose purpose is other [than the doer] or which originates from feelings of love for others, provided that this state is acquired and not natural. They have said so because everybody knows that morality is equivalent with willpower. It is morality when a person is in control of or learns an action, in contrast to a natural action. Moral action is a non-acquired action; that is, it is an action whose root is natural and non-acquired feelings. So, the difference of this theory with the first and second views - which originates from a single theory - is that this theory, like also the other two, holds that moral action is any action whose purpose is other [than the doer] or its origin is feelings of love for others, but one element is added in the definition and that is its being voluntary and acquired.

Be that as it may, this definition, in spite of all these modifications, is not a comprehensive definition because if we particularly mention the definition of natural action and moral action, we will find a third alternative, and that is, a person performs some actions which are neither natural nor originating from feelings of love for others. Shall we consider them part morality or not? You can see that in books on ethics - old and new - fortitude and patience are regards as part virtuous morality. None other than the doer is involved in them. That a person has a formidable spirit of fortitude, iron willpower, and strong determination in facing difficulties is an excellent disposition, yet this has nothing to do with anyone else. So is the case of things which are labelled immoral traits such as jealousy and nemesis. There is no doubt that jelousy is not a natural action; it is an illness of the soul; the purpose is not also love for others. On the contrary, the purpose is to bring harm to others. So, we have no option but to also modify the first definition and to say that moral action includes both good and bad, and then when we say that moral action is any action whose purpose is other than the doer, it means that its purpose is either good for others (good morality) or bad for others (bad morality). Moreover, it cannot be corrected. [Take] injustice [for example]. One commits injustice but his objective is not to harm others; his objective is to gain personal benefit even though for the sake of his benefit, he brings harm to others. So, is this bad? Is it a natural action which is neither good not bad?

Let us deal with other definitions. The initial definitions are popular and widely known and they cannot be attributed to a particular person or school of thought. Perhaps Aristotle, as he regards human being as naturally civil, has considered moral action to have been originating from feelings of love for others.

Kant's View

Another theory on the criterion for moral action maintains that the criterion for moral action is the sense of responsibility or the dictate of conscience, and this is the view of Kant, the renowned German philosopher who among the European scholars occupies the same position of Shaykh al-Anṣārī[1] among the later jurisprudents and *uṣūlīs*[2] most of whom consider themselves to be his students. Kant has a particular about the human being. He has a strong belief on 'moral conscience'. He even believes that God cannot be proved through rational proof but through moral conscience. He himself believes in God through moral conscience. Perhaps there is no philosopher in the world who is like Kant in believing in the primacy of moral conscience, and it is said that this statement of his is engraved in the frontpiece of his grave:

> "Two things fill my mind with ever-increasing wonder and awe, the more often and the more intensely the reflection dwells on them: the starry heavens above me and the moral law within me."

He believes in the conscience inspiration, saying thus: "In his conscience a person feels certain things as a duty

---

1. Shaykh Murtaḍā ibn Muḥammad Amīn al-Anṣārī al-Shūshtarī known as *Murabbī al-'Ulamā'* (Teacher of the Scholars) (1781-1864/1281 A.H.): a preeminent jurisprudent of his age and the author of a number of well-known treatises on jurisprudence and its principles such as *Al-Rasā'il*, *Al-Makāsib* and *Farā'iḍ al-Uṣūl*. [Trans.]
2. In contrast to the *Akhbārīs*, the *Uṣūlīs* are the Muslim jurisprudents that favour the use of *ijtihād*, i.e. juristic derivation of laws applicable to new conditions, the assessment of *ḥadīth* to exclude traditions they believe unreliable, and obedience a *mujtahid* as obligatory when seeking to determine Islamically correct behaviour. [Trans.]

or do's and don'ts. 'Don't oppress' is an intrinsic matter in the conscience of a person. Not to tell a lie and to be honest, to love others, and not to commit treason are a set of orders which is intrinsically there in the human conscience, and the human conscience itself commands a person, saying 'Do this and do that'."

He [further] says, "Any action which a person does on the basis of unconditional obedience[1] and conscience – in the sense that I do it solely because my heart dictates me to do so, my heart order me, my conscience urges me, and there is no other purpose or motive – [is a moral action."] It is in contrast to the first view which holds that the purpose must be other [than the doer]. This view's approach is so-called introspection. That theory is extrospection while this theory is introspection. It maintains that an action is a moral action when it assumes the form of pure obedience to the conscience without taking into consideration any condition or motive such that if a person is asked, "Why do you do this?" he will say, "It is because my conscience urges me to do so." It is for the sake of nothing else other than what the conscience dictates. If you say, "I do this one for the sake of some other purpose," it (this theory) will say, "It is no longer 'moral'." This person (Kant), therefore, regards the performance of intrinsic and conscience duty as the criterion for moral action provided that this performance

1. He particularly uses the description 'unconditional'.

of duty is undertaken unconditionally. He takes morality just in the conscience only. He believes in the conscience and intrinsic inspiration. Of course, what he says is correct to a certain extent. We thus read in the Holy Qur'an:

﴿ وَنَفْسٍ وَمَا سَوَّاهَا * فَأَلْهَمَهَا فُجُورَهَا وَتَقْوَاهَا ﴾

> By the soul and Him who fashioned it, and inspired it with [discernment between] its virtues and vices. (91:7-8)

When the following holy verse was revealed, a man named Wābiṣah came to the Noble Messenger (S).

﴿ وَتَعَاوَنُوا عَلَى الْبِرِّ وَالتَّقْوَى وَلَا تَعَاوَنُوا عَلَى الْإِثْمِ وَالْعُدْوَانِ ﴾

> Cooperate in piety and God-wariness, but do not cooperate in sin and aggression. (5:2)

Before having the opportunity to pose his question, he was asked by the Noble Messenger (S) thus: "Shall I tell you what you want to ask? You came to ask me what *birr* (piety) and *ithm* (sin) is." He said, "Yes, O Messenger of Allah. Incidentally, I have come for that purpose." It is written that the Holy Prophet (S) placed his two rings on the chest of Wābiṣah and said:

يا وابِصَةُ اسْتَفْتِ قَلْبَک، اسْتَفْتِ قَلْبَک

> "O Wābiṣah! Ask it to your heart. Ask it to your heart."

In other words, God has endowed the discernment of piety and God-wariness as well as sin in human nature, and there is no need for a person to ask about intrinsic questions from somebody else; he must rather ask his heart and conscience. He must get the answer from there.

Now, I do not want to elaborate the discussion as there are many issues involved here. This is one view.

Based upon the first three theories, morality pertains to the subject of love but based upon this view, morality pertains to the subject of duty.

We have another theory about the moral criterion [of an action] and that is the famous theory of innate goodness and badness of actions. We know that there have been some people who believed in the innate goodness or badness of actions and this is correct in a particular sense. Of course, its explanation varies. It is said that beauty or goodness are of two types. We have tangible goodness and rational goodness. In the same manner, we have aso imaginary goodness, and tangible goodness is of many types. Goodness means beauty, and beauty has no definition. It is discernible yet indescribable. Tangible goodness may possibly be visual; it may be auditory; it may even be touchable; it may be tasted; it may be smellable. We have also rational goodness. Certain things are beautiful and attractive from the point of view of reason. The quality of beauty can be understood from its attractiveness. That which engenders love and attraction in a person and draws him toward it and urges him to appreciate and be pleased about it is 'beauty'. It is said that some actions are innately beautiful while others are innately ugly and unpleasant. In the same manner, some faces are intrinsically beautiful while others are ugly. To do good to others is inherently beautiful. To be just is inherently beautiful. On the contrary, their opposites such as telling a lie, injustice and all the things considered morally undesirable are inherently ugly. [According to this view,] therefore, the criterion for moralness is the beauty of actions – that is, rational beauty which the intellect independently and directly perceives.

This definition is far more comprehensive those definitions, including that of Kant. But if we regard beauty as the criterion, the issue of rational goodness and badness will be discussed, and of course, it will not be that easy. According to this theory which is more discussed among the Muslims, morality pertains to the subject of beauty and elegance. Based upon the two theories, nay the first three theories, morality pertains to the subject of love; based upon the theory of Kant, it pertains to the subject of duty, and based upon this theory, it pertains to the subject of beauty, though rational beauty; it also pertains to the subject of reason as well as beauty, but rational beauty.

Plato's View

There is another theory here which is close to the view of Plato. It holds that morality pertains to the subject of beauty. It is necessary to explain it to you:

In my book *'Adl-e Ilāhī* (*Divine Justice*), I have mentioned that justice (*'adl*) is defined in three ways. One is equality; the other is "to give what is due to every right owner" (*i'ṭā'u kulli dhī ḥaqqin ḥaqqah*); the third one is balance and equilibrium. If we consider the third definition which is balance and equilibrium, justice shall be equal to beauty because beauty is a kind of equilibrium.[1] Plato believed that there are various potentials and talents in a person, and he is correct [in saying so]. Others have also said so. There are natural talents in a person; there are supernatural talents; there are tangible talents; there are rational talents. It is said that just as a person is good-looking if he is bodily proportionate, he is also spiritually beautiful if his potentials and talents are nurtured in a balanced way (such that each of the faculties is satisfied to a specific extent, nor more or less, and both extremes are avoided).

As you can observe, the issue of going to both extremes is extensively discussed in our books on ethics and then it is said that good morality is the moderate morality. Plato also talks about 'moderate' but his view is more incline to [the issue of] beauty. He says that a person with moderate morality, moderate potentials and proportionate talents, someone whose everything spirituall speaking is to its own extent, nothing more or less, is spiritually beautiful. To be moral means to acquire or possess spiritual beauty. He [also] says that outward and physical organs are beyond our control and they are already perfected in the wombs of our mothers. That which is within our control

1. In the book *Jāmi' al-Sa'ādāt* (*The Collector of Felicities*), the late Narāqī has discussed justice as pertaining to the subject of beauty.

is the spiritual faculty. Physically, man is actually (*bi'l-fi'l*) born in this world. As he comes out from the womb of his mother, he is physically actual; in other words, his body is already complete at birth though it continuously grows. Spiritually, however, it is a bit more behind. That is, for the human soul the world is like the world of the fetus for the human body. Mullā Ṣadrā also remarks that for the soul, this world is like the world of the womb for the fetus. So to speak, the soul is being shaped here. The other difference is that the bodily organ which is formed in the womb is beyond our control; we had no power to make ourselves white or black [complexion], male or female, good-looking or ugly. Neither did we have any duty then. In this world, however, the control is in our hands. The pen and paper of destiny are at our disposal to draw our own spiritual face and organ, lay the foundation of our existence in this world and mould ourselves. (Of course, these [ideas] are not those of Plato; I express these following his remarks. He has only dwelt on the issue of beauty.) As such, it is we who must mould ourselves. How could we mould? How could we mould ourselves spiritually in the best possible manner? We are obliged to mould ourselves in the most beautiful manner possible, and we shall be raised up in the other world the way we moulded ourselves here.

﴿ يَوْمَ يُنْفَخُ فِي الصُّورِ فَتَأْتُونَ أَفْوَاجًا ﴾

> The day the Trumpet will be blown, and you will come in groups. (78:18)

Under this holy verse, we have read in the narrations and traditions (*aḥādīth*) that only one group shall be raised up in the form of humans because the people there [will be raised up] according to their intentions and inward nature; that is, their ourward forms will follow their inward forms and traits. Pious people will be raised up as humans because they remain humans, while other people will be raised up [differently]. One will be raised up as monkey; another as pig; yet another as dog; someone as termite; another as cat; some will be raised up as something without similarity to any animal because they have moulded themselves in such a way.

﴿ وَجَعَلَ مِنْهُمُ الْقِرَدَةَ وَالْخَنَازِيرَ ﴾

> And He turned some of them into apes and swine. (5:64)

Regarding this subject, therefore, which we mentioned while dealing with the view of Plato, there is no doubt that in this world a person mould himself and he is duty-bound to mould himself. In this new philosophy called 'existentialism which emerges in our age, there is an expression which is the same with our expression from the lexical perspective. In terms of meaning, they are two different things but the meaning they mean we also mean elsewhere. These expressions are 'primacy of existence' and 'primacy of essence'. They (existentialists) say, "We advocate the primacy of existence" but what they mean is that a person must design his own essence; man's existence takes precedence over his essence. In other words, every person must build his own nature – "What nature I should have" – and it is correct [to say so] up to this extent.[1]

Plato who believes in morality as pertaining to beauty says that if a person cultivates all the potentials given him by God, the Exalted, proportionately, evenly and moderately without going to extremes such that he cultivates each faculty to a given limit – and this limit can be found in the very nature of the human being – and to the extent necessary, and not more or less than that, then he will become a human being who is beautiful spiritually and inwardly. Why do you become attached to some individuals? What is attachment or devotion? You can see, for example, a 25-year old youth – in the prime of his youth and at the peak of his sexual urges – becomes devoted to an 80- or 90-year old and is pleased looking at

---

1. [A few minutes prior to the next session about the same subject the following points are mentioned:] This philosophy gives the meaning of primacy of existence. Existentialism refers to the school of thought that advocates the primacy of existence. Of course, this 'primacy of existence' in human being mentioned here is different from the 'primacy of existence' (*iṣālat al-wujūd*) which we refer to in our philosophy. This is one thing; that is another thing. That refers to the entire universe while this is exclusive to the human being. Moreover, this is a specific concept about the human being and we do not call it 'primacy of existence'; we call it in another way. This primacy of existence which Sartre says is the exact opposite of the primacy of essence which says that the essence of every existence other than human – inanimate objects, plants and animals – [takes precedence].

his countenance. Everybody had seen the late Āqā Burūjirdī[1] (may Allah be pleased with him). He was really such a man who was pleasing to look at. He was a ninety years old man. What is that attraction called 'devotion' (*irādah*) which draws a 25-year old youth toward a 90-year old man? It is discernment of a kind of beauty in his soul which engenders this attraction. How about the Holy Prophet (S) himself? In him were fused outward and inward beauties, and he possessed the highest degree of spiritual beauty. Ibn Abī'l-Ḥadīd narrates that the Quraysh infidels in Makkah called the Muslims '*Ṣubāt*'. *Ṣubāt* is derived from the root word *ṣabwah* which means 'love' and 'devotion'. It is said that he was in love with this man. They were so attracted and devoted to the Holy Prophet (S) that they were labelled 'lovers'. What was this? There was something in him which was other than physical that attracts [a person].[2] Plato also believes that morality pertains to beauty, but the view which I mentioned prior to this and holds that morality pertains to beauty maintains that the beauty of action refers to the innate goodness or wickedness of actions. He says

---

1. It refers to Āyatullāh al-'Uẓmā Sayyid 'Abd al-Ḥusayn Burūjirdī (1292-1380 A.H./1875-1961), a prominent contemporary Muslim scholar who trained many scholars including Muṭahharī, Bihishtī, Lankarānī, and Muntaẓirī; wrote about 40 books and treatises in jurisprudence (*fiqh*) and its principles (*uṣūl al-fiqh*), *ḥadīth*, philosophy, and logic; and became the sole reference authority (*marji' al-taqlīd*) of the Shī'ah world. [Trans.]
2. [There was about a minute of interruption in the audio tape recording.]

that some actions are innately beautiful while others are ugly. The beautiful person is he who desires everything beautiful. A person is beautiful because he desires beautiful action and a person is ugly because he desires ugly action. This view, however, says that essentially the centre of beauty is the human soul itself. Accordingly, an action is beautiful as it emanates from a beautiful soul and an action is ugly as it emanates from an ugly soul. The centre of beauty, therefore, is the human soul. This is another theory on the criterion for what is moral - that moral action is that action which emanates from a well balanced and moderate soul.

I will also mention another criterion. In a future session[1] I will more or less give my final judgment on them, God willing. In this session we shall only present the theories.

The Muslim Philosophers' View

There is another theory which can be inferred from the statements of Muslim philosophers. They regard the intellect - free intellect or intellectual freedom - as the criterion for morality. You cannot usually find in their books this subject which I mention in this way, and we have inferred it from the statements [of Muslim philosophers], especially those of Ṣadr al-Muta'allihīn. This theory is based upon the same principle of immaterial soul (*rūḥ al-mujarrad*).

1. [The audio tape recording of this session is unfortunately not available.]

These gentlemen believe that the essence of human being is his faculty of intellect; the essence of human being is his intellect, and his ultimate and real perfection and felicity is intellectual felicity. What does it mean by intellectual felicity? It means Divine knowledge (*ma'ārif*). In other words, at the highest level ever possible for him, the human being is supposed to be acquainted with Divine knowledge and discern the world of existence as it is. You can observe that whenever they define 'wisdom' (*ḥikmah*) from the perspective of purpose (*ghāyah*) instead of subject (*mawḍū'*), they say:

صَيرورَةُ الْانْسانِ عالَماً عَقْلِياً مُضاهِياً لِلْعالَمِ الْعَيني.

That is, "The human being could become an intellectual world like the actual world." Of course, an ordinary person cannot grasp its details, and no one can grasp them except the holy personages (*awliyā'*). An ordinary person can grasp according to [the level of] his intellect an overview of the system of the universe as it is from the beginning up to the end; he can grasp the general levels of existence of the universe from the Necessary Existence (*wājib al-wujūd*) up to the Primary Matter (*hayūlā'i ūlā*). The more Divine knowledge about God, His Attributes and Actions – and there is nothing other than these – of a person becomes, the more perfect he is and the more he possesses real bliss and intellectual felicity.

Then they say that the human intellect has two dimensions. One is theoretical dimension which is upward-leaning and wants to discover the truths.

Another is downward-leaning and wants to control the body. Many things up to this level are written in books. Then they ask, "On what basis should this intellect's regulation of the body?" You have heard that the foundation of morality according to the Muslim scholars is justice (*'adālah*)? Have you ever thought why they regard justice as the foundation [of morality]? Its root is as follows. They have said that morality is that [base] nature should not be in control of man's existence. In other words, it should not be desire, anger or any of the natural faculties; neither should imagination or the faculty of imagination [be in control]. What should be in control of man's existence is the intellect, and if the one in control is the intellect, it will do so with justice. That is, it is the same justice which Plato mentions in another way. In this regard, these [philosophers] say that the intellect satisfies each of the faculty or potential without going to extremes. What is wrong if a faculty is given an extra freedom while another faculty is a bit more restricted? If we ask Plato, "What is wrong with that?" he will say, "It will destroy [the existing] beauty." But why do the likes of Mullā Ṣadrā say that there should be no excesses in the faculties and potentials? Do they also say it so that [existing] beauty would not be destroyed? No. [Instead,] they say that if this is done, the intellect's freedom will be eliminated and this is the crux of the matter. If the intellect wants to be in control of all faculties such that none of which could go beyond its limits, the only way is to place all these faculties against each of them; desire vis-a-vis anger; anger vis-a-vis desire, so much so that these faculties would undermine or be on guard of each other. In this way, the intellect can be control with utmost ease. They regard justice and moderation as the intellectual disposition because if a person is moderate in terms of character, what the intellect dictates could easily be implemented. Once the dictate of the intellect could easily be implemented, it will never disturb the soul and once there is no disturbance to the soul, it is only then that person could physically attain perfection and excellence.

According to them, therefore, morality means moderation and striking a balance among the faculties, but what is the purpose of this moderation, by the way? Is it for beauty? No. They are not concerned with beauty. Accordingly, there should be moderation so as for the intellect and soul – and the essence of the soul of the intellect – to have absolute control over the body, instead of having a faculty beyond control. For example, one of the instincts of a gluttonous person is the instinct of eating which goes beyond limit and is out of control of his intellect. These [faculties] must all be controlled so that his intellect could freely give command to the body and [its] faculties and say, for example, "Come here; go there; use it up to this extent; use it up to that extent; do not use up to this extent" [and in sum,] the intellect could have an absolute command over the body. According to them, the foundation of morality is traceable to justice and equilibrium, but equilibrium for what? It is for the freedom of the intellect. And in reality, according to these theosophers (*ḥukamā'*), morality pertains to the subject of justice in one sense, and pertains to the subject of the dominance of the intellect, in another sense, and whenever we say freedom, we mean intellectual freedom.

Russell's View

There is another theory which is pursued by the likes of Bertrand Russell. Since they are materialists, thinking about the universe materially and regarding the human being as materialist being, they say that these claims that the goal of the action is other [than the doer] and feelings [of love] for others are lies and mere lip-service. Everyone has no feelings [of love] for others at all; everyone is only after his own interest. Never could a person does something for others and does it for the sake of somebody else. Kant has said, "[This is] moral conscience." We have no moral conscience at all. [Or he has said,] "Sense of duty." There is no sense of duty. Conscience is indeed a lie. The other one has said, "Beauty of action." We cannot understand beauty or ugliness in action. Yet another one has said, "Beauty of the soul." We cannot grasp 'beautiful or ugly soul'. Another one has said, "Immaterial intellect and immaterial soul." We do not believe at all in immaterial soul. We say, "So, do you believe in morality or not?" He says, "Yes, I also believe in morality (because one cannot deny morality)." We say, "So, on which basis do you explain morality?" And incidentally, he himself is one of the towering figures in ethics and some have been duped by his words, thinking him to be humanitarian, and I have thus said time and again: "The philosophy of this person is contradictory to his slogans. His slogan is humanitarianism yet he makes anti-humanitarian remarks in his philosophy. In Russell's philosophy, humanitarianism is sheer lie. We ask, "What is morality?" He answers, "It is a combination of cleverness and profit-oriented foresightedness. All schools of ethics regard profit-orientedness as against morality except [the school of thought of] Russell who says that morality must be built upon the edifice of profit-orientedness, though a clever and foresighted profit-orientedness, and that a person wants to gain personal profit through foresightedness can be moral. How?

He says that the intellect is at the service of the human nature. The intellect is a light for human being. Light is at the disposal of the one who possesses it. To whatever direction he wants to bring it, it illuminates his way. A person utilizes his intellect to serve his interests. The intellect is meant to serve a person's interests. The scope of human intellect must be very broad; neither should it be so weak that it can only perceive its immediate front. If it wants to perceive just its immediate front, it becomes profit-oriented; it becomes individualistic; it becomes selfish. [Accordingly,] there is no need for us to combat self-centredness and profit-orientedness. We say, "Be profit-oriented but be foresighted at the same time. Be clever. Lengthen the scope of your intellect. Be conscious of the reactions to your action. If the scope of foresightedness is long, the individual interest could be reconciled and synchronized with the collective interests and social welfare, and this could be moral. Let me cite an example. He says, "Let us assume that I observe that my neighbour has a good milch (milk-producing cow). There is no doubt that initially my profit-oriented instinct dictates that I have to steal my neighbour's milch. This is very natural for a person. But I have reason; I have intelligence; I know that this action will not be devoid of a reaction. If I steal my neighbour's cow, tomorrow he will also steal my cow. I who want to serve my interests will realize that if I encroach upon the interests of others, they will also encroach upon my interests; I therefore say that expediency dictates that neither you nor I [should steal another's cow].

Bāyzīd and God

There is a story which 'Aṭṭār[1] has also expressed in poetry. Of course, it is a fiction. It is narrated that one of

1. Farīd al-Dīn Muḥammad ibn Ibrāhīm al-'Aṭṭār al-Nayshābūrī (1145?-1221?): a Sufi Persian poet, whose most celebrated work is *Manṭiq al-Ṭayr* (*The Conference of the Birds*), a poem consisting of 4,600 couplets (two successive lines of verse that rhyme, forming a single unit). [Trans.]

the Sufis whom they call '*sulṭān*' was talking to God when he was once in his realm of mystical unravelling (*'ālam al-mukāshafah*). Accordingly, God told him, "O Bāyzīd! Do you want me to disclose to the people your inward reality (*bāṭin*) so that none of your students will be left and follow you?" Bāyzīd replied, "O God! Do You want me to expose to the people Your extraordinary mercy so that no one will be left obeying Your words?" God said, "Let it be; neither you nor I will ever reveal anything!"

The Story of a Government Employee and his Co-worker

One of our friends thus narrates, "It was the first day of *Ramaḍān*. I was fasting then and I just became acquainted with a co-worker. He was also fasting then. After an hour or two hours of work, he told me, "Friend, I want to tell you something." I said, "Please." He said, "I really ask your apology for telling you this, but I deem it necessary to tell you this. What I am going to tell you is part of my bad attitude. I have such a bad attitude that in the month of *Ramaḍān* when I am fasting, I get angry – I get very angry. And when I get angry, I say whatever I want to say. I do curse; I do insult. In this month of *Ramaḍān*, I may be audacious toward you. If ever that happens, please forgive me; it's fasting [month]; it's my attitude." This friend of ours retorted, "This is amazing! On the first day of the month of *Ramaḍān* this man informed us in advance. Now, we were supposed to hear insulting remarks from him for the whole month of *Ramaḍān* because on the very first say, he told us his attitude. I told him, 'What a timely reminder! Incidentally, my attitude is the same, nay worse than yours. When I get angry while fasting, you may see me picking this inkwell and throw it to your head.' My co-worker said, 'Amazing! What a very bad attitude! So, it is better for us to be careful of each other's feeling.'"

Russell says that such is the issue of morality among people, [and notions such as] love of fellow human beings, others as the goal of action, immaterial soul, immaterial intellect, and sense of duty [are meaningless]. A materialist person will think except that the world is material and the human being is also a material being. Man pursues nothing but his own interests. He must only enhance his cleverness, and in this way, he will see that whenever he wants to violate the rights of others, others will react in kind. He who throws a clod deserves to be hit by a stone. Once I throw a clod, I have to expect a hundred stones to be pelted at me. So, I have to behave courteously toward others.

As such, he regards morality as pertaining to intelligence. The more a person is ignorant, the more he is unaware of the reactions to his action and the more he is [only] concerned with his individual interests. And the more he is aware and intelligent, the more he is conscious of the reactions [to his action]; the wider is his scope of considerations; his considerations extends to his old age; he takes into account his next generation; in order for his children not to suffer, he tries his best to reconcile his interests with those of others. Morality, therefore, signifies rational and clever selfishness, and the root of morality must be traced from cleverness and intelligence. Accordingly, according to this person, in order for us to bring good morality into the society, we must always make the society more conscious and aware and make the people more acquainted with the consequences and repercussions of their actions and works. In this way, better morality can be found among the people. Socrates also held such a view, and in the words of Imām 'Alī (A.S.) we can also see this expressed in a different way:

عَلِّموهُمْ وَ كفي

"Teach them (people) and it is sufficient."

Socrates used to say, "Make the people knowledgeable and good morality will emerge." Of course, he was saying this on a particular foundation, just as the saying "Teach them and it is sufficient" is based upon another foundation. The knowledge he refers to means awareness of the reactions. [That is to say,] "Let the people understand the repercussions of an action, and everything will be fine."

According to the theory of Russell, further training pertains to the subject of teaching and upbringing pertains to the subject of education.

Criticism of this View

We have said that Russell's theory is against humanitarianism and contrary to his claims. This theory has uprooted the foundation of morality. According to his theory, morality can only be 'morality' when a person is concerned with the negative reaction of others toward his interests. In other words, according to this theory, a weak yet intelligent person does not do anything contrary to morality because if he does so, others will trample upon his interests multiple times. A person who sees himself as strong as others will not do anything contrary to morality because others are as capable as he in advancing their interests against his.

Then, let us tell Russell: Morality, in its highest level, is that which controls the strong. According to this theory, the injustice of the strong is not immoral (and this is the main fault of Russell) and what Nixon does in Vietnam or the Middle East is not immoral, because he has taken many things into consideration; he knows that he is so powerful and he could plunder whatever he wants; the force that could undermine his interests simply does not exist. Once morality is equated with intelligent profit-orientedness, this intelligent profit-orientedness is meant for the weak and one whose power is in a sense equal with those of others, but it is something else for the strong and powerful. If the powerful is certain that the weak canno react to his action, whatever he does is 'moral' and not immoral, because it is an intelligent and well-calculated profit-orientedness. Therefore, once Israel shots down a Libyan airplane, if it is absolutely sure of its force and that of America [which supports it] and that the other party is weak and cannot retaliate in kind, for Russell it (Israel) does not do anything immoral. As such, O Russell! For what purposes is this sense of humanitarianism of yours as expressed in the streets against the Vietnam War and others? It (America) is powerful and it pursues this policy as dictated by its power, astuteness and understanding that no one could dare to react decisively. You yourself have permitted yourself to do so.

وصلّي اللّه علي محمّد وآله الطاهرين.

"And may Allah's benedictions be upon Muḥammad and his pure progeny."

Chapter 12: Communist Morality and Russell's School of Morality

I shall to [theories about] morality which are put forth more in our time. One of them is the so-called communist or Marxist morality. This school of thought has its own moral system, and every school of thought must formulate a set of criteria for morality that responds to such questions as to what purpose that it believes in human value, what kind of action it regards as 'moral' and what kind of action it regards as 'immoral' or 'anti-moral'? In this school of thought there is a criterion for morality and that is society's evolution – an evolution which is explained on the basis of the evolution of the means of production. The Marxist school has a logic which is the same famous logic of Hegel, the dialectic logic; it has a philosophy and worldview which is a materialist worldview, materialism which was particularly prevalent and widespread in the eighteenth century, and one of the so-called leftist students and advocates of Hegel named Feuerbach[1] revived it. In [his] materialist philosophy, Marx[2] in reality is a follower of Feuerbach, but Feuerbach's logic has not been dialectic logic. Marx has synthesized that dialectic logic with materialist philosophy, and out of that evolutionary or polemical materialism (as they call it) or dialectical materialism.

In the same manner, this school of thought has a distinct theory regarding [the nature of history which is based upon] the primacy of the economy. It holds that the original nature of history is constituted by economy and it is called 'historical materialism'. Apparently, this term has been originally coined by Engels.[3] Historical materialism means that history has materialist nature, and its other part is sociological. Like also in the philosophy of history component, in the sociological

---

1. Ludwig Andreas von Feuerbach (1804-1872): a German philosopher and anthropologist whose thought was influential in the development of Marxist dialectic. [Trans.]
2. Karl Heinrich Marx (1818-83): a German philosopher, political economist, historian, political theorist, sociologist, and communist revolutionary, whose ideas played a significant role in the development of modern communism and socialism. [Trans.]
3. Born into a wealthy family in Bremen, Germany, Friedrich Engels (1820-1895) met Karl Marx with whom he was in agreement on the materialist theory of history, in France in 1844, and thereby the two became close friends and collaborated on a number of works, the best-known of which is *The Communist Manifesto* (1848). [Trans.]

component society is classified as infrastructure and superstructure, and [accordingly,] the infrastructure of society consists of the economic and production relations, while the superstructure pertains to all other things. Of course, other components of the Marxist school of thought are related to economic issues. That is, it has really economic nature – the very area of expertise of Karl Marx. In other words, he was an economist and he was an authority and theoretician in economics. Although this theory was already held by other economists before, perhaps he was the one who developed it further. It is about the question of work and value, maintaining that value only comes into being from work and that capital to production makes no value. Surplus value (any profit that the capitalist earns), therefore, does not belong to him but rather to the worker. This is a distinct theory on work and capital.

As a matter of course, the other issue is the question of communist morality – how does this school of thought promote something 'moral' and [at the same time] condemn something 'moral'? It can be said that in this school of thought – although this term might not have been used by himself, one can make such a conclusion – the only criterion for morality is evolution. In other words, every action which brings the society forward, leads the society to development – which is not possible except through a revolution – or catapults it to perfection, is 'moral'. Whatever it wants, in whatever form or manner, and every action which hinders the society's advancement is 'immoral'; no matter what it wants. Of course, if we say this in its general form, it is something which perhaps no one wants to oppose. That is, every school of morality in spite of declaring a criterion other than evolution, its contention is that the evolution of society depends on moralit; the same morality which I mention. Although they have not mentioned evolution as the criterion, no one denies that the morality he promotes is anti-development; he rather claims that the said morality is a prerequisite and precondition of development. We must, therefore, see what this theory which says that evolution or development is the criterion specifically wants to say and in reality, we must see what its view about development is and in which way development could be achieved. And this is very important.

Dialectic Logic

In this school of thought, the logic in general is the dialectic logic and dialectic logic regards these principles as governing all phenomena: the the principle of contradiction is not the way others refer to but rather in its specific sense. In other words, it is the principle that every thing has its opposition or negation within itself, and it is for this reason that there is an internal conflict within; it is dynamic; it is in a state of motion; it is not static. So, its second principle is the principle of motion.

This very motion is also a product of contradiction – a contradiction which originates from within and not a contradiction of an external thing with the phenomenon. Motion leads to a series of gradual changes; rather, motion means gradual change. But every gradual change ends up to a sudden change in the sense that every change initially takes a quantitative form; that is, there is an increase in the number and volume. For a certain time, this numerical and quantitative increase continues; gradually it reaches a level which [ends up in qualitative change]. In other words, gradual change ends up in sudden change, or expressed differently, quantitative change always ends up in qualitative change.

Hegel has cited a well-known example. If we heat water, it will gradually become warm. From zero degree it becomes one degree, five degrees, fifty degrees, ninety degrees; it thus gradually changes. As it reaches 100 degrees, however, it will undergo a sudden change and that is, the water will turn into steam. In other words, the quantitative change will turn into qualitative change; that is, from 100 degrees up, its nature will essentially change; that is, from formerly a fluid matter, now it becomes gaseous; its nature changes. As the effect of this change in nature, naturally the laws which used to govern it – for example, the laws pertaining to fluidity for its being fluid – are no longer applicable. Another set of laws, for instance, laws pertaining to gases, shall govern it. That quantative change ends up in qualitative change is the result of this contradiction, because we have said that it is the product of motion and motion, in turn, is the effect of contradiction. As the degree of heat does up, and in other words, as quantitative change increases, it means that internal contradiction also intensifies. That quantitative change turns into qualitative change means that this contradiction or conflict reaches its optimum point, and at the ultimate point, the antithesis which originates from the thesis itself (as we say that every thesis has its own antithesis) prevails and as it prevails its being antithesis comes to an end. This revolutionary state which comes into being, has actually brought about a third state. The first state, in reality, is the state of production; it is the same initial moment when a thing comes into being. The second state is the state of growth of a thing; it is the sate of a thing's encounter with its antithesis. And the third state is the state of qualitative change; it is the state in which the thesis and antithesis assumes a third form which is the perfect form.

The course of nature, therefore, always follows the same process. Something comes into being while its antithesis is embedded within itself. The conflict between thesis and antithesis comes into being. This conflict leads to motion, and in the end, these two are combined in a higher level, which the same qualitative change. When there is combination, the subsequent state is the more perfect form of the earlier state [and in other words,] is the developed state.

Evolution of Society

The same thing also happens in society. In whatever stage it is, society has antithesis within, and this will lead to conflict and motion, and in the end, it will result in the society's qualitative change; that is, it will end up to a revolution in society and transformation of the society's social system into another one, which is inevitably more perfect compared to the previous social system. This in turn will generate its own antithesis within; conflict will arise again and in the end, there will be a qualitative revolution and then a society with a higher level will come into being. The root of all these, in reality, is the means of production and relationships of production. Society comes into being under a certain condition with specific means of production.[1] Subsequently, a kind of conflict within this society, which in reality is the conflict between the infrastructure and superstructure, will gradually emerge, and this conflict will eventually end up in a revolution. We must always take into consideration that society is persistently divided into two classes: the class which is dependent on the previous condition and the class which is dependent on the new means of production. The class which is dependent on the previous condition wants to preserve the previous infrastructure which is suitable to the previous means of production,

1. Means of production refer to the tools with which man bring into existence his means of living.

and the other class is that which is dependent on the new means of production and which wants to build the new infrastructure for the society.

Now, every action which is to the benefit of the class dependent on the previous society is 'immoral,' no matter what form it is expressed and what name is given to it. If you say that in this city where there are people who are needy, poor, unprotected, hungry, occasionally die of hunger, and sick, there is nothing better and much moral than that I fill the stomachs of some hungry poor and indigent people, provide clothing to the naked, and cure the sick, it will be said, "No, this is not enough; you have to see the outcome of this action of yours. Will this action of yours expedite the revolution in society (in which development means revolution and revolution means development), or will it delay the occurrence of revolution? If this action of yours expedites the revolution, then it is 'moral' and it delays the revolution, it is 'immoral'. On the contrary, if you think there is no action worse and more immoral than a given action, you will be told that it is such. For example, let us assume that they are oppressive and unjust people and I can do something to stand in the way of their acts of oppression. It will be said that this is not enough to say that your action is good. We have to see what effect it will bring to society in the end. There are many instances when actions which you consider to be moral and good actually delay the occurrence of a revolution, and a delayed revolution means a delayed development. For example, if your efforts in feeding the hungry, covering the naked, and curing the sick are expected to bring peace of mind to the deprived people and tone down their anger toward the ruling class, then these are bad actions. Let there be further instability and undersirable conditions so that the deprived be more stimulated and get angry. As you want to stand in the way of the oppressor, its result is for the oppressed to keep quiet. Let him commit acts of oppression so that this oppressed would oppose him more. Let there be more disparity between them; let there be more distance between them so that revolution would soon occur, and the society will not experience development except through a revolution. So, this is the crux of the matter. Now, we have reached the main point.

The Meaning of Evolution According to Marxism

We have said that if we say that this school of thought regards evolution as the criterion for morality, there is no objection – and it is correct, as such – for there is no school of morality which at least believes that the criterion is anti-development. Every school [of morality] believes that its criteria for morality are those of development. So, what is the peculiar thing in this school [of morality] for having such a claim? Of course, this question is relevant, and thus, we have to explain it in detail. This school views evolution or development in a peculiar way. Accordingly, development has no meaning except revolution which originates from internal contradictions within society. Other schools [of morality] believe in gradual reforms and gradual development. One school believes that if I render an iota of service to the society, the same amount of step is taken toward development. If I do an iota of moral act, the same amount of step is taken in favour of development. There is a time, for example, when we want a tree to bear fruits and a time when we want a pot to explode; these are two different actions. If we want a tree to bear fruits or a baby to be born, elaborate acts of care and supervision are required. The more we take care of a tree – to be protected from [extreme] heat, pestilence and aphids, to be always irrigaged on time, to be always provided with sunlight, to be provided with fertilizer whenever needed, and to be always cultivated whenever needed (in short, a set of gradual acts of care is given) – it will bear fruits the sooner and better. In the same manner, the more a fetus inside the womb is taken cared of, the healtheier and safer will it be born. There is a time, however, when we want a pot to explode. If we want a pot to explode, we must fill it with some amount of water; we have to close each of its openings. Then we have to heat until it boils and as it continues to boils, this will lead to the explosion of the pot. If we make an outlet – even a small one – of the pot, this will prevent its explosion.

It is so different, therefore, when we want to bring about qualitative and essential transformation – as they call it – on a thing and with respect to society we must have such a view and say that it has a nature which never passes and will never pass from one stage to another peacefully. Caesarean operation must always be done; one must pass a stage in a violent, revolutionary and explosive manner and proceed to another stage; inevitably, it is like that. Development – all forms of development – lies on this.[1] In essence, the evolution of society shall not happen except through its explosion, and explosion, in turn, shall not happen except through conflict and contradiction reaching its optimum point, and if conflict and contradiction wants to reach its optimum point, two types of action must be undertaken: one is no less than resistance and the other consists of other actions that will lead to resistance; that is, fomenting unrests, propaganda campaign, and even undertaking operations. The wrath of the people must be intensified so that explosion would occur in the future.

Revolution as Criterion of Morality

In reality, therefore, it must be said that in this school [of morality], the criterion is revolution and not development or evolution. And if ever we say 'development,' it is because in this school, development shall not take place except through a revolution, and it does not believe in any

1. As to what they regard as the infrastructure, for the moment it makes no difference on the issue of morality, whether we consider it infrastructure or superstructure.

development other than this. It is here that all moral criteria shall be changed. Which one is 'moral' – honesty or dishonesty? It says, "If dishonesty will hasten the revolution, then [it is] dishonesty, and if honesty will hasten the revolution, then [it is] honesty." [Which one is 'moral' –] trustworthiness or treachery? It says, "It is that which will hasten the revolution." [Which one is 'moral' –] self-sacrifice or self-preservation? [It says,] "It is that which will hasten the revolution." [Which one is 'moral' –] peace or war? [It says,] "It is that which will hasten the revolution." Naturally, this school [of morality] is a school whose value is one-dimensional. One of the distinctive features of this school is that it has a single value, and in this school, there is no issue about conflict of values which is an important question in ethics and which has been raised even before and discussed even now, and it is even a hot issue in a theory newer than communism, i.e. existentialism.

Concerning the conflict of values, one example is being cited. Let us assume that a youngster lost his father in childhood and he, a lone child, is with his mother who is in difficult conditions. She became widow at a young age and she never married again. She deprived herself of comfort and worked as a maidservant, for example. She strived very hard to bring up this child. Now, this child grew up and this mother enjoys looking at the fruit of her, say, twenty years of labour and efforts and for the first time in her life that she is thinking of taking a breath. That is, this mother has sacrificed her entire life and all her hopes and aspirations for the sake of this child, focusing on this single goal, and this child is the sole goal of this mother. On the other hand, let us assume that the country of this child is facing an existential crisis as it is under foreign invasion, and this so-called motherland is asking for help, asking for volunteers to fight against the enemy, and if the patriotic youth do not fight with the enemy, it will invade [their land].

Here this youngster is caught between the demands of two mothers and he is in a state of intrusion (*tazāḥum*) as the *Uṣūlīs* call it – intrusion of values. The motherland says, "Go to the battlefront." The real and actual mother says, "Do not go." This mother pleads to him not to go, thus: "You are everything to me." The other [mother] says, "Go forth." This in itself is a kind of moral conflict; it is an inner debate. That is, there are two conflicting and intruding dictates of the conscience here, and this question is raised: which mother he would give affirmative response?

In the schools of thought which put morality under emotion, for example, individuals experience this state of intrusion and conflict of values. Here there are actually two conflicting emotions, viz. love of mother and love of the country, feelings toward the mother and feelings towards the country, or expressed in another way, the rights of his mother toward him and the rights of his country toward him. Now, which rights take precedence, the former or the latter?

Since this school [of morality], however, has a single value and gives no value to anything except one and that is social revolution, [the question of the conflict of values is not raised.] It says, "Which one could be of help to the revolution, the revolution in the way we describe it (class-based revolution): your going [to the battlefront] or your not going [there]? Choose the one that could be of help to the revolution. And it is not possible that both your participation [in the battlefront] and non-participation are of help to the revolution. It is a one-value school [of morality], and therefore, no other moral criterion can prevail there. For example, it is possible that someone might have been a lifetime revolutionary comrade, rendering service to communism. Then a time comes that his superior or at least, one who is more influential than him suddenly supposes or concludes that his steps were taken for the sake of the revolution but recently he holds an idea which hinders or stands in the way [of the revolution]. They will just easily execute him; that is, they will eliminate him. There is no more difference between this person and that person who had fought for this ideology for fifty years. [According to this school of thought,] human being does not have more than one value and his value is determined by the revolution, and if this one value is relinquished, it is not immoral to eliminate one million people who do not subscribe to this value or who have lost it. In fact, it is not even immoral to eliminate two-third of the people on earth, for there is no other criterion other than this.

This is also a school of morality which is mentioned with particular label at the beginning and which says that the criterion is development. This is a very interesting criterion and it seems as though other schools believe in a kind of anti-development morality. But if we take into account its specific implication, it says that the criterion is the revolution, and this stems from a specific sociological viewpoint and historical philosophical perspective which its advocates hold, for they believe that history has not advanced except through revolution, and in the future it will not advance also except through revolution. Development, therefore, lies in revolution and anything other than this is anti-development and must therefore be anti-moral.

Primacy of the Individual and Primacy of the Society

The communist morality must be discussed in two ways: one is the general approach which involves the discussion on the primacy of the individual and the primacy of the society. Basically, one may possibly do not accept development as the sole criterion [for a moral action]. We have development of the individual and development of the society. Sometimes, there is conflict between these two types of development. That is, conflict between the rights of individual and the advancement of society happens. We may possibly do not believe in any right for the individual and we may not believe in the primacy of the individual, giving preference only to the society and saying that the individual is not part of the equation. In fact, according to some [thinkers] such as Durkheim,[1] the individual is essentially a nominal matter; that which is real is the society. Everything belongs to the society and the individual has nothing of his own. Though incomparable, it is like the logic of the Qur'an concerning God that the individual has no right of his own in relation to God:

﴿ إِنَّ الأَمْرَ كُلَّهُ لِلَّهِ ﴾

> Indeed the matter belongs totally to Allah. (3:154)

Even the individual is for Allah and belongs to Him, and if ever he possesses anything, it is such that he who belongs to God has possession as possession of God; that is, in relation to one another, the individuals have rights and possessions, but they have nothing in relation to God.

I remember a story. Abū Firās[2] was a proficient Arab Shī'ah poet. Apparently, he lived during the fourth century A.H. and approximately a contemporary of Fārābī. He belongs to the Hamdanids who were lovers of lilterature and strong patrons of poets and men of letters.

---

1. David Émile Durkheim (1858-1917): a French sociologist who formally established the academic discipline and, with Karl Marx and Max Weber, is commonly cited as the principal architect of modern social science. [Trans.]

2. Al-Ḥārith ibn Abi'l-'Alā' Sa'īd ibn Hamdān al-Taghlibī (932–968 CE), better known by his *nom de plume* of Abū Firās al-Hamdānī: an Arab poet and member of the the noble family of the Hamdanids, who were rulers in northern Syria andUpper Mesopotamia during the 10th century. [Trans.]

Although their kingdom was not that vast, it was so significant in terms of quality, and for this reason, after finishing his studies in Baghdad and other places, Fārābī went to Mosul [which was then ruled by the Hamdanids] and considered them better than the caliphs in Baghdad. He passed away there and Sayf al-Dawlah al-Ḥamdānī[1] led the burial prayer for him. At any rate, the Hamdanids were among the patrons of poetry and learning among the rulers, and in most cases, figures such as poets and the like were many in their royal court.

One day, Sayf al-Dawlah al-Ḥamdānī was sitting with poets and men of letters. He said, "I have composed a couplet and I think no one could complete it except Abū Firās." The couplet he composed is as follows:

لَک جِسْمي تَعُلُّهُ فَدَمي لا تُطِلُّهُ

That is, addressing his Beloved (Lord), he says, "This body of mine belongs to you and You always let me suffer; so why don't You spill my blood all at once?!" Abū Firās immediately responded as if quoting the Beloved's reply, thus:

قالَ ان کُنْتُ مالِکاً فَلِي الْامْرُ کُلُّهُ.

That is, "He said, 'Am I not the King? You yourself say,

---

1. 'Alī ibn Abū'l-Hayja 'Abd Allāh ibn Ḥamdān ibn al-Ḥārith Sayf al-Dawlah al-Taghlibī, more commonly known simply by his honorific epithet (*laqab*) of Sayf al-Dawlah (*Sword of the Dynasty*): the founder of the Emirate of Aleppo, encompassing most of northern Syria and parts of western Jazira, and the brother of al-Ḥasan ibn 'Abd Allāh ibn Ḥamdān (better known as Nāṣir al-Dawlah). [Trans.]

'This body of mine belongs to You.' If I am the Owner, then the discretion is mine.'" The clause *Faliya'l-amru kulluh* alludes to this Qur'anic verse:

﴿ إِنَّ الأَمْرَ كُلَّهُ لِلَّهِ ﴾

> Indeed the matter belongs totally to Allah. (3:154)

This is a very elegant line:

قالَ انْ كنْتُ مالِكاً فَلِي الْامْرُ كلُّهُ.

Nowadays, there is such argument regarding society. There is a set of sociological theories which basically does not believe in the individual's primary, discreation, freedom, and right vis-à-vis the society. Within the context of society, individuals have rights and responsibilities toward each other, but this is meaningless in relation to the society.

Freedom and Equality

According to this school of thought, therefore, the criterion is the advancement of society. Anything that stands in the way of its advancement must be eliminated. Other schools of thought, however, do not subscribe to this notion. Some regard as absolute the primacy of the individual while others believe in the primacy of the individual although not in absolute sense. As such, concerning the issue of freedom and equality, this enigma always lingers: Freedom and equality are two human values which are in conflict with each other. That is, if the individuals are free, equality [among them] will cease to exist, and if equality is supposed to be implemented, then there is no option but to limit freedom. It is because individual human beings are not like products of a company which have no difference with each other after being manufactured. Instead, one may have more skills while another has fewer skills; one may be physically strong while another is physically weak; one may be full of initiative while another has no initiative at all; one may be lazy while another is hardworking. If we want to open equal opportunities for all in society, then naturally some will become winners while others will be losers, due to their laziness or inability, as the case may be. Whether we like it or not, freedom will bring about inequality. If we want to implement equality, however, then we have not option but to give certain things which belong to A and give the same to B.

This is like the case of horse racing field. When the horses want to run together, there are two conditions. There is a time when we want the horses to run like the military horses. We group them together; they must be lined together; their speed must also be the same; and naturally, each group must control its own horses. In this case, all the horses move in synchrony. As a hundred military horses move together - if, for example, they move in groups of ten with an interval distance of 10 meters - even after an hour of running, none of these horses could overtake the rest in each group. Here, however, the freedom of horses shall be restricted; many of them might become unruly as they want to run faster but the rider will not allow because they are supposed to run together in synchrony. Yet, there is also a time when the issue is that of freedom and competition like in horse races. There, naturally, one may lag behind while another is ahead. If we want, therefore, to give freedom to the horses, then there will be no equality and synchrony, and if we want to generate equality and synchrony, then there is no option but to get rid of [their] freedom. Freedom belongs to the individual and equality to the society. In the Western Bloc the emphasis is given on the individual freedom, and naturally, equality is trampled upon and uprooted. In the Eastern Bloc, the stress is on equality and [in the process,] freedom is undermined. There is no equality in the former while there is no freedom in the latter, and these emanate from two distinct philosophies. Of course, the important question is this: Is it really a case of either/or – either the development of individual or that of society? Is it either the success of individual or that of society? Or, there is a natural way and that freedom – that natural human right – has a specific limit which if it exceeds, is no longer to be considered freedom, and that development is also dependent on this extent of freedom; that is, a third school of thought. Now, this is a separate discussion.

Criticism of this Theory

At any rate, my point here is that if someone would say that the criterion is development, it is questionable because in this case, we have given all preferences to the society and we deny the individual any sort of primacy and we cannot be single value-oriented. The development of society is one of the values. Individual development is another value in itself. As such, sometimes there is conflict between these two values, viz. social value and individual value. Firstly, therefore, from this perspective, the communist school of morality is questionable or debatable. That is, this principle cannot just be easily accepted that the criterion is the development of society, that one [must be] single value-oriented, and that the individual has no [real] value. Secondly, granted that we regard the development of society as the criterion, whether the sole criterion or one of the criteria, we cannot accept that development solely depends on a revolution or qualitative changes, as they call it; that is, except through a revolution, the society cannot advance forward. In fact, it cannot be said that the revolution is definitely the path to perfection. Oftentimes, revolutions occur without necessarily giving any form of perfection to the society. In any case, this issue is expressed in the form of a general philosophical principle that nature always undergoes perfection through the shift from quantitative changes to qualitative changes, which mean the revolutionary path, and this is applicable neither to the nature of non-human [animal] nor to that of human being. If we plant a graft of a tree on the ground, when do these qualitative changes take?! As it moves, you must therefore believe that in the first stage it takes the form of a thesis and then an anti-thesis will be developed within as it continues to move. Moreover, it cannot also be accepted that it moves due to its opposition to itself (anti-thesis). Now, granted that we do accept up to this point. We, for example, plant a pears seedling on the ground. This seedling will gradually undergo its process of growth until it becomes a young pears tree. It will bear fruits for many years then it will become old. It will not undergo any qualitative change until it dies. Thus, as this seedling moves, according to you, it has passed the stage of thesis and anti-thesis; that is, the stage of rule and its opposition. But the stage of fusion or synthesis which we did not see must happen. If you say that this tree in its entirety is the stage of thesis and its antithesis is the moment when it dies and its synthesis is when another tree comes into being, then we ask, "What was then the motion during that stage? It was in motion for twenty years. You say that there will be no motion until there is no antithesis from within."

Neither non-living nature, therefore, nor living nature has such a law. How can the periods of life of a person to be born be reconciled with these three stages?! There is no such a thing.

The second objection, therefore, is that this hypothesis is based upon the assumption that the sole path to development in both nature and society is revolution. And since this theory cannot be confirmed in this way, it follows that this [system of] morality cannot also be confirmed.

As such, there are two objections [to this school of morality]. The first objection is that we do not accept that the development of society is not the sole criterion, because this matter is based upon the principle of the primacy of society and the nominal nature of the individual, and this [notion] is neither scientific nor real. Even if we regard development as the criterion, therefore, we are not single value-oriented; individual criteria also exist. Secondly, granted that we regard development as the sole criterion, we do not accept that development is always through a revolution. Very limited and exceptional cases cannot be the proof that the entire nature is such, especially by considering the fact that actual observations run contrary to this hypothesis.

Russell's School of Morality

Another [system of] morality is that which Bertrand Russells proposes, and he has mentioned this theory in numerous books. One of those books is the book *The World that I Know* in which he has allocated a chapter on the discussion of morality. Another is the book *Marriage and Morals*. Although his discussion is limited to sexual ethics, his general theory becomes clear. In my opinion, it is also mentioned in his book *Scientific Worldview*. There are two other books which I cannot recall at the moment.

Russell's morality is so-called rational morality in the

sense of acuity. In reality, because of this materialist thinking of his, he does not believe in any criterion of morality. He does not believe in Plato's notion of goodness and virtue. Neither does he subscribe to Aristotle's notion of moderation nor to Kant's notion of conscience morality or sense of responsibility. He says, "Man is a being who has been created to be inherently profit-oriented. Other than the pursuit of his own profit, everything else is empty rhetoric. Do not believe that man is looking for something else other than his own profit. On the other hand, in society we need a set of good relationships which we have called 'morality'. We say, 'Let us observe the rights of each other. Let us respect each other. Let us perform our social responsibilities.' Performance of our duties and responsibilities, observance of the rights of others, respecting others and whatever man needs in his social life as 'morality' are such." Then he says, "Morality is that we must do something so that these principles become dominant in society; individuals must all believe in these principles that the rights of others must be observed; they must perform their duties; they must respect each other, and the like." You want to anchor them on a non-materialist foundation. Why should we observe the rights of others? It is because this is what virtue calls for, or because duty and responsibility dictate so. He says, "No. These notions have no basis or foundation. The fact is that one's interests also lie in doing so. We must let human being understand, thus: 'You must pursue you own interests and happiness, and your interests lie in this. You are mistaken in thinking that if you trample upon the right of another person, you gain something, or if you do not perform your duty, you benefit something, or if you do not respect others, you earn something.' These are all mistakes. Man's intellect or intelligence must be enhanced and he must be endowed with foresightedness. A person who thinks that his interests are served by trampling upon the rights of others, this is because of his nearsightedness; he can see what is near in his front but cannot see what is far, without paying attention at all to the reactions. Man must be informed of all the reactions and repercussions."

Let me cite this example. Imagine that some people live together in a room. Due to laziness or any other reason, each one may possibly not give importance to the condition of this room, yet at the same time, expecting it to be always clean and orderly. But it can easily be realized by everybody that the interest of each of them can be served by performing their duty toward this room. Man can easily realize this fact. Once I understand that my individual interest lies in this, you will also understand that your individual interest lies in the same. Others will also understand that their individual interests lie in the same. Naturally, all of them will do the same because human being is profit-oriented.

He cites an example, saying thus: "Initially, I may

possibly think that if I will steal the neighbour's cow, I will gain something, but when they let me realize that if I steal my neighbour's cow, that neighbour of mine will steal my cow and another neighbour of mine will steal my donkey, for example, and instead of gaining something, I will lose multiple times. Obviously, I will not steal my neighbour's cow so that he would not retaliate in kind, and this is very natural. We must, therefore, only let man enhance his intelligence and inculcate in his mind that what is called 'morality' refers to the things which encompass others' gain.

This is another school of morality which, in reality, denies moral values. That is, the criterion, once again, is profits. Yet, it is always said that morality is that which is in conflict with one's interests, and the action of the one who gives preference to moral value over [personal] interest is 'moral' but this school [of morality] says, "Why do you believe in contradiction between [personal] interest and moral action and then say that man is intrinsically in pursuit of his interest but on which basis one can do a moral action? And then you want to state a criterion or standard for it, and you say something for each of them. This is not so. Moral action is that which guarantees [personal] interests in the long run while immoral action is that action in which a person only considers what is in the short run."

We shall cite another example. A child who wants to go to school only thinks in a short run. For this reason, he is only concerned with today and he is unhappy for going to school: "I have to remain there for four hours. I will be deprived of these plays and entertainments that I enjoy." He sees himself between enjoyment and inconvenience – today's enjoyment and tomorrow's inconvenience. He is not intelligent enough to see the repercussion of his action: "If I do not study today, where this non-studying will lead to and where this studying will lead to?" He does not understand but his parents do understand. They desire what is good for the child. The child also desires for what is good for himself, but he looks at his interest in a smaller extent while his parents look at the same in a wider scale. As such, the parents' profit-orientedness ends up on enduring such deprivation and suffering which is the suffering in studies, but as the child is short-sighted, he does not want to do so.

[According to this school of morality,] all moral actions are as follows: I must tell the truth; my [personal] interest lies in telling the truth. If I tell a lie, others will tell a lie to me. I must be trustworthy; if I do not want to be trustworthy, others will also be not trustworthy and this is surely harmful for me; thus, my [personal] interest lies in becoming trustworthy.

In reality, Russell's contention is a negation of morality as a value, because he has implemented morality in the context of profit. Thus, the first objection to Mr. Russell is that the kind of morality he proposes is devoid of sublime value and sacredness and it is nothing above profit; in fact, it is profit itself. And this is contrary to the slogans that Russells himself gives. One of those whose slogans are contrary to their own philosophy is Russell. He had presented himself to the world as a man of humanitarianism and lover of fellow human beings, and yet his philosophy is essentially against it; his philosophy is that of profit-orientedness. So, all of Russell's values for peace are traceable to himself: "Why am I who live in London against the war in Vietnam? It is because my [personal] interest lies in doing so." What you are doing, therefore, is devoid of any value.

Secondly, this proposed morality is beneficial only when the powers involved are equal, such as the case of the two neighbours: "I will not steal my neighbour's cow because my neighbour will [also] steal my cow. When two equal forces face each other or a weaker force faces a stronger force, these considerations will be observed well. But when one party is overwhelmingly stronger and the other is weak and this stronger party knows that the weak party cannot advance its interest even for the next one hundred years, morality will not demand it to do so. As such, if, for example, Brezhnev faces Carter, morality dictates Carter must be 'moral' because he has an equally strong rival like Brezhnev. In the same manner, Brezhnev must be 'moral' too because he has an equally strong rival like Carter. But when these two are dealing with much weaker nations, morality never dictates that [they must be 'moral'] because they know that weak nations could not gain enough power within the next one hundred years [and stand in their way]; in fact, these [two] will not allow them to gain power in the first place, and thus, they are sure of that. In this case, what can be expected from this system of morality based upon profit, such as Russell's?! In essence, morality is meant to stand in the way of the powerful with utmost power and strength:

أَوْلَى النَّاسِ بِالْعَفْوِ أَقْدَرُهُمْ عَلَى الْعُقُوبَةِ.

> "The most capable of pardoning is he who is the most powerful to punish."[1]

On the other hand, the second foundation of morality which is based upon profit is the equality of powers; that is, it is only applicable when there is equality of powers. When I face a rival who is at least having strength or force equal to mine, I will never threat to kill him because he may also threat to kill me. If I could most probably kill him, he could also most probably be able to kill me; so, naturally, I will never attempt to do so. Or, it is also like the story of the employee, along with his officemate, who says in the end: "So, it is better for both of us to be careful with each other." That will be the case when two persons are equal in strength or power. But if they were not equal, then morality will not be applied. This [system of] morality, therefore, is not morality at all; it is a negation of morality.

In reality, the meaning of Russell's philosophy is as follows: Relinquish morality because morality is identical with the value of acquiring power, and there is nothing

---

1. Imām 'Alī, *Nahj al-Balāghah*, Saying 49.

above personal interests and animality. Morality means sense of humanity, and humanity means value above animality and action above personal interests. Russell's argument implies that morality has no foundation, but the conclusion from morality which you can arrive at you can also get from teaching by letting the people understand that the interests of everybody could be served in such a way. And you have seen that this argument can be faulted by saying, "Yes, such can be said to the people who are equal in strength and power, but this morality is not applicable to anyone who has an overwhelming power. As a matter of fact, he shall be persuaded to go against morality because, after all, the criterion is personal gains. The former will be compelled to be 'moral' while the latter has no need to be such.

Chapter 13: Question of the Self in Ethics

﴿أَلَمْ تَرَ كَيْفَ ضَرَبَ اللَّهُ مَثَلًا كَلِمَةً طَيِّبَةً كَشَجَرَةٍ طَيِّبَةٍ أَصْلُهَا ثَابِتٌ وَفَرْعُهَا فِي السَّمَاءِ * تُؤْتِي أُكُلَهَا كُلَّ حِينٍ بِإِذْنِ رَبِّهَا وَيَضْرِبُ اللَّهُ الأَمْثَالَ لِلنَّاسِ لَعَلَّهُمْ يَتَذَكَّرُونَ * وَمَثَلُ كَلِمَةٍ خَبِيثَةٍ كَشَجَرَةٍ خَبِيثَةٍ اجْتُثَّتْ مِنْ فَوْقِ الأَرْضِ مَا لَهَا مِنْ قَرَارٍ * يُثَبِّتُ اللَّهُ الَّذِينَ آمَنُوا بِالْقَوْلِ الثَّابِتِ فِي الْحَيَاةِ الدُّنْيَا وَفِي الآخِرَةِ﴾

> Have you not regarded how Allah has drawn a parable? A good word is like a good tree: its roots are steady and its branches are in the sky. It gives its fruit every season by the leave of its Lord. Allah draws these parables for mankind so that they may take admonition. And the parable of a bad word is that of a bad tree: uprooted from the ground, it has no stability. Allah fortifies those who have faith with an immutable word in the life of this world and in the Hereafter. (14:24-27)

At the outset, let me greet you all on this occasion of the noble birth of the greatest martyr in the way of truth and justice, Imām al-Ḥusayn ibn ʻAlī (A.S.). Last year, in such a night and place we briefly talked about the topic "The Main Pivot in Islamic Ethics" as appropriate to the time and place. Meanwhile, in terms of the occasion, I chose the topic because the issue of self-respect is a prominent chapter in illustrious life of Ḥusayn ibn 'Alī (A.S.), and in terms of the venue, it is because this is a sacred place; it is a centre of teaching and learning, and it is most appropriate to have an educational and moral discussion. It also seemed to me tonight that I have to discuss another topic which is appropriate to both the occasion and venue, related to training, education and ethics, and at the same time, an exposition and elucidation of one of the chapters in the life of Ḥusayn ibn 'Alī (A.S.). And perhaps it would be appropriate to have given the title "Moral Discipline" to this topic but I shall deal with another topic which is an introduction to that topic, and that is "The Question of the Self in Ethics" which is an important chapter and in fact the first chapter in [the books of] ethics. What does it mean by the question of the self? Firstly, as you know, not to mention some methods and systems of morality which do not give much importance to training and social-educational practices, nay even oppose them and advocate human being's return to 'primitive nature' – and for the meantime these are not our concern and their theories are also deemed rejected – other schools of morality, after all, regards as necessary and essential a sort of morality, a particular approach in ethics, and a specific system of training. One will say, however, that so-and-so educational approach and moral system is good while another person will suggest another approach or system.

Why the Human Being Is in Need of Moral and Educational System?

Now, in human life, why morality, training, developing habits (which are known as 'second nature'), and nourishing second nature and superficial characters in the human soul which are called 'disposition' (*khulq*) are necessary and how did they become necessary? This in itself is a separate story; it is a chapter and it is related to the human constitution, and that is, it seems that human being has been created defective in terms of the instincts. Why he is created defective. By the way, there is nothing defective in the creation. This means that in terms of the instincts and natural traitsm every animal is equipped according to its life status in nature. God, the Blessed and Exalted, however, has created human being in such a way that although his potential in terms of evolution and advancement is more than that of any other animal, in terms of the instincts and primary natural traits which are necessary and essential for him, he is so weak and defective:

﴿ وَخُلِقَ الإِنْسَانُ ضَعِيفًا ﴾

For man was created weak. (4:28)

And this potential is indeed embedded in human nature for man to choose and prefer for himself the training method and disposition that is necessary, and teachers and trainors have to come and complete or perfect this defect which seems to be present in nature. This in itself is a separate story.

This is the point of this statement of the Noble Messenger (S):

بُعِثْتُ لِاُتَمِّمَ مَكارِمَ الْاَخْلاقِ

"I have been sent to perfect excellent moral traits."

That is to say, "I am supposed to perfect the acquired traits which human being needs for his felicity and grant them to him." Muslim scholars have a [related] terminology in the principles of jurisprudence (*uṣūl al-fiqh*). They say that we have some rules which state that a law and its supplement (*mutammim*) must be forged separately. In the nature of that law it is not possible for that law to be forged at once along with its supplement; it requires subsequent forging (*mutammim al-ja'l*). This is a philosophical key and it is impossible other than this. Man's humanity has no other way other than that initially he has been created with such a defect, then educational and moral tools shall come to the forth in order to remove this defect or weakness and he will attain the highest point of his power of thinking and willpower. [Human being, therefore,] is in need of a moral system.

Two Types of Morality

We know that those who propose morality are of two types. The foundation of philosophy of one group is based upon selfishness and egoism; self-aggrandizement;

survival of the fittest; and promotion of the self. They do not believe in more than one pillar or foundation, and that is the efforts for self-preservation. The foundation of their morality is 'selfishness'. An example of it is the morality which Nietzche proposes, and even the communist morality is also like that. Its foundation cannot be other than interests – personal interests as such. In other words, the philosophical foundation of communism does not give the possibility of developing its own [system of] morality and bring a degree higher than that of the foundation of selfishness. Moreover, other moral and educational systems which exist in the world, the terms they have coined and the values they have promoted – [moral values] such as justice, honesty, truthful, trustworthiness, and the like – all these morals are a sort of campaign against selfishness. When a person is told, "Be truthful and do not tell a lie," it means that whenever personal interest could be served, for the sake of personal gain, do not relinquish honesty. Honesty is a kind of trampling upon the 'self'. It is the same when a person is told, "Do not be hypocritical;" "Do not steal;" "Be just;" "Be fair-minded;" "Be impartial." All of these virtues, which are called 'moral virtues,' are a sort of campaign against selfishness. In other words, unless a person is in this station wherein he sets aside himself and so long as there is no kind of self-sacrifice and altruism, it is impossible for him to be able to abide by the moral virtues. As such, in ethics the issue of the self is of prime importance.

The Root of aDherence to Moral Virtues

Well, what is the foundation or root of this point? What should be done so that a person abide by the moral virtues vis-a-vis personal interests and would have faith or belief that he should set aside his personal interests for the sake of honesty, truthfulness and justice? What is supposed to be the foundation of morality – a kind of morality that must campaign against selfishness and at the same time, be logical, has basis and not hollow? This statement is attributed to Alexis Carrel:[1] "In the world, how much interest is hidden behind the curtail of such words as chastity, piety, truth, and justice!" In other words, these are hollow words; they are veils covering 'selfishness' and as there is no truth in it, its inside is empty; it is like walnuts or almonds which have peels but no seed inside. Now, what must be done? Of course, there are two options. One option is for those who do not have clear mind in the sense that their power of discernment is weak. So many baseless concepts could be imparted to a

---

1. Alexis Carrel (1873-1944): a French surgeon and biologist awarded the Nobel Prize in Physiology or Medicine in 1912 for pioneering vascular suturing techniques, who, in his *Man, The Unknown* (1935), claimed the existence of a "hereditary biological aristocracy," arguing that 'deviant' human types should be suppressed using techniques similar to those later employed by the Nazis. [Trans.]

person by means of inculcation and speech. Sometimes, superficial feelings are created in him. Due to these superficial feelings, occasionally self-sacrifice or altruism may possibly be performed, but this has no basis or foundation. In the jargon of the logicians, with only the slightest analogical predication (*tashkīk al-mushakkak*) it will crumble. For example, a soldier is so much trained in the barracks; that is, he is under the influence of inculcation and indoctrination such that he is really attached to a particular water and soil. But if someone comes and talks to him, putting into question his notions, all these will crumble because all of them are mere inculcation without having any basis or foundation. And even if no one comes to put these into question, as his level of understanding improves, he reads more, becomes more knowledgeable, becomes more intelligent, and becomes capable of analyzing an issue, he will come to realize that all those things inculcated in him – "For the sake of such-and-such goal, offer your life; sacrifice your own happiness; set aside your enjoyment; give everything you have" – [have no basis at all.] As he reads four books, it will become clear in his mind, and he will ask, "Why? For what purpose? Is it other than that I should desire everything for myself? Well, why should I sacrifice myself? For what purpose?" As he becomes ready to pose these whys, you will see that this inculcative training will be totally shuttered.

The reason why the more the world become more

informed, the more it becomes faithless and its abidance with moral principles becomes weaker is that in most cases, the moral principles which are taught to humanity are devoid of any logic, support, credibility, and basis, and they are founded on a set of inculcations. A person is inculcated in the family; he emulates his parents; the same is true in the school. As he goes to school and thinks about moral principles, although he always support these moral principles, saying that social justice is so-and-so; honesty is so-and-so; trustworthiness is so-and-so; freedom is so-and-so, as he reflects he knows that these words have no basis. He says, "On which basis or criterion that because of four words, I would come and set aside my personal interests? For what reason that I would set them aside?" Once he ponders, these would come to his mind. This is the very reason why the community of the learned does not subscribe to moral concepts. Morality that the people had in the past, apart of that of a few pious which I will mention later, their morality is based upon something strong which the Qur'an describes, thus:

> ﴿ أَلَمْ تَرَ كَيْفَ ضَرَبَ اللَّهُ مَثَلًا كَلِمَةً طَيِّبَةً كَشَجَرَةٍ طَيِّبَةٍ أَصْلُهَا ثَابِتٌ وَفَرْعُهَا فِي السَّمَاءِ* تُؤْتِي أُكُلَهَا كُلَّ حِينٍ بِإِذْنِ رَبِّهَا وَيَضْرِبُ اللَّهُ الأَمْثَالَ لِلنَّاسِ لَعَلَّهُمْ يَتَذَكَّرُونَ ﴾
>
> Have you not regarded how Allah has drawn a parable? A good word is like a good tree: its roots are steady and its branches are in the sky. It gives its fruit every season by the leave of its Lord. Allah draws these parables for

> mankind so that they may take admonition. (14:24-25)

And in a succeeding verse, it is thus said:

﴿يُثَبِّتُ اللَّهُ الَّذِينَ آمَنُوا بِالْقَوْلِ الثَّابِتِ فِي الْحَيَاةِ الدُّنْيَا وَفِي الآخِرَةِ﴾

> Allah fortifies those who have faith with an immutable word in the life of this world and in the Hereafter. (14:27)

This is one of the bases, foundations or roots of their morality, and no power had been able to take this morality away from them. Yes, apart from them, most of the people [used to learn] moral concepts through imitation, inculcation, hypnotism, and the like. They used to be so captivated by whatever was inculcated in them. But the intelligent one is less likely to believe in such words, and this a serious threat to morality. Now, what should be done? If mankind totally relinquishes morality, naturally this is exactly the very extinction of humanity. No matter how we tell a person, "Sir, for the sake of the community, do this and do not do that," for him this is unacceptable and he will say, "In this ocean, what is the effect of something true I am going to tell? But a lie that I would tell, I will do so for the sake of myself. Once he thinks, he will realize that there is no logic behind; it has no support; it is devoid of any basis or foundation.

Knowledge of God as the Foundation of Morality

Some say that morality has a basis. It is thus said:

اوَّلُ الدّينِ مَعْرِفَتُهُ.

> "The foremost in religion is the knowledge of Him (God)."

In the same manner, knowledge of God is main pillar of humanity, and sense of humanity and morality without the knowledge of God has no meaning. That is, no spiritual matter without having a set of spiritual assumptions as its bases has any meaning. It is mere empty rhetoric for someone to come forward [and promote morality] for the sake of humanity. I have not seen any logic sillier than that of Bertrand Russell. This man is materialist in thinking and yet he persistently says, "Come and do such-and-such for the sake of humanity." Once the basis is outside the framework of human spirit, how could one talk about humanity? How is it related to me? The other person in my front is just like a tree or sheep [in the logic of Russell]. This [morality] has no basis or foundation and it can never have one. Regarding the logic of religion, I will tell later how it has a foundation and how experience and experiment have proved its accuracy, and how strong moral disciplines have created and will also create iron willpower.

A mistake is committed along this way and that is to say, in the jargon of the seminarians, thus: "The occurrence of a thing is the proof of the possibility of its existence." How could you claim that there is no discipline and morality in a society which is devoid of the knowledge about God and religion? Today, we can observe how disciplined and reasonable the enlightened society of today is. They are civil people who do not go beyond their rights. Now, there are nations in the world that never tell a lie although they are not concerned with spiritual matters. We have gone and seen. We have seen the European and American nations. Those who are not religious also refrain from telling a lie, hypocrisy, deception, stealing, and treachery. It is obvious, then, that morality could be formed and 'selfishness' be uprooted with leaning toward faith and knowledge of God. You have heard a lot this argument. I have also heard it a lot and perhaps for sometime I used to believe that such a thing is possible, but now let me cite you an example.

Types of the 'Self' and 'Self-worship'

1. Personal 'Self'

When a person submits to selfishness and self-worship, he recognizes a personal 'self' for himself. Some people really live alone; self-worship and all wicked traits relation to self-worship (various forms of aggressions, injustices and immoralities) can be found in them. Their only consideration is themselves and none else. They have made a circle whose centre is only themselves and whose periphery does not go beyond their personal 'selves'; they have drawn a circle in which their selves are inside and all others are outside it. They want everything for themselves. This is the weak type of self-worship.

2. Familial 'Self'

Sometimes, however, the radius of self-worship is a bit larger, in the sense that it is self-worship but the radius of the 'self' is sometimes broader. As the self-worshipping person gets married and has some children, as he enters their home, you can observe that he is a just man with his family; he is completely just with his children; in fact, he is even selfless and altruistic, and he never commits treachery to his children; he really does not tell a lie to them and he does not commit deception with the intention of treachery to them. You can see so many individuals who are so good at home and within their respective families. But when the same individuals go out, they want to do anything for the family. Although all wicked traits emanating from self-worship do not exist in the family, they do exist outside the family, and since the unit becomes bigger, the greed and activity involved also become bigger. One would repeatedly tell a lie outside for the sake of the family; he would commit deception for the sake of the family; he would be hypocritical for the sake of the family; he would entice people for the sake of the family; he would commit murder for the sake of the family. All of these are [a manifestation of] the self. You can observe that this 'self' has become a bit bigger; the unit has been changed; otherwise, self-worship is self-worship after all. You can see people who, when inside the house, are just, but outside the house they are unjust and swindler, being unreliable in transactions. Can you regard them as moral people? It is said, "You do not know how so-and-so a person is upright! When he brings home a kilo of apple, he will weigh each of them and distribute the same to the children according to the amount appropriate to each of them. He does not mind if there will be nothing left for him. I had been in their house and I saw how just this person is toward his children. But this is not the totality of morality and moral virtue. If this person goes outside the sphere of his famility which is the sphere of his 'self' that becomes bigger, and he still possesses those virtues, then it is clear that he is moral. Once you observe, however, that outside the family which the sphere of the bigger 'self' this same person steals, cheats, tells a lie, does injustices, and violates the limits, [then you should know that self-worship also exists but] this 'self' is 'familial self'. Are the robbers who form a group treacherous to each other? While committing robbery, they are in good terms with each other, but they are not like that with others. Wherever part of the world you go, in most cases you will see groups being organized that engage in robbery or other forms of cheating; sometimes, they take control of the affairs of people; after all, they are bands. A band does not tell a lie to its members; they provide accurate to each other. But the same individuals are unjust and aggressors in relation to the outsiders. It cannot be said that the individuals who are good within their own band are upright, virtuous and morally meritorious.

3. National 'Self'

Sometimes, we can see that the 'self' becomes broader, becoming even bigger than a band; it becomes a national self. That is, the unit becomes the nation itself and the members of that nation are included, just like the family member who is truthful to his fellow members in the family. He is trustworthy in relation to his own nation; he does not steal within his nation. In reality, he does to steal from himself; he does not tell a lie to himself; he does not do injustice to himself; he does not commit murder against himself; he does not commit any of the wicked acts. Yet, this 'person' or in other words, this 'self,' becomes bigger; his 'self' becomes the nation. Whenever the spirit of the nation depends on telling a lie, all immoral things emanating from self-worship (with a broader scope) can be expected from him. [It is rooted in this way of thinking that] today we can see a person not being unjust toward another person while nations commit the worst kinds of injustices toward other nations while not considering these acts to be evil. You can see leading figures of Europe being proud of themselves for the oppression they have committed against colonized nations. The same person who is so just and trustworthy within his nation and who is not possible to commit the least amount of treachery and immorality in his city, region, or country would say that these concepts are meaningless in reference to another nation. In this very book which is recently featured in the newspapers under the title *Jang-e Jahānī* (*World War*), a moral concept, viz. justice is highlighted. The author thus says, "Although these things are true to individuals, they are not applicable to nations." He is correct; this is exactly the logic behind. All good traits and moral virtues (integrity and honesty, peace and harmony, justice, sincerity, and protection of weak nations) are correct, if advantageous to that nation, otherwise they are not correct.

Gustave Le Bon's Statement

In the later part of Gustave Le Bon's[1] famous book *Islamic and Western Civilization*,[2] there is a chapter about the reasons why Eastern nations, as they are supposed to do, do not welcome Western civilization. He mentions the reasons. The first reason is that they themselves are not ready. The second reason is that "Our lifestyle is not compatible with their living condition. Their life is a simple one. We have articificial needs. Our civilization is more compatible with our condition compared to theirs. They have simply life while our life is more artificial." He continues, "It seems that we hide this." He then says, "This is an unjust pattern of behaviour that the Western nations have had toward them." He then mentions a subject on what they did in America; what they did in the

1. Gustave Le Bon (1841-1931): a French social psychologist, sociologist, and amateur physicist. [Trans.]
2. Most probably it refers to Le Bon's *La Civilisation des Arabes* (1884). [Trans.]

Oceania; what they did in China; what they did in India. He particularly mentions the story of wars known as the Opium Wars in which in order for the British to dominate over the Chinese, they came and introduced opium to the Chinese thereby making them addicted to it. The vigilant Chinese government realized what tragedy they (British) wanted to bring there and so it defended its people. They fought and killed each other until finally, due to the superiority of guns and gun powder, they succeeded in bringing opium. It is true that Britain used to profit 15 million pounds every year, but according to statistics, every year six hundred thousand people would die due to addiction. He then says, "When the British dispatched Christian missionaries to the Chinese, the latter said, "What a surprise! On one hand, you used to bring us opium and sent us to perdition, and on the other hand, you are dispatching missionaries to call us toward faith and piety!"

Two Types of Struggle Against the 'Self'

What should be done then so that man's morality be truly humane morality; morality based upon humanity and humanitarianism; in other words, how can the 'self' be really eliminated? We have to state also that in Islam, elimination of the self does not mean that, but there is the development of the self and advancement of personality but in such a way that the human personality is one with that of the entire world. There is personality up to that extent; up to that extent that this personality is simple, elegant and global.

به جهان خرم از آنم که جهان خرم ازوست
عاشقم بر همه عالم که همه عالم ازوست

> I belong to the pleasant world as the pleasant world is from Him.
> I am in love with the entire world as the entire world is from Him.[1]

But that kind of struggle against the self which is negative in meaning [does not exist in Islam]. This 'self' means limitation or setting a border. A person believes in a demarcation and always wants to sacrifice any outsider for the sake of the insider. This is selfishness, and there are two ways to struggle against the self. One is to weaken or extinguish it; the same thing the the Hindus and Buddhists do, and more or less also prevalent among some Muslims. This is wrong according to Islam. Moreover, let us expand the border of the self until it encompasses the entire humanity and until it encompasses everything in the world. In other words, its scope must extend to infinity and nothing else will remain outside it. This is not a struggle [against the self] with negative sense. In Islam, therefore, while struggling against the self, protection of the rights and limits of the self and defending it are obligatory. The speech I delivered last year about self-respect pertains to a kind of

1. Shaykh Muṣliḥ al-Dīn Sa'dī, *Kulliyāt Sa'dī, Mawā'iẓ, ghazal* 10, 724

preservation of the self, but preservation of the self from which immoral traits do not emanate. In Islam, it is exactly the same and [the notion of] the self is broad. The perimeter of Islamic ethics is not limited to specific individuals or territory; it knows no boundary even for the Muslims and non-Muslims; that is, it is not that inside the boundary of Islam aggression is not permissible but outside this boundary aggression is considered necessary. Islam does not even permit aggression and oppression toward non-Muslims. Of course, it regards retaliatory punishments as permissible (both Muslim and non-Muslim in relation to one another) but aggression is not identical with retaliatory punishments.

God as the Foundation of Moral Virtues

Once we deal with religious training, we will see that these concepts are no longer empty concepts; they are solid concepts. Truth, justice, peace, co-existence, chastity, piety, spirituality, honesty, rightfulness, and trustworthiness – all these are solid terms, having foundation, basis and logic of their own. The crux of the matter is what logic we have to obtain for morality. Can we find sound logic for morality other than the path of the knowledge of Allah (*ma'rifat Allāh*)? No. The basis and credibility of all these concepts is the knowledge about God. If there were no faith, [morality] is like an empty banknote. Initially, it is possible that some people may not understand but it has no basis or foundation. Were the French not the first people to have made universal declaration of human rights? But where was this declaration during the First and Second World Wars?! Where was it during the [French] occupation of Algeria?! Were there not human rights [in Algeria]?! Was it other than that a nation wanted to exercise its own right [to self-determination]?! It was nothing other than this. During that time, what acts were not committed?! Did they show mercy to the women? Did they show mercy to the children? Did they show mercy to traces of civilization? Did they show mercy to libraries? Did they show mercy to cultural institutions? Did they show mercy to houses of worship? (You can see during our own time.) Why? It is because it has no basis. The Holy Qur'an has this declaration:

﴿ وَمِنَ النَّاسِ مَنْ يُعْجِبُكَ قَوْلُهُ فِي الْحَيَاةِ الدُّنْيَا وَيُشْهِدُ اللَّهَ عَلَى مَا فِي قَلْبِهِ وَهُوَ أَلَدُّ الْخِصَامِ ﴾

> Among the people is he whose talk about worldly life impresses you, and he holds Allah witness to what is in his heart, though he is the staunchest of enemies. (2:204)

There are some people who, when you listen to their talks; when you read their writings; when you examine their declarations; when you peruse their books, you will be so impressed, thus: "What a reasonable nation it is! What a truthful nation it is! How excellent these declarations are!" They also emphasize, thus: *"He holds Allah witness to what is in his heart."* But you do not know what he would do with impunity once he acquires power:

﴿ وَإِذَا تَوَلَّىٰ سَعَىٰ فِي الْأَرْضِ لِيُفْسِدَ فِيهَا وَيُهْلِكَ الْحَرْثَ وَالنَّسْلَ ﴾

> And if he were to wield authority, he would try to cause corruption in the land, and to ruin the crop and the stock. (2:205)

That is, once he is the helm of his own obstinacy and selfishness, you will see that these words which senseless and meaningless for him have no effect there; he wants the world to be under his dominion. He wants to cause corruption in the land and to destroy the human race, crops and habitations. In religion, the self has no boundary; that is, moral virtues know no bounds, and religious ethics does not distinguish the religious from the non-religious. Let us first read a verse of the Qur'an in *Sūrat al-Nisā'*:

﴿ يَا أَيُّهَا الَّذِينَ آمَنُوا كُونُوا قَوَّامِينَ بِالْقِسْطِ شُهَدَاءَ لِلَّهِ وَلَوْ عَلَىٰ أَنْفُسِكُمْ أَوِ الْوَالِدَيْنِ وَالْأَقْرَبِينَ إِنْ يَكُنْ غَنِيًّا أَوْ فَقِيرًا فَاللَّهُ أَوْلَىٰ بِهِمَا فَلَا تَتَّبِعُوا الْهَوَىٰ أَنْ تَعْدِلُوا ﴾

> O you who have faith! Be maintainers of justice and witnesses for the sake of Allah, even if it should be against yourselves or [your] parents and near relatives, and whether it be [someone] rich or poor, for Allah has a greater right over them. So do not follow [your] desires, lest you should be unfair. (4:135)

This is the teaching of religion, and regarding this teaching we have so many stories and narratives, which I shall not deal with due to time constraint.

In *Sūrat al-Mā'idah*, when the Muslims were about to enter Makkah [during its conquest] – the same Makkah [whose people] brought sufferings to the Muslims; the same Makkah that broke some teeth of the Prophet (S) (during the Battle of Uḥud); the same Makkah expelled the Prophet (S); the same Makkah that killed loved ones of the Prophet (S) – the Qur'an has the following command:

﴿ وَلاَ يَجْرِمَنَّكُمْ شَنَآنُ قَوْمٍ عَلَى أَلاَّ تَعْدِلُواْ اعْدِلُواْ هُوَ أَقْرَبُ لِلتَّقْوَى ﴾

> And ill feeling for a people should never lead you to be unfair. Be fair; that is nearer to God-wariness. (5:8)

That is to say, "Behave within the bounds of justice. Never mind if they were Muslims or non-Muslims, enemies or not. Do not take this into consideration. The basis of moral virtues is God. Abide by the moral virtues for the sake of God. [The believer (*mu'min*) is he who in moral virtues] does not recognize relatives, family members or kinsfolk; he does not recognize a local fellow; he does not recognize a fellow member in a band; he does not recognize any party. He does not set as boundary even religion itself for moral virtues. He broadens the perimeter of the self to infinity; everything belongs to us. (Every dominion is our dominion as it the dominion of our Lord.) All belong to us.

Imām al-Ḥusayn (A.S.) and Moral Virtues

One chapter in the life of Ḥusayn ibn 'Alī – which I shall mention and pass by – is this one, and it is a very important chapter. You all know the history of Ḥusayn ibn ʻAlī – in what condition he commenced his uprising, under what pressure and injustices were then prevalent. Be that as it may, whenever the issue was that of morality, was he willing to go beyond the limits even against the enemy? Never. Muslim ibn ʻAqīl was trained by him; he was a Shīʻah; he was his soldier. He had the best of opportunities to kill Ibn Ziyād but at that very moment he was aware that Islam is opposed to that kind of struggle, not considering this kind of struggle to be chivalrous. He was asked, "Why did you not go out of this closet (when Ibn Ziyād was off guard) and put an end to his evil acts toward the Muslims?" He said, "At that very moment, this saying of the Prophet (S) came to my mind:

الْايمانُ قَيدَ الْفَتْك.

That is to say, "Faith does not allow a Muslim to go beyond limits even against someone outside the bounds of religion. This is unmanliness and cowardice; I cannot do so."

The enemies came while extremely thirsty. [Some of his companions] said, "Let us take this opportunity and cut to them the supply of water." The Imām (A.S.) said, "Let us never do so. This is not our way of struggle to cut off the supply of water to them; let us give them water; let us give water to their horses." They suggested that it was then the most opportune time to wage war. The Imām (A.S.) said, "That is true from the perspective of our chances to be able to kill them. But how about from the perspective of the truth and law? They have not yet attacked us. They are Muslims and we are Muslims too. Unless they attack us, we shall not fight them in self-defence." Look at this moral discipline. It is the same morality whose edifice is the knowledge about God. This morality cannot be shaken by anything. Personal interests, love of life, self-preservation, protection of the family, political leadership, and caliphate cannot shake its foundation.

Even during that bloody day of *'Āshūrā'*, one of the most wicked among them would approach from the rear to stage a surprise attack, without knowing that the formation of the date trees and dug-up trenches would make it impossible to do so. He got mad and started making verbal abuse. One of the Imām's (A.S.) companions said, "O son of the Messenger of Allah! Allow me to shot an arrow and send him to perdition." The Imām (A.S.) said, "It is not permissible for us unless they start the war. They have to start it first and then we will fight in self-defence." This moral discipline gives no more room for the 'self'; neither is there any room for 'personality'; no family [consideration] is involved there; local belongingness is of no moment there; there is no such thing fellow city dwellers or countrymen there; there is no connection to the land and territory there; race and nationality have no value there; even some degrees higher than humanity are involved thre; it is universal.

As such, the issue of the self cannot be resolved except

within the framework of religion. The communist morality, Nietzche's morality, and Machiavellian morality – each of them is a [system of] morality may be useful in certain limited conditions and in essence, it cannot be considered a school of morality; it is reactions – violent reactions under certain circumstances. While expanding [the perimeter of] the self, Islam regards the protection of the rights of a person as obligatory. It is thus stated:

﴿ لا يُحِبُّ اللَّهُ الْجَهْرَ بِالسُّوءِ مِنَ الْقَوْلِ إِلا مَنْ ظُلِمَ ﴾

> Allah does not like the disclosure of [anyone's] evil [conduct] in speech except by someone who has been wronged. (4:148)

While having such a broad perspective, we must also defend our rights. Now, there is a time when in society such a Christian, or Muslim society that follows these Christian beliefs and does not defend the rights its members, they would come and establish a [system of] morality on the basis of self-defence and protection of this aspect which they consider. Initially, they are so supportive and so long as they are in the world of the oppressor and oppressed, they advocate such a school of thought. But as they take the helms of world affairs, there should be no more opposition which they call 'antithesis', and as a result, they could not do anything. Do not believe that a basis, logic, support and credibility other than the knowledge about God could be found in the world for the moral concepts; for these things that they are mentioning; for justice, truth, peace, humanity, honesty, and rightfulness.

One reason why knowledge abot God, faith and spirituality will never cease to exist in the world is that mankind is in need of morality. In this age of science when moral virtues can no longer be promoted through emulation and imitation, it must be done through logic and foundation. The world and human society must be either there or not there.

If it does not exist and was non-existing, then there is nothing. But if human society is supposed to remain, then it is in need of morality and it is in need of an all-dimensional morality and not communist morality; morality that takes all aspects into consideration; morality that has basis, foundation and pillar, and this is impossible except through religion and spirituality.

﴿ أَلَمْ تَرَ كَيْفَ ضَرَبَ اللَّهُ مَثَلًا كَلِمَةً طَيِّبَةً كَشَجَرَةٍ طَيِّبَةٍ أَصْلُهَا ثَابِتٌ وَفَرْعُهَا فِي السَّمَاءِ * تُؤْتِي أُكُلَهَا كُلَّ حِينٍ بِإِذْنِ رَبِّهَا وَيَضْرِبُ اللَّهُ الْأَمْثَالَ لِلنَّاسِ لَعَلَّهُمْ يَتَذَكَّرُونَ ﴾

> Have you not regarded how Allah has drawn a parable? A good word is like a good tree: its roots are steady and its branches are in the sky. It gives its fruit every season by the leave of its Lord. Allah draws these parables for mankind so that they may take admonition. (14:24-25)

See how God draws a parable: A word of truth, a pure word, a substantial word like a formidable tree whose roots are deep on the ground and whose branches are extended to the sky. It always bears fruit. It is not meant for only one season; it is always 'spring'. It then states, "*Allah draws these parables for mankind.* That is, God draws a parable and this parable is for human society: If human society wants to be fresh and have branches, leaves, fruits, and shade, that is not possible without having a root.

﴿وَمَثَلُ كَلِمَةٍ خَبِيثَةٍ كَشَجَرَةٍ خَبِيثَةٍ اجْتُثَّتْ مِنْ فَوْقِ الأَرْضِ مَا لَهَا مِنْ قَرَارٍ﴾

> And the parable of a bad word is that of a bad tree: uprooted from the ground, it has no stability. (14:26)

That is, "The parable, however, of many baseless talks is that artificial trees which are only 'tree' in form. The concepts are very clear but they have no basis.

﴿يُثَبِّتُ اللَّهُ الَّذِينَ آمَنُوا بِالْقَوْلِ الثَّابِتِ فِي الْحَيَاةِ الدُّنْيَا وَفِي الآخِرَةِ﴾

> Allah fortifies those who have faith with an immutable word in the life of this world and in the Hereafter. (14:27)

God fortifies the faithful in this world and in the Hereafter with fixed word, with firm and substantiated speech whose root is in the depth of [human] soul. No one can take them away from firm speech, as was the case of Ḥusayn ibn 'Alī. That which he said during the first day was the same with what he said during the last moment.

ولا حول ولا قوة الّا باللّه العلي العظيم.

> "And there is neither power nor might except that of Allah, the Exalted and Mighty."

Bibliogerphy

The Holy Qur'an.

'Abd al-Wāḥid Al-Āmudī, *Ghurar al-Ḥikam wa Durar al-Kalim*, (Qum: Daftar-e Tablīghāt-e Islāmī, 1366 S.A.H.).

Abū Ja'far Muḥammad ibn Ya'qūb al-Kulaynī, *Uṣūl al-Kāfī*, vol. 3, (Tehran: Dār Kutub al-Islāmiyyah, 1362 S.A.H.).

Abu'l-Qāsim Pāyandih, *Nahj al-Faṣāḥah*, edited by Ghulām Ḥusayn Majīdī Khānsārī, (Qum: Anṣārīyān, d).

Aḥmad ibn Yaḥyā Bilādhurī, *Al-Ansāb al-Ashrāf*, (n,d).

'Alī ibn Asākir, *Tārīkh Damishq*, (Beirut: Dār Iḥyā' al-Turāth al-'Arabī, 1421 A.H.).

Ḥusayn ibn 'Alī ibn Shu'ba al-Ḥarrānī, *Tuḥaf al-'Uqūl 'an Āl al-Rasūl*, (Qum: Daftar Intishārāt Islāmī, 1404 A.H.).

Ḥusayn Muḥaddith Nūrī, *Lu'lu wa Marjān*, (n,d).

Ḥusayn Muḥaddith Nūrī, *Mustadrak al-Wasā'il wa Mustanbaṭ al-Masā'il* ,(n,d).

Imām 'Alī, *Dīwān Mansūb beh Amīr al-Mu'minīn (A.S.) (Collection of Poetry Attributed to the Commander of the Faithful)*, (Qum: Intishārāt Payām Islam, 1369 S.A.H.).

Imām 'Alī, *Nahj al-Balāghah*, trans. Fayḍ al-Islām, (Tehran: Ḥeydarī, d).

Jalāl al-Dīn Muḥammad Mawlāwī, The Mathnawī of Jalālu'ddīn Rūmī, ed.Reynold A. Nicholson, (Tehran: Suād Publisher, 2002).

Khwārizmī, *Al-Maqta al-Ḥusayn*,(n,d).

Muḥammad Bāqir Majlisī, *Biḥār al-Anwār*, vol. 41&45&43&46&75,

(Tehran: Dār Kutub al-Islāmiyyah, 1362 S.A.H.).

Muḥammad ibn 'Alī ibn Shahr Āshūb Sārawī Māzandaranī, *Manāqib*, vol. 4, (Tehran: n, 1316 S.A.H.).

Muḥsin Amīn, *Fī Riḥāb A'immah Ahl al-Bayt*, (n,d).

Mullā Muḥsin al-Fayḍ al-Kāshānī, *al-Maḥajjat al-Bayḍā'*, (Qum: Daftar Intishārāt Islāmī, 1417 A.H.).

Mullā Muḥsin Fayḍ Kāshānī, *'Ilm al-Yaqīn fī Uṣūl al-Dīn*, (Qum: Bīdār, 1418 A.H.).

Muṣṭafā Āl al-I'timād, *Balāghat al-Ḥusayn* , (n,d).

Sayyid Ibn Ṭāwūs, *Luhūf 'alā Qatlay al-Tufūf*, (Tehran: Jahān, 1348 S.A.H.).

Shaykh 'Abbās Qummī, *Mafātīḥ al-Jinān*, (Qum: Dār Uswah, d).

Shaykh 'Abbās Qummī, *Muntahā'l-Āmāl*, (Tehran: Payām Āzādī, 1379 S.A.H).

Shaykh 'Abbās Qummī, *Bayt al-Aḥzān*, (Qum: Anṣārīyān, 1390 S.A.H.).

Shaykh 'Abbās Qummī, *Nafas al-Mahmūm*, (Qum: Dalīl-e Mā, 1389 S.A.H).

Shaykh 'Abbās Qummī, *Safīnat al-Biḥār*, vol. 1&2, (Tehran: Farāhānī, 1363 S.A.H).

Shaykh Muṣliḥ al-Dīn Sa'dī, *Kulliyāt Sa'dī*, ed. Muḥammad 'Alī Furūghī, (Tehran: Intishārāt Dūstān, 1379 S.A.H.).

Index

A

G

H

I

J

K

O

P

Q

R

S

T

www.ingramcontent.com/pod-product-compliance
Ingram Content Group UK Ltd.
Pitfield, Milton Keynes, MK11 3LW, UK
UKHW012251290726
14090UKWH00016B/596

9 781911 361015